This memoir by Dan Bowman is a page turner, an amazing record of Dan's remarkable memory. He records in great detail events he recalls from his sighted years up to age 12 in vivid color, as well as his more black and white memories of the decades that followed. Dan's boundless curiosity, courage and persistence is evidenced by his tackling complex challenges including learning to use Braille, mastering the pipe organ, learning the original Biblical languages, piano tuning and technology, building an intricate miniature water wheel, and much more. His humility is grounded in his understanding of and commitment to Mennonite-Anabaptist understandings of the Christian faith.

ERWIN H. REMPEL, Retired Senior Executive, Mennonite Mission Network, an Agency of Mennonite Church USA

Daniel L. (Dan) Bowman, 80, of Harrisonburg, Va., may be blind, but is very much in touch with the world around him. Having completely lost his sight at age 12, Bowman has not let that physical disability hamper an aggressive pursuit of personal and career endeavors over the years—vocational rehabilitation counselor, piano technician for 36 years, accomplished pianist and organist and skilled wood craftsman, and above all, devoted husband to wife Ferne and three adult daughters and their families.

Dan's memoir describes his longstanding commitment to using his God-given talents to help others, from making beautiful music to tuning pianos and contributing other works of his hands to the annual Virginia Mennonite Relief Sale in Harrisonburg. He chronicles an "eye for detail"—his homes, persons who stepped in at the right time in his critical growing-up years, his academic and spiritual growth. Get to know this inspiring, humble man.

JIM BISHOP, retired public information ...nce writer/photographer

Dan Bowman invites us into the vivid, sensory world of a curious, mechanically-inclined farm boy growing up in a Mennonite community of the 1940s and '50s. When he loses his sight at age twelve, his world, instead of constricting as one might expect, opens up, offering enticing new possibilities. With honesty and complete lack of self-pity, Bowman takes the reader along on his eventful journey. His pluck, curiosity, and many gifts shine through what could be a sad story but instead becomes a hymn of joy for the richness of life.

KATHIE WEAVER KURTZ,
retired pastoral counselor

WATCH THE DOCUMENTARY:

"A Good Blinder" is a 30 minute documentary on Dan Bowman's life produced in 2017 by Professors Shaun Wright and Mike Grundmann of James Madison University.

This can be viewed on YouTube at:
https://www.youtube.com/watch?v=1T8_UnWTq0I

A DVD copy for $25 can be ordered at:
mikegrundmann@gmail.com

Daniel L. Bowman

From

SIGHT

to

INSIGHT

A Mennonite Farm Boy's Adventures
Through Blindness to Living
and Seeing Without Vision

———————

BY DANIEL L. BOWMAN

From Sight to Insight

*A Mennonite Farm Boy's Adventures Through Blindness
to Living and Seeing Without Vision*

by Daniel L. Bowman
1578 Hawthorne Circle
Harrisonburg, VA 22802
Phone: 540 574-3892
Email: danbow1941@gmail.com

Library of Congress Control Number: 2021947158
International Standard Book Number: 978-1-60126-759-7

Masthof Press

219 Mill Road | Morgantown, PA 19543-9516
www.Masthof.com

TABLE OF CONTENTS

DEDICATION

To the memory of my Grandma Laura E. Wenger. Grandma Wenger took a special interest in me as I went into blindness. From her very meager resources she bought me a portable Underwood typewriter. She is the first adult for whom I developed a sense of solicitous caring. I looked forward to checking in with her every time I came home on break from the school for the blind. When she died, I felt the loss keenly.

ACKNOWLEDGEMENTS

Gratitude! Where can I find enough words to express all the gratitude that has been stirred up in me by writing this memoir!? I trust that the reader will see throughout the book that I am acknowledging many people in my life as essential to the rich and full life that has fallen my way. "Thanks be to God for every one of you! And thanks to each of you for your role in my life!" I'll mention three persons who precipitated the specific decision to write and coached me along the way.

My brother Bernie, one day in the midst of many voices urging me to write, got serious and insistent, "You need to write. People need to hear your story." This was a considered opinion. I thought things over carefully, then capitulated to the task. Then I began to smile—back when I was age seven and Bernie was ten months old, I spied his cute little face peering across the top rail of his crib with an expression clearly begging me to play with him. I dragged him out over the top rail, letting him flop onto my chest. I stood him on the floor and held his chubby little hands. He took a step or two; I stepped back still holding his hands, and he kept walking! "Look, Mom!" I yelled. "He's walking!"

Then there's Laurie Kutchins, an oft-published poet and professor of English at James Madison University. I always ran overtime tuning her piano because we liked to talk and talk about many ideas. She made me fully aware of what I only half-knew previously, that it was blindness that really opened the world of books and ideas to me. Her insight on this shows in the title of this book, *From Sight to Insight* ...

I'm especially delighted to have this opportunity to say publicly to my wife, Ferne (Lapp), "THANK YOU for these 54 years of life together, and, at this particular time, THANK YOU for your support, encouragement, and coaching during this writing project. It's been wonderful!" And, folks, it does get better with age!

I also want to thank Bill Gates and the people at Freedom Scientific (Clearwater, Florida)—Bill Gates for the microcomputer and word processor, Freedom Scientific for JAWS, a workable screen reader for the blind. I do not, cannot, write out a paragraph in linear fashion, one sentence after another. Rather, I sculpt and build the paragraph till, when I listen to it with the screen reader, it accurately speaks my mind and has a nice, natural flow, not jerking the mind around. You call it "editing"; I call it building or sculpting. The word processor and screen reader made it possible for me to write.

Last of all thanks to Masthof Press for transforming my manuscript into a book and for their marketing and distribution.

INTRODUCTION

Around age seventy-five I must have reached the age for wrapping up and taking stock. The notion of writing down my life story began getting hold of me. One source for the notion is what Ferne, my wife, and I have been reading. We spend a lot of time after supper reading together—book after book after book, and for the last while most of these have been personal memoirs. So, "Well, OK, maybe I can tell a good story, too."

Another source for the impulse to write has been friends and acquaintances who've begun urging, "You need to write! Your story is interesting. It would sell."

My three brothers, Eldon, Jim, and Bernie, had already published their memoirs; a sister, Miriam Haarer, had published a collection of Bible stories told in her special way; and Ferne, my wife, had published her memoir. (These books are listed on page 344.) So now my whole family is leaning on me, "Dan, it's your turn!" OK, OK, it is time for me to write!

Admittedly, those kinds of reasons aren't the compelling impulses that make a good story. As I got into the project, though, I began to see that, indeed, my stories might be helpful to folks figuring out how to live well without vision. Parents and teachers of visually-impaired children might find my stories useful. Folks dealing with the ways their young people react to their religious heritage, and folks who like human interest stories of ethnic Mennonite color might also be interested. People who like to ponder life's big issues might find some grist for thought. So, here are some of my stories.

Not nearly all of me, the good or the bad, is in this book. In this memoir project, I have become conscious of the fact that often it is the really personal details that helps sell a book. But I have not told all. Sometimes it's because wisdom—I hope that's what it is—has overtaken me. Sometimes it's because of lack of time, energy, or space. And sometimes it's just because I don't want to.

We nine children of Millard and Oma Wenger Bowman grew up in the 1940-70 world of Virginia Conference Mennonites. This world was centered around Shenandoah Valley family farms and around Eastern Mennonite College in Harrisonburg, Virginia.

We all were "raised in the nurture and admonition of the Lord" (Ephesians 6:4, KJV) but our reactions and feelings toward Mom and Dad and toward our Mennonite heritage as a whole have been very different. Consequently we will write very different memoirs. This surprises some folks—"You all grew up in the same family environment, why did you all turn out so different?" Those who understand the ways a child grows into adulthood with a mature mind understand that these different outcomes are normal.

I have come to see that loss of vision at age twelve set me up in relationship patterns with Dad and church elders that reduced "normal teenaged head butting." But more significantly, the seven years I spent at VSDB (Virginia School for the Deaf and the Blind, Staunton, Virginia) for grades six through twelve set me on a track to relate to and wrestle with my religious heritage in ways different from my sibs and Mennonite peers. While many of my peers back home were beginning to question and test and toss out chunks of our Mennonite heritage, I was in a state-run boarding school, where I had to figure out all by myself how to explain and defend and live out my Mennonite ways and beliefs. In this strange new world, the name "Mennonite" was an unheard of, unpronounceable, funny word. Dad had acquainted us nine kids with the Anabaptist Mennonite story, and I discovered it told very well among at least some of these new friends—I could get them to listen at least a little bit before waving me and my funny religion aside. I just didn't experience much of that "Mennonite shame" my friends talk about. Several adults in that VSDB world did try to show me the errors of my Mennonite ways, but I pretty much held my own.

As I began sorting through memories—what to omit, what to emphasize—I was taken aback with the way memory pictures from the seeing years were qualitatively different from those from the blind years. Age twelve, for me, is the great divide between seeing and not seeing. My memory pictures before age 12 are in bright, vivid colors; those after age 12 are clear and detailed but colors are less interesting or not even there. The contrast is as striking as when you move back and forth between two photo albums, one in color and the other in black and white.

Instead of dismissing this discovery with a casual, "Well of course, how could it be otherwise," I began exploring the phenomenon. From my own experience as a blind person who once had vision and from general reading in brain science I deduced the following:

> In the normal process of moving about and comprehending the world around us, our brain sets up mental constructs, which we think of as memory pictures. Colors are, of course a part of these pictures. The brain of a blind person also sets up memory pictures.

These pictures in a blind brain may or may not include colors. If colors are present in the picture, they are spliced in from memories from the seeing days. These spliced-in colors are not as vivid as those directly experienced as part of the particular visual memory. I am trying to underscore this: *In a given memory picture, colors brought into that memory picture from memories of another time are less vivid than colors directly experienced as part of the memory in question.* That observation may seem so trite as to be pointless, but it has become important to me.

So it is, as I began rummaging around in my childhood memories, the seeing years, I was surprised, then practically breathless at the colorful beauty of these scenes. It was and still is like the joy of finding things that were long lost and longed for, though the longing was long ago forgotten. As I began writing, I was soon reveling in the sensory fun of recreating these scenes in English prose for others to "see." The reader will probably notice I have included more details from my seeing years than an editor might recommend for a memoir about living without vision. But I did also include lots of details from the blind years for the fun of recreating and reliving those scenes, too. Writing this memoir has been fun!

This book is a memoir, not an autobiography that documents details in scholarly fashion. It is stories and MEMORIES of life experiences that shaped me. Knowing full well how memories can play games with you, I have been ever on guard against including stories where the memory details won't settle down into an account that "rings true" in me. I have avoided fiction. In some cases, I have gone to considerable length to verify factual details with external sources and persons. Any factual mistakes that remain are mine.

Some of my stories have extended dialogs in quotation marks which would seem to mean exact reproductions of conversations from long ago. In some cases, as with Mrs. Stubbs' tirade to a misbehaving boy in her classroom, or Mrs. Kiracofe's weeks-long pleading with me about going to Curtis Institute, I am indeed presenting those lines as virtually exact quotes. These are not tape recorder verisimilitude, but they are very accurate reports of what was said.

In other cases, as in the story of the cabins and slaves in first grade, I use adult words and concepts to express accurately what was going on in the mind of a six- or seven-year-old. I know of no other way to get the TRUTH that is in the child's mind across to the reader, and, oh yes, a young child can have adult-size thoughts and feelings well before he has adult-size words to frame and express them.

After writing out those very earliest memories at the beginning of the book (from age fifteen months), I came upon news stories reporting that "science" has concluded that the child's brain before age two is physiologically incapable of processing and retaining true memories into adulthood. Well, my response to that is, "That means science hasn't finished figuring out how the brain works and when it starts working." (Actually, don't tell anybody, I do have some memories from well before those stories, but I don't want to embarrass folks.)

To protect the privacy of some individuals in these stories I have changed their names.

Now at age 79 as I conclude the book, the following scene from Virginia Woolf's novel, MRS. DALLOWAY[1], perfectly sums up this writing experience:

The compensation of growing old, Peter Walsh thought, coming out of Regent's Park, and holding his hat in hand, was simply this: that the passions remain as strong as ever, but one had gained—at last!—the power which adds the supreme flavour to existence— the power of taking hold of experience, of turning it round, slowly, in the light.

Yes, in writing this book I have taken one experience after another and turned it round in the light of insights and wisdom that has come with old age. I like some of what I see, yawn at some, and regret some.

A LOOK AHEAD

When I got off the school bus that day—sixth grade in October 1953—I knew something was very wrong with my vision. As I started up the lane to the house, I could see where I was going, sort of, but things were distorted and I was scared I would trip on something. I'll never forget—I'm lying on that old sofa just inside the kitchen door. My vision is getting even crazier and distorted now. There are rainbow colors when I look at windows and ceiling lights.

It's time for Eldon and me to do our afternoon chores— he's supposed to feed the turkeys in one half of the turkey house and I do the other half. "Mom," I say, "I don't think I can do the turkeys with my eye like this."

Mom responds, "Eldon, you're gonna have to do all the turkeys this time."

Eldon protests loudly, "Mom, he can too do his share of the turkeys. Make him come and help!"

Now wait a minute here…! But, well, I realize I could get out there to the turkey house OK, and if I really had to, I could help with the feeding. But that place is dimly lighted and I could easily trip over the feeders. Besides, this situation by now has me really scared—and hey, am I not going to be allowed to be sick?! I mean, after all, what self-respecting farm boy wants to pass up a chance to get out of his chores? I fire back at Eldon, "I cannot see good enough to do those turkeys!"

"Yes, you can!" he fires back.

"No, I can't!"

"Yes, you can! Mom, make him come and do his chores!" El-don sees that I'm looking straight at him while we're arguing and fig-ures he can prove that I can see well enough to do my chores—"OK, where am I sitting?" he challenges.

Shoot, he's gonna trap me! I know full well where he is sit-ting—I can see his distorted image sitting over there in that chair and besides, I can hear where he is. But if I answer correctly he's gonna say, "See, you can too see well enough to do your work." So, I'll have to improve on the facts in order to convince both him and Mom—"You're sitting over there," I say, and point to the wrong side of the room.

"Well why are you looking this way then," he triumphs.

Umph!—he's got me. I mumble something like, "I thought you were sitting over there (pointing to the wrong side of the room), but you sound like you're sitting over there (pointing to the right place)."

"Mom, make him come and do his work!" he triumphs again.

Mom ends the argument, "Eldon, you go on now and do all the turkeys."

Eldon did go on out that evening and do my chores along with his. When he went out, the truth finished settling over me that I was sure enough in trouble, real trouble. Eldon tells me the gravity of the situation settled over him, too. I'll tell you now, the reader, in the weeks and months after that argument, Eldon became a really neat brother alongside as I learned my way into living without vision!

1

MY FIRST MEMORY CLIPS AND
THAT OLD HOUSE WHERE I BEGAN

What better place to start my story than with my starting memories? My very earliest memories are like short video clips.

The right front wheel of the buggy is going round and round, crunching against the gravel on the dirt road. The horse's rear end is jiggling up and down and slightly side to side, and his scraggly tail occasionally flicks as his hooves trot out a steady clop, clop, clop, clop, into the afternoon. The sun is filtering through the trees making a speckled shadow pattern on everything. The grey-brown wooden dashboard of the buggy is up at an angle in front of me, and the wooden floor is down there. I sense the sort of closed-in feeling from the buggy's top. My hands explore the deep holes where the upholstery buttons are pulled way down into the black seat cushion. Mom is beside me, on my left, and Dad is on the other side of her, holding some strings going out to the horse (the reins).

"Where does that memory come from?" I asked Mom in 1999, three years before she died. "Is it a dream or for real?"

"Why Daniel!" she exclaimed. "We did go for a buggy ride one Sunday afternoon! You remember that?! Daddy got his Granddaddy Eli Bowman's buggy and borrowed a horse from a nearby farmer and we went for a ride. It was a Sunday afternoon before Eldon was born."

Before Eldon was born! That means that buggy ride occurred before I was 15 months old, and I remember it like yesterday. We were not horse and buggy people. That buggy was old; it was my great-granddaddy's means of transportation.

My next memory clip is just as vivid.

I'm standing in front of the old wood cookstove. Baby Eldon is tied in a rocking chair with a towel or something across his lap. He's yelling at the top of his voice and rocking that chair like mad. Mom is at the kitchen sink, working in a hurry, all frazzled.

A bit later in 1999 I said to Mom, "There's another old memory I need to confirm with you," and told her about Eldon tied in a rocking chair. She reacted with the same astonishment as with the buggy ride—"Why Daniel! I did tie him in a chair so I could get some things done. And you remember that?! I had completely forgotten that!"

A third very early memory—Eldon and I got up one morning and found that we had a new baby sister. I would have been almost three years old. A formal announcement had evidently just been made—"Her name will be Shirley Ann." *I wanna see this baby, but there's so much busyness around the crib I can't see!* Then at some point Aunt Fannie (a community aunt, not a family aunt) herded Eldon and me over to the crib. *She's insisting that we look at our baby sister.* Aunt Fannie must have been changing the diaper and wanted Eldon and me to see things before finishing up. *That's Baby Shirley lying there, all red, with boney skinny little legs flailing! Hey, her bottom! Oh my, her bottom is different from mine!* Over the next several weeks I mulled over the business of naming babies—some names were girl's names and some were boy's names. *How did they know when to give a baby a girl name and when a boy name?* Eventually I concluded, *baby bottoms are different, so people know whether to give the baby a girl name or a boy name.* I also wondered what about a name makes it for girls or for boys. I never figured that out.

Mom and Dad, that is Millard Bowman and Oma Frances Wenger, were married at Bishop Sam Rhodes' home on a SNOWY Valentine's Day in 1940. Dad's brother and his new wife, Uncle Durward and Aunt Barbara, were the only guests; they were the witnesses. The snow canceled the honeymoon. So, Mom and Dad spent their first night, and indeed the first 12 years of their marriage in Mom's girlhood home.

This was the Daniel P. Wenger farm located near Cook's Creek Presbyterian Church northwest of Harrisonburg, Virginia. The current address is 3784 Mt. Clinton Pike, Harrisonburg, 22802. Mom's father, Daniel Wenger and his third wife, Mom's stepmother, Laura Suter Wenger, along with Mom's three older unmarried sisters also lived in that house. These sisters: Lena, Annie, and Edna, were getting along into spinsterhood (a term they used back then). Annie, nine years older than Mom, had practically raised Mom as a daughter since Mom's mother, Emma Heatwole Wenger, died when Mom was age seven. The wise reader will be taking note of these living arrangements. When I was around age 12, I heard Dad telling a friend, "There came a time when Oma and I had to tell her sisters, 'From here on we will be making our own decisions.'"

I was born into that household in April, 1941. I got lots of attention and Mom got lots of help from her older sisters; they were doting aunts. Eldon came along in July, 1942. Aunt Annie's, our term for those older sisters, moved out soon after Eldon was born. Now Mom was left with two diaper babies and no help from doting aunts. Hence it is that Eldon got tied in a chair so Mom could get some things done.

That Wenger house, built around 1900, where Mom and the first eight of her nine children were born, and where I began—I need to tell you about that house; if you don't care for description, just skip ahead. It was a plain, foursquare brick structure with a slate roof. It was set into the south flank of a hill such that the basement opened out on ground level at the front while the second floor opened at ground level at the back. Some folks see that house as artless and boring, but those of us who know how certain marks of wear and tear got there and who generally have it stuffed full of memories see it as charming and special.

From the road, the house looks like a three-story building with a ground level porch, a second story with a balcony-like front porch, and a third story with a door that opens onto that balcony roof. The woodwork on the balcony railings and posts, window frames and doors were white against the red brick and gray slate roof. Our living room and kitchen were on the second floor; our bedrooms were on the third floor. The floor plan of the top two floors featured a hallway and staircase running from front to back with two identical rooms on either side. The two rooms on each side of the hall were connected by a doorway, which made possible one of those "circles" that kids love—and did we kids ever run (and ride) round and round that circle.

Once Dad ran round and round that circle, too, from the living room into the kitchen, out into the hall, back around into the living room, and round again, and again, his face getting redder and redder; he was chasing one of his naughty kids. When the kid was finally caught and correction administered, Dad was out of breath. (Some of us think that naughty kid got more correction than necessary.)

The first floor, basement level, had two rooms arranged across the front of the house, one on either side of the staircase.

These were Grandpa and Grandma Wenger's living room and kitchen. Each room had a wonderful Dutch door that opened out to the ground level porch and front yard. With these Dutch doors you could open the top half while leaving the bottom half closed, a very nice arrangement for controlling sun and breezes. At the foot of the stairs between those two rooms was a recently added bathroom—just a toilet and wash bowl. This was installed for Grandpa's convenience, but we kids used it when possible to avoid the cold outhouse or those awful "toilies" (chamber pots).

The main front porch was like a balcony; a full flight of steps at the west end ushered guests from ground level up to the second-story front door. From this porch you could survey the countryside near and far—Mom's flowers around the yard, the hats on people below you, the pond in the meadow down front of the house, the galvanized windmill off to the left with its wheel always turning to face into the wind, Uncle Paul's and Uncle Jake's houses across the road, and Mole Hill off to the southwest.

One really neat thing about this porch was the several missing slats in the railing—we kids could climb through those openings and hang onto the railing while walking outside the railing along the porch edge—about 8 feet above the ground. Mom never stopped us and none of us ever fell. I do remember worrying about little Jim and little Bernard—they were too little to be going outside that railing. Eldon and I tied bailer string or something across those openings to keep them from copycatting Eldon, Shirley, and me.

This front porch had a standing seam tin roof, and, believe it or not, at the front end of the third-floor hall was a door that opened right out onto that porch roof! There was no railing up there; you simply stepped out onto the tin roof and saw to it that you didn't get too near the edge! Why that door was put there I never heard. Were they planning to eventually put a third-floor balcony up there? The women of the house did go out there to shake out rugs and bedding. They also put corn and beans and apples and such stuff out there to dry. When the door wasn't locked, we kids would go out there to better survey the country-side, or more likely just for the thrill of being up so high. I more than once heard Mom calling, "Now Daniel, you stay back from that edge."

Eldon tells me several different times he went over to the east end of that roof, reached out and took hold of the down-spout and then shimmied himself up and over the main gut-ter, getting clear up onto the slanted slate roof of the house—to retrieve balls, he says. I'm queasy now thinking about this, es-pecially Eldon coming back down over that gutter and sliding down the downspout.

To my recollection Mom never forbade these roof-top excursions, but I don't think she ever saw Eldon going up that downspout onto the main roof. They just kept that door locked—most of the time.

Back down on ground level and under the second-floor porch was a smooth concrete slab serving as a ground level porch. Those two Dutch doors opened out here and made a very nice entrance to Grandpa and Grandma's rooms. Eldon's and my footprints are in the concrete over at the west front corner; mine is the deeper one. Outside Grandma's kitchen door was a wood-en plank bench with a plank back, made, I understand, when the house was built. I taught myself how to use Grandpa's old brace and bits by drilling holes, shallow holes, in its seat—and no one reprimanded me! From that lack of scolding I did begin to con-clude it was OK or even good to learn to use tools. On nice days Grandpa would sit out there in his rocking chair, shaded by the upper porch. He kept his chair turned sideways so we kids could ride back and forth on our trike or pedal tractor. At the east end of this porch was a huge snowball bush planted there by Mom in 1931 when she was seventeen. Several years ago, two of my sisters took cuttings from that bush and now have thriving snowball bushes of their own.

The cellar, as we called it, was just behind Grandpa and Grandma's kitchen and living room; it ran across the entire back of the house. All sorts of canned goods sat on shelves. A clutter of tables, drying racks, food containers including Grandma's cookie jar, and a pie safe lurked in the cool shadows. Of most interest to me was the cream separator, solidly anchored to the middle of the concrete floor. You had to crank it to get it started and then turn on the electric motor. When you had it going you poured fresh milk from the barn into the bowl at the top and out one spout came a stream of rich creamy milk and out another spout came a stream of pale watery milk. Over at the west end of this cellar sat a water pump and big pressure tank—the heart of the waterworks for the whole farm; Dad installed that system when he came to the farm. The motor for that pump had a nasty growl when it turned on and always made me jump.

The back porch, at second-floor level, was just several steps above the ground. From that back porch you could run in the back door, straight through the hall, and out the front door onto the high front porch. The most interesting feature of this back porch was the screened-in window box at the kitchen window—it served as a refrigerator when the weather was cool. Mom would open the window from inside and set crocks of lard and hominy, along with jars of jelly and other stuff out there. A wood box with odds and ends of kindling sat by the back door. We older kids learned to brush our teeth out there—we took our toothbrushes and cup of baking soda water to the west end and spat over the railing.

Underneath this porch the soil was a soft red clay, just right for boys to dig in—and we did! There was just enough head clearance to sit and work comfortably, and it was always cool under there. A long running project was "the hole!" We dug and we dug, we excavated and we excavated. I had no idea, and still don't, what the hole was for. Years later when someone gave our daughters a picture book entitled, *A Hole is to Dig,* I understood the simple, profound truth—a hole is to dig!

The attic was a huge wonderland of dusty old treasures. Mom's old school notebooks were up there with her neat hand-writing and very neat drawings for biology and geography classes. Her geography textbooks were of particular interest to me—my present knowledge of world geography and of Bible land geography began there. Mom would sometimes let us have things we found up there, but more often she would tell us to put it back.

The attic windows, one in either end, would easily open and close like the other windows in the house. Adults would sometimes throw trash out these windows and later clean up the mess from down on the ground. Once I found a big dusty old cloth bag and took it over to the west end and dumped the contents out the window. Well, the contents were goose feathers—lots of them! Wow, what a beautiful midsummer snowstorm! But whoa here, those weren't just any old goose feathers. That was Mom's supply of goose down for making feather pillows! Mom was not happy! We kids to this day recall that Mom almost never spoke in anger. She didn't speak in anger this time either; she didn't spank; she didn't lose her cool; but there was no doubt I was standing before clear, unquestionable authority: "You will clean that up—all of it." I did—all of it, including those little flecks of white stuff scattered in and over a nearby bush; I got very tired. But I must not have gotten it all—that bag was not as full when I finished as when I dumped it. (Recently, Eldon told me he was partner in this project.)

A most interesting feature of this house was the cistern-based water system. There were two cisterns at the east end of the house, one at the upper back corner and one at the lower front corner. A complex system of downspouts crisscrossed the east wall of the house bringing the water from the slate roof to the cisterns. With several butterfly valves set in the spouting you could direct the water to either system or out onto the ground. When it began to rain, you were supposed to first let the water run out onto the ground for a while; any debris, such as bird droppings, would then be flushed from the roof and out of the way. Then you set the butterfly valves to run the water into, say, the lower cistern in summer or the upper cistern in winter. Throughout the year, then, you could have warm water by drawing from the lower cistern and cool water by drawing from the upper cistern. In her later years Mom told me that system really worked.

On top of each cistern stood one of those classic galvanized "G E M" cistern pumps with a hand crank in front and a spout off to one side. These pumps should be ranked alongside galvanized metal windmills as a triumph of economical water handling equipment before electrification. Inside the galvanized metal housing was a continuous chain that ran up over a ten-inch sprocket on the crank shaft; on that chain were two-inch rubber "sucker" disks every ten or twelve inches. A two-inch diameter galvanized metal tube hung straight down under the pump into the water. The continuous chain with the sucker disks ran up through this tube, over the sprocket wheel at the top, back down into the water, and back up through the tube. You turned that sprocket wheel with the hand crank that traveled the chain round and round, pulling those sucker disks and water up through the tube. The water was discharged into a little reservoir box at the top end. From that box, the water poured out the spout on the side of the pump. It was a delightfully simple and effective system. When the sucker disks were in good condition, by turning the crank you could get a surprising gush of water from the spout and fill a bucket quickly. When the sucker disks were in poor condition, you had to crank a lot to get a little. Over time those rubber disks did get rotten and brittle, prone to crumble away, especially with the touch of little exploring fingers. I loved to take off the top hood to look and explore inside—and crank, and crank, and crank, and finger those rubber disks.

That house was Mennonite plain and solid. It, along with the remaining farm outbuildings, represented self-sufficient state-of-the-art farm technology of the late 19th and early 20th century. It was prosperous but its glory was in the past. That house and farm is where I began, and it is where my first "sense of place" is deeply rooted. My marks are on the place and its hooks are deep in me.

2

FARM BOY—HAPPY YEARS, FLOWERS AND UNFORGETTABLE SCENES

My roots are sunk deep and permanent in that Daniel P. Wenger farm near Cook's Creek Presbyterian Church northwest of Harrisonburg. The most vivid of my early memories are Mom's flowers. Though I would be turning into a rather ornery farm boy whose chief interests were things mechanical, those colorful flowers impacted me more deeply than anything else on the farm. Scenes of the front pasture with the pond and windmill are a close second place.

Purple irises filled a long wooden flower box on top of a stone wall at the east edge of the front yard. I distinctly recall getting up from my afternoon nap in an upstairs bedroom, no more than age 3, slipping QUIETLY down the stairs and out the front door. I carefully closed the screen door behind me, trying not to get Mom's attention—I didn't want to hear, "No, Daniel, you didn't sleep long enough yet. You go back up to bed." I crept down the front porch steps and across the yard to the irises. Pushing my nose into the purple flowers, I could plainly see on the petals, close up to my nearsighted eyes, little beads of water with rainbows shimmering inside—a spring shower had just passed through and the sky was now deep blue with white clouds and bright sun making the water drops come alive. The iris fragrance filled me to the core of my little soul.

Pink, very pink, climbing roses that were very fragrant, totally engulfed the east end of a woven wire fence that ran across the front yard. *Why must so much beauty be tucked into nasty thorns like that?* Just outside that fence was a stone retaining wall. In the middle of the fence was a yard gate that opened out to three or four stone steps that went down from the wall into the front pasture. Between the fence and that retaining wall, grew daffodils; they had yellow trumpets ringed with white petals standing in clusters of narrow green leaves. We liked to talk into those trumpets, pretending they were mouthpieces to those old crank telephones.

A little ways down in the pasture and a bit to the east, sort of in the middle of nowhere, were more clumps of the same daffodils; their foliage and flowers were more lush and vibrant than the others, their colors oh so vivid. One warm spring day on my way up to the house after getting off the school bus I thought I would just go over there and stretch out on the lush green grass amidst those flowers and, well, maybe meditate a while—or do whatever passes for meditation for a 7- or 8-year-old boy. The quiet beauty of that little area was really drawing me in. Suddenly my shoes broke through that lush grassy sod into the stinkenest muck you can imagine! Then I saw why the daffodils and grass in this spot were so lush and vibrant—they were thriving on the "lush stuff" oozing from septic system laterals in that area. Some of the lateral tiles had worked too close to the surface! I thought I would never get that stink off my shoes. The proximity of so much beauty with such stink was a point for a small boy to ponder for a long time.

Snowball bushes crowded the front yard gate, one on either side, and one more snowball bush stood at the east end of the lower front porch. That one is still there, planted by Mom at age 17 in 1930. Several of my sisters still have snowball bushes started with cuttings from that bush.

In the lower end of the east yard near Mom's hotbed, stood bushes of pink and white and dark red peonies. I would nose into those blossoms, trying to keep the big black ants off my nose. I inhaled with all my might. The beauty and fragrance of those flowers made me yearn for something but I knew not what.

Along the east side of the house and around two sides of the wash house stood tall stalks full of red and pink hollyhocks. Shirley, Eldon, and I learned from our cousins how to make cute little women and men by picking various sized buds and flowers off these stalks and sticking them together with toothpicks.

White day lilies and orange tiger lilies bloomed in profusion in various clumps around the wash house and inside the backyard white picket fence. Mom let us pick these at will—mostly they ended up on the kitchen table as big sprawling arrangements in a canning jar.

To the left of the backyard gate stood a big lilac bush, deep purple and fragrant. I tried to inhale their beauty, too. There was another lilac at the west side of the front yard down front, against the picket fence. Under it were bluebells and, I think also, lilies of the valley.

Long partial rows of marigolds held their place in the garden amidst the rows of more important vegetables. Morning glories grew in the sweet corn rows. Mom also planted snap dragons and other flowers in the garden.

There were pear trees, one in the front and one in the backyard, but I don't recall pear blossoms. Dad rigged up a swing in the back pear tree where we swung and twisted the ropes and spun ourselves dizzy amidst all those flowers. That backyard tree was good for climbing, too.

Indoors Grandma Wenger had lots of African violets that sort of annoyed me—I thought, "If they're gonna be that pretty they need to be bigger!" I thought the same thing about the bluebells under the lilac bush out front.

And there were those other unofficial flowers—daisies, Queen Ann's lace, red and blue clover flowers, blue weed, and, if Dad didn't get the thistles hoed in time, thistle blossoms.

Dandelions! Oh the dandelions—those dandelions put on a wonderful show each spring in the front pasture. Spring weather would carpet the pasture in green. Then there would be several days when the entire pasture was a solid carpet of bright dandelion yellow. Then came several days when the carpet was dandelion puffball gray—a bright luminous gray almost as pretty as the yellow. In a few days the pasture was once again green grass. I looked forward to this every spring.

The pond in the middle of this front pasture was as fascinating as Mom's flowers. Its colors and mood constantly changed to match conditions in the sky above. Sometimes, depending on where you were standing, the sky blue in the water would shade toward the greens and browns on the banks. Sometimes lazy, white clouds overhead would be mirrored in what seemed to be perfectly clear blue water. Then again you might see lowering stormy skies in the pond. Two or three times I saw a spectacular show produced by what I now understand were weather fronts caused by tropical depressions or hurricane activity off the East Coast or in the Gulf of Mexico. Once we got off the school bus into the middle of one of these shows. Walking by the pond on the way up to the house, I realized the whole world in these moments was different. Banks of roiling black and gray and white clouds were hurrying across the valley, very low, churning, tumbling and rolling. The sun, somewhere off the edge of this scene, was low enough to give an eerie brightness to the underbellies of these wild clouds. This in turn gave an eerie light to everything on the ground—the green grass, the pond, even the galvanized metal windmill across the way. The air at ground level was perfectly still and pleasant, very balmy, while it was obviously wild and stormy up there! Those stormy clouds were mirrored in the pond, but it seemed far deeper than just a surface reflection—the water was luminous; the whole pond seemed to be rolling and tumbling and churning deep down, just like the clouds overhead.

The whole scene was wild and wonderful, positively exhilarating! I felt I would burst with the wild joy of it all! I wanted to run, or do cartwheels, maybe even dance, but oh well—I suppose I was thoroughly Mennonite. I had no clue how to dance or otherwise express such wild joy. Later in high school literature, a teacher was explaining epic poetry, specifically "Beowulf." He said many ancient peoples were powerfully moved by events in nature. When he said that, I remembered that pond under the stormy clouds and understood perfectly well!

One day a gorgeous double rainbow put one foot smack down in the front pasture, right down on the ground beside the windmill. Eldon and I could plainly see the exact spot. We knew about the pot of gold that was supposed to be at the end of the rainbow. We knew it was mythical, but Eldon wanted to see what was REALLY there—he was already a budding scientific investigator. We were about eight and seven years old. He started down through the pasture while I waited and watched from the farm lot between the house and the barn. I saw him, bright and clear, the sun on his back, going down across the green grass. Gradually his image kind of faded into a mist; then his hazy form was striding along purposefully in the midst of rainbow colors; then he disappeared. (I suppose he walked out the far side of the mist.) After awhile his hazy form came striding back through the colors and out of the mist. He came back up the hill with the air of one who had just confirmed that a myth was a myth. I knew I'd better not ask if he saw any gold.

"That rainbow kept moving away and staying the same distance in front of me no matter how far I walked," he said. "Nobody ever gets to the end of a rainbow." I could see he was intrigued with this finding but I also thought he seemed a little disappointed that the spot where the rainbow had so clearly stood minutes before was, on close inspection, so ordinary.

I said, "I saw you walk straight into and back out of that rainbow right where we first saw it. For me up here, it didn't move a bit." We had just learned a basic scientific fact about rainbow perspective.

Mom's ducks put on their own show in that front pasture around and on the pond. She housed and fed them in an old "duck house" in that row of outbuildings at the back of the lot between the house and the barn. These ducks were very white with bright orange feet and beaks, and very black eyes. When Mom let them out in the morning they would head straight down the hill toward the pond—but not in a rush like a flock of hungry chickens. They quickly fell into a long line, a long diagonal line as formal and precise as a line of soldiers, but they waddled along like so many funny ducks—fifty, sixty, maybe seventy of them. A small lame one always brought up the rear.

On the pond under a blue sky with white clouds they made the classic greeting card picture of ducks on a pond—quaint, sentimental, and unforgettable. More than once I wished I could sit on the water so comfortably like those ducks and move about so casually. At feeding time in late afternoon, Mom would call the ducks from up at the duck house. The ducks, way down on the pond, would answer with a chorus of crazy quacking and come scrambling out of the water. But again, there was no pell-mell rush for dinner; they would fall into their straight, diagonal line and march up across the field. The precision of that line of white ducks coming diagonally across the green grass was unforgettable—their orange feet duck-stepping along almost but not quite in unison, their orange beaks tilted slightly up and heads moving almost but not quite in unison, The little one bringing up the rear, struggling heroically to keep up but always managing. (I don't know if these ducks merit inclusion in my story, but there they are just for anyhow.)

The windmill on the Wenger farm stood over a well by the east line fence overlooking the pond in the front pasture. (I'm wondering as I write this whether the reason "they" later wanted to drain that pond was fear that seepage from the pond might contaminate the well water.) This was one of those classic galvanized metal windmills that began appearing on American farms in the 1880s and continued in use through the 1940s when electric power reached the farms thanks to Roosevelt's rural electrification program. Some farms, particularly out west, still rely heavily on these windmills. Grandpa's windmill was almost certainly an Aermotor brand. It pumped water to two reservoirs up near the barn.

Eldon and I never tired of watching that windmill running, now lethargic, now fast enough to make things rattle and screech. The big tail fin or "vane" on the back kept heading the wheel this way or that to keep it facing into the wind. Finally, just watching all this from the high front porch wasn't enough, so, around ages five and six, we went down across the pasture with the set purpose of climbing the windmill tower and checking out the stuff at the top.

As we approached the windmill, I began to be aware how big and tall that thing was. I had been around the windmill before, but its size and height somehow never really registered with me. It was the shadows on the ground that made things different this time. The sun was up about 45 degrees, say around 9:00 a.m. Somehow I realized that, if my shadow there on the ground was the same length as I was tall, then that windmill's height had to be the same as its LONG shadow right there on the ground beside me—that thing was TALL! Furthermore, the shadow of the wheel going round and round on the ground was HUGE! The wheel's blades made a revolving pattern of alternating light and shadow over me that started to feel like when you stand on a foot bridge looking down at the water flowing under you—suddenly you feel like you and the bridge are sweeping up the river while the water is standing still. I actually got a little dizzy standing in those moving shadows.

Eldon, always the monkey, went straight over to the ladder that was fastened to one leg of the windmill; he quickly got himself past those FIRST HIGH RUNGS (that were supposed to keep kids off) and started up. I followed—*Hey, this is easy, and fun!* Then I noticed Eldon's shadow out there on the ground, about halfway up the shadow ladder. *And there's my shadow starting up after him!* I kept looking up at the real Eldon and back down at the shadow Eldon. The fun was changing to nervousness. Then he and his shadow disappeared over the edge of the top platform. Now my shadow was way out there on the ground, halfway up the shadow ladder. I looked straight down—*Oh my, that's a long way down there!* My grip on the ladder tightened. I looked up—*Oh my goodness, there's that wheel up there just over me! It's huge and going round and round! That thing's like a queen, serene and regal, totally indifferent to little scared me clinging down here to its leg, turning a little this way and that like it's busy presiding over the countryside. It's so huge! It's scary!* I closed my eyes and clung to the ladder a few minutes, then started back down. I remember making sure I had a SOLID grip on the next rung before letting go of the previous rung, and I tried not to be looking around. Finally, I was down on solid ground—the good earth was pushing up under both feet!! I backed off from the thing and was quite content to wait for Eldon to come down. Finally he did come down and commenced to tell me of all the machinery up there. Seeing for myself was (and still is) much to be preferred, but this time I was quite content to settle for his secondhand report!

(After writing the above account and rereading it a year or more later—I get butterflies in my stomach all over again!)

Comparing notes with Eldon and with our first cousin, Boyd Burkholder who still has an Aermotor windmill like ours, I've concluded the wheel on our windmill was probably 10 feet in diameter and the top platform was about 30 feet from the ground. Those measurements aren't all that impressive to me now, but I was a little kid then and that was my first close up encounter with such large structures and moving machinery—the shadows showed me how large those things really were—I was overwhelmed.

That reminds me of another time my senses were overwhelmed by a close encounter with large moving machinery—the water wheel at Stoltz's Mill on Singer's Glen Road. Whenever we went to Great-Granddaddy Eli Bowman's house near Singer's Glen, we kids crowded to the left side of the car to see the wheel on that mill. Sometimes we got lucky—"Look, look, it's running!" We wished and wished Dad would stop and let us get a close-up look. Finally, one day he did stop and, after some business inside, he led us along the front of the mill and around the corner to see the wheel. Suddenly, right there in front of me, just a few yards ahead, was this HUGE wheel (actually, just 18 feet or so in diameter). At first it seemed to be rolling right at me, but then I saw it was turning in place. The troughs or buckets on the wheel were going down and down. Water was cascading down over the buckets seeming to come right at me but then dropping down and down out of sight. My eyes were drawn down and down into a roaring watery chasm below the wheel! I felt like I was going headfirst straight down in there!! I was never so viscerally scared, before or since! I nearly fell over. That imagery became the stuff of my bad dreams for several years.

Dad saw that some of the other kids were scared, too; he herded us back to the car and drove off. Well, I digressed...

FARM ANIMALS

I was talking above about Mom's ducks—she also kept geese, and yeah, they had a nasty disposition! A board fence ran from the barn between the two reservoirs and their respective pumps over to Dad's shop. That fence was a perfect perch where a small boy could take part in farm life, that is, watch the comings and goings of those geese, and also sheep, chickens, cattle, horses, cats and people around the pumps and barn. But those geese spoiled the fun of that perch by going MERCILESSLY for my bare toes. A goose doesn't just give a light pinch or peck like a hen does when you reach under her for her eggs. That goose gets a good, firm hold on your toe and commences to jerk-yank-wiggle-twist as though he/she is entitled to it!

Among the sheep was a buck that was also not friendly—I remember lying flat on my back on a pile of rocks with that buck sheep standing over me. I was crying; Dad came and shooed the buck away and picked me up.

The cats—lots of barn cats; well, they were nice and cuddly after I learned you had to be nice to them first. I had to learn by means of cat scratches that if you want a creature to come to you, play with you, and be nice and cuddly—you have to EARN their trust first.

For a time, Eldon and I had the chore of feeding Dicky, an orphan lamb. At first this was fun—he was so cute and playful. All too soon, though, he got big and rough, really rough! He would butt the bottle we held for him. Lambs do that—butt their mother's udder while feeding, hard enough at times to lift her hind end off the ground. Dicky would really knock us around with his head—it was amazing how quick and hard he could shove and butt. We would hold the bottle to him through a fence and even then we stood to one side so he couldn't jam the bottle into our tummy and maybe knock us down. I remember wondering how poor Mother Sheep puts up with that. Eldon reminds me that we dreaded feeding Dicky so much that one morning we deliberately stayed in bed way longer than usual hoping that someone else would feed him. Finally, around nine o'clock we went downstairs; first thing Mom said was, "Boys, go feed Dicky." Duh! We had given up breakfast and all that good morning time and still had to feed Dicky. When Dicky went to market, we were happy.

The cows—were so quiet and tranquil, rarely hurrying, usually just quietly grazing along or lying in some shade comfortably chewing their cud. I liked hanging around in the milking stable when Mom and/or Dad did the milking—by hand. That milking stable, in the lower level of the barn, had 7, 8, or maybe 10 stanchions equipped with a head locking system. When all was ready, you would open the stable door; the cows would hurry in and put their heads through the stanchion opening to get at their feed. Each cow would always go to her own place in the row. You would then quickly close all the openings by sliding a long overhead rail to the left; that closed each window around each cow's neck to hold her in place for milking although it did allow enough freedom for her to feed.

While milking, Mom and Dad sat on little one-legged stools. Though I tried many times I never figured out how you keep your balance on those things. It was amazing how fast they could fill bucket after bucket by just pulling and squeezing on those cows' teats. And it was fun watching the cats lap up their share of the milk that was poured into their pan—I got down close to watch the cupping action of their tongues. I believe it was cousin Mary Louise Ours that taught us how to make drinking straws from wheat straw found everywhere around the barn. Mom cautioned me not to make those drinking straws from the bedding straw there in the stable.

I learned to stay back from the cow's rear end—she could accidentally (I presume) smack you upside the face with her dirty ol' tail while swatting for flies. Also, you might get splattered when she let go that other stuff. Mom would just laugh and say, "You better stay back!" If a cow got to kicking during milking (they sometimes did lose their bovine tranquility), you just tied one end of a rope around the offending hind foot and the other end to the wall behind her. That way you could milk her regardless of her opinion on the matter. When milking was finished you would leave the stable and go around to the end of the row of stanchions and lift the lock from the stanchion rail. When the cows saw you there at the unlocking position, they would all pull their heads back against the stanchion windows; the top rail, being unlocked, would then slide back to the right thus freeing all the cows. They would back out in unison, mill around a bit (you didn't want to be in the stable at that moment), and hurry on out.

Once when I was around age 10, I was herding the cows through a gate from the pasture into the barnyard at milking time. Suddenly, to my complete surprise, one cow decided she wanted nothing to do with this round up. She turned and charged straight at me with her tail high heading for the open gate behind me. Her bovine tranquility was clearly suspended for the moment! I started to head her off but thought better of it as I realized she was coming to a full gallop. I sort of turned to the left and flopped backward to the ground just as she sailed right over me. The sight of a huge cow from the perspective of lying flat on your back looking straight up at her underside as she flies through the air over you, legs outstretched, is unforgettable! I was quite impressed with the view of that cow's belly and the pink color of the skin between her hind legs and her udder. I suppose somebody else rounded her up for milking; I sure didn't. After that incident I would look at those nursery rhyme pictures of the cow jumping over the moon with informed interest.

And, oh yes, there were the chickens—while still quite young Eldon and I had to feed and water the chickens and gather eggs. In one of the chicken houses, getting the feed from the feed barrel was problematic. We were supposed to use a hand scoop to get the feed from the barrel and put it into the feeders where the chickens could get at it. But, when the feed got low in the barrel, we simply couldn't reach it. I don't know if Dad was unaware of this difficulty, or did he just figure we would solve the problem on our own. Well, we did—I climbed into the barrel, and, standing knee-deep in the feed, I would fill the scoop, and hand it over the top to Eldon who then dumped it into the feeders. He would then hand the scoop back to me for a refill. When finished, I would just climb out, dust off my pants (and shoes, if I wasn't barefooted) and get on with farm boy life. Mom never let on about me getting so dusty.

At one point I began noticing how mean and cruel the roosters were. They kept jumping onto the backs of the hens, and it looked like they were really working them over. It looked to me like the poor hen would just hunker down and endure things until he got off and went elsewhere. The hens' backs were getting raw and bloody. I started yelling at "those mean ol' roosters" and chasing them off. Then, one day Eldon quietly relayed a message from Dad: I should just leave those roosters alone; they were supposed to be doing that. Well, OK, but I was still concerned about the hens' sore backs. (In those days, I didn't know that chickens look so bedraggled when they're molting.)

Then there was the day I stooped to look into a nest for eggs. Right there before my astonished eyes I saw an egg being delivered into this world! I already sort of knew where eggs came from but I never dreamed a hen's back end would actually stretch open like that! You can imagine my thoughts for a long time after that when eggs were served at breakfast.

Dad farmed with horses (Tom and Bob) till he got his Case tractor in 1945 when I was age four. Those horses were so big and smelly. I just stayed back out of the way. They would sometimes toss their heads in a way I instinctively knew meant they had a mind of their own and might be impatient or irritated. Sitting here now, remembering the way Ol' Tom looked at me, I think maybe he didn't like children.

Upon writing that last paragraph I began wondering if maybe Tom had reasons for not liking children. So, I called Eldon. "Yes, Ol' Tom had reasons to not like you," he said. He then proceeded to drag the following completely forgotten scene into vivid memory: Eldon and I and Ol' Tom were there in the lot in front of the chicken house. I got to tossing rocks at Tom's heels. At first he just sort of ambled out of the way. I persisted. Suddenly he kicked out both hind legs—high and hard. Eldon says from where he was standing, he could see clearly that Tom's heels went higher than my head; he missed me only because I was short—oh my! (There's another story of me and Ol' Tom; you'll find it later.)

One day Dad was harnessing up and hitching Ol' Tom to a one-row cultivator plough to work the garden. Presumably to keep Tom happy, he handed him a big ear of corn. Tom took that ear crossways in his mouth, the ends sticking out either side, and commenced to roll and crunch on it. Soon he dropped the empty cob to the ground. That made an impression on me— *what a mouth!*

When Dad got the horse and cultivator to the garden, he called me to come and ride the plough. *Oh goody, this'll be fun!* But it wasn't. I quickly caught on this was no joy ride for me; I was there to be extra weight to help hold the plough down. The ride was bumpy and jerky. The horse got sweaty and smelly; Dad got sweaty and smelly; and I was between them—in the corn rows—where there seemed to be no fresh air. It was hot. When Dad heaved and grunted and jerked and thumped the plough on the ground to turn horse and plough around at the end of the rows, I had to hang on for dear life. Despite the bumping and jerking, I was aware of a glimmering of pride in that I was actually making an important contribution to man-size work. Riding that plough right there in front of Dad I could see plainly how hard the ploughman has to work—and I've never forgotten that. Despite that glimmer of pride, I was glad enough when Dad let me jump off. Eldon remembers taking his turn—and he liked it no better.

BASICS OF CONSTRUCTION LEARNED EARLY

From my earliest years, construction, renovation, and repair projects about the farm drew me to the scene like a magnet. I was enthralled with the tools and equipment as well as the project itself. These occasions always included a litany of admonitions from Dad like: "Now, Sonny, you can look but you gotta keep your hands off." Or, "You children can watch but you have to stay back out of the way. We don't want you getting hurt." Or, "I told you to stay out of the way! We can't work with you around here like that."

The first such project was the new bathroom downstairs and the nice concrete floor for the ground level front porch just outside that bathroom wall. I happened to come across Dad and Uncle Menno Suter hunkered down with their heads together, struggling over a hole they were making, I believe, below ground level in the concrete footer below the brick wall. They were using a heavy section of pipe as a battering ram to break through the concrete. They were sweating and grunting and grumbling and fussing. Only later did I comprehend they were installing the sewer line for that new bathroom for Grandpa.

Then there were men all around, pouring concrete into that whole area beneath the second-floor front porch. Some of the guys wearing boots were wading and slopping around in the wet concrete as they distributed it here and there with shovels. I wanted to jump in and play too—I loved the feel of that wet cement—but Dad made Eldon and me stay back out of the way. Then the men began smoothing the concrete by stroking the surface with hand-held trowels, swinging them in big sweeping circles. Suddenly I spied Uncle Oliver with his trowel right out there in the middle of the concrete, but, wonder of wonders, he wasn't sinking in; he was staying right up on top! Then I saw he was squatting on a board, which had been laid out across the still mostly wet concrete, and from there he could reach the far side with his trowel.

Somehow Eldon and I knew that any concrete project had to include footprints of any children who happened to be present. We must have been told to "just be patient, it's not time for that yet." I remember waiting and waiting and hoping they wouldn't forget. Finally Dad called Eldon and me over and showed us, one at a time, just where he wanted us to put our foot. I was surprised and delighted with the cool, damp cement, squishing between my toes, forming around the heel, caressing the arch; I started to squash my foot down hard. Dad grabbed my foot—"No, Sonny, not so hard!" Then Eldon put his foot on the assigned place, but he obeyed Dad's instruction to press lightly. Those footprints are still there—and mine is the deeper one! The size of those prints confirms my sense that Eldon and I were somewhere in the 1-3 age range at the time. I never forgot those lessons in how to work concrete, including how to help children leave their footprints for posterity.

The second "life learning project" began when Uncle Menno brought several carpenters to install a new hardwood floor in Grandpa and Grandma's living room downstairs. I was five or so at the time, Eldon a year younger. I took note of the tar paper (or some such thing) they first put down on the concrete subfloor; that was to keep the moisture from rotting out this new floor like it did the old one. Then they put down two-by-two's to serve as floor joists. Then came the hardwood flooring boards—this was my first exposure to nice, newly planed, fresh smelling lumber—the smooth wood texture, the light tan color with darker grain patterns, the smell of it—I was in love with wood for life. I was right there in the middle of things, Dad's

litany about staying out of the way ringing in my ears. I took
in how the boards fit together with tongues and grooves. I liked
how the carpenters made the nails invisible by driving them in at
an angle in the groove and then driving the head further in out
of the way with a nail set; the tongue of the next board fitting
into that groove would then conceal the nail hole.

Outside I walked up to where a carpenter had a number of
boards laid across a pair of sawhorses. I reached up to finger the
boards and get a closer look at the grain patterns in the wood.
Suddenly—WHACK! The carpenter on the other side of the
boards had reached across and whacked the back of my hand
with his hard knuckles; it hurt. I looked up into a quiet, angry
face that was trying to avoid eye contact. Eldon had been warning me, "Those men are getting mad at you."

Dad saw this and immediately assigned me, and Eldon
too, to some specific area—"You boys may watch from here but
you dare not get any closer. If you don't listen, I'll send you in
to Mom."

My unspoken thought—*How's anybody supposed to see anything from here?*

Finally, back in the living room, it was time to fit the last
floorboard into place against the wall. The board, of course, was
too wide. When I walked up, the carpenter was preparing to cut
the board lengthwise to fit the space. He placed a small block of
wood against the wall and held a carpenter's pencil against that.
Then he moved the block and pencil along the wall; the pencil
made a line on the board—a curving line that exactly matched
the curving wall. (That wall was old plaster applied directly to
brick and was not at all straight; the board had to be made to fit
the contours of the wall.) Next he took the board outside and
worked a long time with a small hand held saw cutting it end to

end along the curving pencil line. When he took it back inside, wonder of wonders, it fit right into place! Many times during our remaining time at the Wenger place I reexamined the fit of that board against that curving wall and was "re-impressed" with the carpenter's skill. By the end of this project, the love of woodworking—the feel and smell of freshly worked lumber, the way wood can be used for so many different purposes, the way wood lends itself to careful fitting of parts, the sheer joy of handling tools—the love of woodworking, I say, was rooted deep in me for life!

GRANDPA AND GRANDMA WENGER

My favorite place in that Wenger house had always been those downstairs living quarters for Grandpa and Grandma Wenger. My earliest memory down there is Grandpa and Grandma at the breakfast table, just inside the east window in the kitchen. I liked the yellow of the rising sun, the yellow of the butter on the bread, and the yellow of the eggs; it was so cheerful. If I would ask, Grandma would give me some butter bread, and sometimes, sugar bread—I was very small then—small enough to be wearing a dress. Now, the new hardwood floor accentuated the quiet and pleasant atmosphere. The smooth wood was a delight to play on—for one thing it felt warmer to the skin on a cold day. Sometimes I would just lie on my tummy and study the grain patterns in the wood. The light color added a subdued brightness to the lighting in the room. That floor was the perfect place for setting up my first Erector Set. Later Eldon and I would come in there after school (before checking in upstairs) and spread the newspaper out on that nice floor to read the funnies.

Grandpa in his armchair and Grandma in her rocking chair were a quiet and peaceful presence. Sometimes Grandma read to us from her old McGuffey readers. Sometimes she let us look at her Bible story comic books—these were Bible stories in comic book format; that's a format I think should be retried today.

Grandpa mostly just sat, quiet and dignified, never grouchy or threatening—not to me anyway; Eldon recalls Grandpa reaching across with his cane and rapping him on the head for some infraction.

I need to tell you more about Grandpa Wenger—Daniel P. Wenger was born April 16, 1870, died March 14, 1948. He was a quiet and devout man, a lifelong member of the Valley Mennonite Community. He frequently contributed money and labor to many church building projects around the Valley. He had eight children with his first two wives, Annie and Emma Heatwole (they were cousins), both of whom died of TB. In 1924 he married Laura Suter next door, daughter of Emmanuel Suter, the potter. Laura's niece, Grace Suter Grove, told me, "We believe he proposed to her in the barn where she was milking the cow." Also in 1924 he bought his first car, a Dodge touring car with two full width seats and a cloth top—a new wife and a new car in the same year! Four years later in 1928, at age 58, Daniel was told by his doctor that he had heart problems and should not work. He reportedly went home, sat down, and never worked again—but he lived another 20 years. Mom told me that about that same time some runaway horses dragged a farm wagon over him and that may have contributed to his precipitous retirement.

The last seven of those sedentary years were the first seven of my years. Hence it was that Grandpa's quiet presence in that easy chair came to be a warm secure space for me!

Grandpa was sedentary, almost passive, yes, but I did see him move quickly, very quickly, four times.

The first time—I was walking down the sidewalk on the east side of the house; I was age 3 or so. I was barefooted. My heel bumped something. I looked down and saw a garden hose—only wait a minute, it moved! Then it disappeared into the grass. I went on down to the front of the house and in to Grandpa in his easy chair. "I just saw a big worm out there," I said, "this big (gesturing with my fingers)!" Grandpa's quiet face came wide awake and alive. He made me repeat my story and show him again how big. He then practically jumped up out of his chair, hurried into the cellar and got a hoe. *Man, his legs were long!* He went around to the side of the house prepared to dispatch a snake. He never found it. For a long time after that adults and kids were mighty careful going by that area.

Second time—It was a pleasant day, I was 3 or 4 years old. I was riding my tricycle back and forth on the ground level front porch. Grandpa was sitting there slouched down and snoozing in his outdoor rocking chair. He had it turned sideways so I could get past easily. After several passes, I wanted to wake him up—you know, I wanted to give him a child's love pat that said in effect, "Hey Grandpa, wake up and notice me!" I meant to tap him on the chest or shoulder on my next pass; I missed and hit him in the face. He jerked awake, his eyes popped open, his glasses went a flyin'; he caught them in midair! It was all so funny to me; I cackled and rode on. I turned around and came back past him. To my surprised amazement he suddenly had me by the arm and brought me to a screeching halt. He leaned toward me with a tired sternness on his face I hadn't seen before. "Don't you do that again," he rasped slowly. I didn't.

Third time—Dad was working in the shop. This time, for whatever reason, Grandpa was there, too. Whenever that shop door was open, I was IN THERE, exploring and rummaging around in any boxes, drawers, or buckets in reach. I would hold up any newfound treasure and ask, "Daddy, what's this?" And then maybe, "Can I have it?" This time, all the way in the back, I found a big paper sack, about as tall as me. I reached inside and found a whole bunch of big candles. I pulled one out—*Wow, I never saw a candle so big!* I liked the heft of it in my hand; it was all waxy. I held it up—"Daddy, what's this?"

Suddenly Dad and Grandpa were both rushing at me, yelling, "No, no, NO, Sonny, NO, NO!!" It scared me so bad I flung that candle with all my might, just off to Grandpa's right. It crashed into shop clutter in a far corner.

Well, those "candles" were sticks of dynamite! Dad had been using dynamite to blast stumps out of the old orchard field. I now know that dynamite, when properly stored, does not explode when jostled or bumped, but it's still a scary thought—I threw a stick of dynamite at Dad and Grandpa!

Fourth time—Around 1946 (I was age five) Dad bought a McCormick Dearing combine. He was preparing to do custom combining. He was busy checking, adjusting things, and pumping a grease gun on all the grease nipples around the machine—he was obviously enjoying his new toy. Grandpa (he had bestirred himself from his easy chair) and I were checking this thing out, too. *Look at all these wheels and pulleys and V-belts and sprockets and chains and levers and what-not!* I was enthralled. Over on the other side Dad cranked up the engine and got it running all nice and smooth. Right there in front of me was this big 18-inch V-belt pulley; it had a connecting rod that connected to a shaker toward the back of the combine.

What was there about that belt and pulley? It consumed my attention. To comprehend and appreciate it I had to get my hands on it. I socked my right hand, palm up, into the crotch where the belt met the pulley—JUST AS DAD EASED FORWARD ON THE CLUTCH LEVER!! He did not fully engage the clutch; he was still just checking and testing things. But the machinery rolled forward just enough to catch and hold my hand between the belt and the pulley. It wasn't hurting much, but I couldn't get my hand free. Grandpa saw all this and instantly yelled to Dad to stop the machine. Dad released the clutch lever; the pulleys and belts rocked back enough to release my hand! Dad ran around the back of the combine, grabbed my hand, and inspected it carefully. There were red marks, but no bruises or broken bones! If Grandpa hadn't immediately yelled to dad, my arm would have been dragged up under that connecting rod and…I probably wouldn't have survived. Dad and Grandpa and I just stood there, all breathless. Dad saw clearly he didn't have to lecture me much about staying back from all such machinery—and to this day I am CAREFUL about belts and pulleys—though I still love them.

There's one other vivid picture of Grandpa I want to include here. Soon after Dad got that combine, he began building a lean-to shed to house it. It was early morning; Dad was trying to get a heavy beam, maybe 20 feet long, properly placed and level across some rocks or cement blocks. Grandpa was flat down on the hard, gravelly ground sighting across the beam to help get it aligned. When Grandpa went to get up, he could hardly manage. Dad immediately ran to him, grabbed his hand and helped him up. The morning sun was low such that I could clearly see both their faces—Dad wore a look of boyishly bashful respect and admiration for his father-in-law; Grandpa was mildly amused and embarrassed about his awkwardness and very appreciative of his son-in-law's help. It was clear to my young mind those two men appreciated each other!

One morning in March, 1948 (I was almost seven), I cut one of those funny face masks from a cereal box and went downstairs to show it to Grandma and Grandpa. To my surprise Aunt Lena, Aunt Marie, and some others were there. Someone quickly took me by the shoulder and explained in a kindly way that it was not appropriate right now to wear that funny face. I took it off and stood around watching. Nobody shooed me off. Then I saw Grandpa, in his undershirt and shorts, sitting on the edge of a bed, looking rather frail and shaky; someone was holding him up. His legs and arms seemed awfully long and skinny. Aunt Marie, I think it was, had a hypodermic syringe and proceeded to give him a shot in his left arm. He was groaning and groaning and groaning; I finally made out what he was saying—"I wanna go heaven, I wanna go heaven," over and over. I then understood he was dying.

ESCAPADES

The Wenger farm was a wonderful setting for lots of childhood escapades, expeditions and projects.

The earliest escapade I recall was Eldon's. Baby Jim was lying in his crib. This crib (nowadays we would say "playpen") that Mom used for most all of her babies was a somewhat narrow homemade thing that stood on tall legs; the top rails were maybe waist high to an adult. I know now the thing had to be rather tipsy, though I knew of no such mishap back then. Eldon, almost age four, got the notion he wanted to love and adore Baby Jim. Being half monkey from the get-go, he must have figured the best way to address Baby Jim was from high overhead. When I turned and saw this, Eldon was standing astride the crib, his feet on the two side rails, straight up over Baby Jim, looking down and jabbering off a long string of loving baby talk to dear little baby brother Jim. His face had that certain look adults get when adoring a baby. Just then Mom came around the corner from the kitchen. With one smooth, emphatic move she swept Eldon from atop that crib and carried him off to the kitchen. As they went out of my hearing she was saying, "I told you…," and Eldon was protesting, "But I forgot…" That scene of a three, not quite four-year-old, standing atop the crib rails adoring his baby brother would make a wonderful Norman Rockwell painting!

The second escapade I remember, and which Eldon to this day dearly loves to tell on me, was, according to Eldon, my insti-gation. Shirley was age two, Eldon four, and I was five. The three of us went bumpity-bumping down the long farm lane with the trike and "little red wagon." Somewhere along the way, the offi-cial reason for this expedition became "to fetch the mail from the roadside mailbox." Well, the mail wasn't there yet. So now, how could we get the mailman to hurry up and come? A wonder-ful solution came to mind—we would ride the trike and wagon back and forth on the road in front of the lane; that would make the mailman hurry up and come! The road was paved with black top; it was delightful how smoothly the trike pedaled and how easily the wagon rolled along even with Little Shirley in it. This was FUN! Our excursions back and forth in front of the lane got longer and longer. Finally we seemed to break loose from some invisible constraint and went on up the road about two tenths of a mile, past Mom's cousin Lewis Wenger's house, to Uncle Jake Wenger's little red brick house. We turned into the front yard and played a little while under some nice low, cool shade trees. Then Little Shirley wet herself. I helped her get her wet undies off and carefully stowed them in the wagon—we didn't want to lose those.

With Shirley now quite content to play there under the trees, Eldon and I found our way back to Aunt Martha's hen house. Now, what do you do with a hen house? You go in, of course. So we did. There were lots of hens, and, wow, eggs lying everywhere! We quickly discovered (Eldon insists I did the discovering) if you smash an egg on the ground in front of a hen, she'll gobble it up like she's starving. We verified this finding with several repetitions. Then we discovered (Eldon insists I was still the creative leader) the satisfying "smack" and bright yellow flash when we threw eggs against the back wall of the hen house. That wall looked ever so much better in bright egg yolk yellow, so our official reason for this visit became "to paint that whole back wall bright egg yolk yellow." Just as our project was progressing nicely, meaning the yellow patch on the wall was getting nice and big, Eldon stiffened and got awfully worried. The door had opened and there was Aunt Martha. Eldon says the thunder cloud on her face told him we were in big trouble. I caught on more slowly. She herded us into the house and set us to playing with a set of rubber bricks that you stuck together a little like modern Lego block. The rubber bricks were fun, but that phone call Aunt Martha made to Mom sounded ominous. So did Aunt Martha's next words, "You all stay right there and play with those bricks till your Mother gets here."

Mom did get there, soon; her usually sweet disposition had an ominous edge to it. She marched us out of there and up the road; goodness, she seemed in a hurry. She carried Little Shirley in one arm and dragged the trike with the other; Eldon and I had to follow with the wagon. Mom informed us, "When we get home y'all are gonna get a switchin'." The sun was hot. That walk, two tenths of a mile, on the hot pavement and up the bumpy lane to certain judgement was not fun! At the head of the lane by the barn, Mom abandoned the trike and wagon and marched the three of us down a steep hill to a wonderful, big, old sycamore tree (which still stands there as of this writing). She quickly had herself a nice switch and turned to me first—me first, I suppose, as the oldest child, but Eldon will surely insist it was me first as the ringleader. When I was reduced to suitable dancing and tears, Mom turned to Eldon. Eldon, being very intelligent, had noticed that when I started crying, Mom quit switching. He therefore saw to it that he was crying before the switch landed on leg; his switching was much less severe than mine. As to Little Shirley—I simply cannot remember if Mom addressed her with that switch; she was, after all, only two and was not in the hen house. But as to sweet innocence on Shirley's part, consider this: Before she died Mom told me, "When Shirley came along after two boys, I was so happy to have me a nice little girl who would behave, but she turned out to be just as big a duck in the puddle as the rest of you."

Several years ago I called Aunt Martha and asked if she remembered Eldon and me in her hen house. She certainly did! She said Lewis' wife, Ethel, called and said she'd better go check her hen house. Ethel had watched these three kids with the trike and wagon going past on the road looking up to no good. When the two boys went into the hen house, she called Martha. I wonder how long that yellow "paint" remained on that hen house wall.

Then there was the day Eldon, Shirley and I were playing with an old tricycle wheel—it was just the hub, the spokes, and the rim; the rubber tire was gone. The bench grinder Dad used to sharpen the knives on his field mower was sitting on the big work bench in the wagon shed. The brand new white 1949 Ford was parked alongside that work bench, maybe three feet over. That trike wheel fit perfectly on the end of the grinder shaft opposite the emery wheel. We would slip the wheel on the shaft and then plug in the motor. The wheel would chatter madly a bit and then start spinning as fast as the emery wheel. After a minute or so it would drop off the shaft and land spinning on the work bench. The metal edges of the rim would bite into the wood of the bench and send the wheel "a flyin' every which way!" The wheel would bounce off the bench down onto the ground and go bounding and ricocheting around the shed making the dirt fly. Sometimes it would bound from the bench over to the side of the car (!) and then down to the ground. We did this again and again and doubled over laughing at the antics of that wheel! I don't know about the others, but I was learning basic lessons about flywheels and angular momentum.

Later that day, or was it the next day, Dad rounded up the three of us and marched us back to that wagon shed. He had a switch in his hand and was clearly about to use it. So what evil had we done? He pointed to the side of the car around the door handle indicating that we were to look at the damage we had done—we had scratched the paint on our brand new white '49 Ford with that trike wheel! He then applied the switch to all three of us. I don't know that Shirley deserved the switch; she did nothing more than laugh at the fun. But for Dad that was complicity. He often said, "If you run with the wolves, you'll have to howl with the wolves." If you must know, you can figure out our ages for yourself—I'm too embarrassed to say. (Hint: I specified "brand new 1949 Ford.")

Maybe here's a good place to interject some comments about Dad's punishments. He usually used a switch. He went for the bare legs; he meant to sting. He never beat with a big stick or leather belt; he never did the pants down, bare bottom thing; he never knocked or kicked a kid around the room—of such things I knew nothing until I heard some of the VSDB kids talking about their home lives. If Dad was angry, you knew it. His "I don't mean maybe..." was menacing. He had no tolerance for infantile temper tantrums. I can't say all his disciplinary sessions were right on target, especially for adolescent and teen-aged kids, but he surely tried to be fair and, as he would urgently add BIBLICAL in his "training up a child in the way he should go." He often quoted the maxim, "Spare the rod and spoil the child." But he also quoted scripture, "Fathers, provoke not your children to anger." I once heard him agonizing with one of his brothers about suitable punishment for a recalcitrant child—in other words, it wasn't easy for him to punish a child, and I know now it isn't easy. Many years later when I thought I had to spank a naughty child, I found myself slapping the side of my leg to gauge how hard not to spank. In a flash I understood why Dad was switching his own leg one time when he approached me for a "session"—back then I saw it as a menacing gesture, but I now see he was actually gauging how hard not to apply that switch. It's also worth noting that Dad's (and Mom's) punishment and discipline became lighter and more relaxed over the years as more kids came along, and we older kids like to remind the younger kids of that fact. OK, enough of that. Back to my story.

DAD—INVENTIVE FARMER AND TOY MAKER

Dad was a very inventive, do-it-yourself kind of farmer. In addition to routine farm work he was constantly repairing and designing and building tools, gadgets and mechanical devices. He installed modern plumbing—meaning digging many ditches BY HAND for running water to the house and many of the outbuildings on that Wenger farm. He designed and built livestock shelters, feeding and watering equipment for the turkeys and modified various farm buildings. In addition to all these projects, he built a number of toys for us kids; and some of these toy projects had to have taken significant time and energy from his other work.

One day I came across Dad painting something a very bright orange on top the living room stove. I climbed up on a chair and pushed in amidst his nervous fussing about watching out for wet paint and not upsetting the little paint can. *Wow, look at that!* Dad had made two wooden locomotives, about 8 or 9 inches long, probably cut from an old 2-by-4. There was a smokestack, sand dome, a cowcatcher, and a peg for a hitch on the back. He was painting them on top the stove because his shop was too cold for painting. When the paint was dry, or almost dry he put four wheels on each engine—roller skate wheels, steel with ball bearings! Boy, did those engines scoot across the floor, and they sure made Mom nervous!

Sometime after that Dad was in the shop fiddling around with angle iron and lots of bolts and nuts and an electric motor. Soon he had himself a wood lathe and was turning out lots of funny little wooden pieces and some larger wheels. Then, two little John Deere tractors showed up on top the same living room stove, freshly painted authentic John Deere green and yellow. They were about 9 or 10 inches long. The 4-inch wooden rear wheels had shiny black tires painted on. Each tractor had a seat, steering wheel, exhaust pipe, air cleaner, a pulley, and a peg for a hitch—all were little wooden turnings from the homemade lathe, all carefully painted black. Those tractors were a beautiful sight for any farm boy! And most amazing of all—the front wheels TURNED! They were ball bearing furniture casters. That made our tractors the envy of our cousins and school friends—the front wheels on their fancy

store-bought tractors DID NOT turn. Eldon and I, and then
Jim and Bernard, played with those tractors a long time. To my
knowledge, that homemade lathe was not used for any other
specific project—at least not by Dad. Eldon and I later learned
basic turning skills on that lathe.

Little wooden propellers on wooden handles showed up
that we would hold out the car window. Dad made the first
one and then Eldon and I learned from our Burkholder cousins
across the road how to make them for ourselves. You start with a
stick of soft wood about five or six inches long and maybe three
quarters of an inch square. You drill a hole in the center, clamp
it in a bench vice, and use a wood file to shape the blades. Then
you put a nail through the hole and drive it into the end of another short stick to serve as a handle. The idea was to grab the
handle and hold the propeller out the car window in the wind.
The propeller would spin like mad, and because they were never
well balanced, the handle would vibrate intensely in your hand,
making it almost numb. We would urge Dad to "go faster," and
he would push the car up to fifty or fifty-five—very fast for those
curving country roads. He enjoyed making those propellers buzz
as much as we did. We also learned that a propeller can really
crack a knuckle if you reach into it too soon after bringing it
back into the car.

Dad's biggest toy project was a pedal tractor and, boy, was
it a dandy! I was around age seven by now. Over several days
or weeks I saw him in the shop cutting and bending and welding various pieces of pipe into something I couldn't recognize.
By bending I mean heavy heaving and grunting and making his
muscles ripple. I was curious about several ten-inch wheels and
some V-belt pulleys lying around there but Dad just kept insisting I stay out of his way.

Then one morning when we came down for breakfast there was a very strong smell of fresh paint and, right there in the middle of the living room, was a beautiful JOHN DEERE PEDAL TRACTOR! It was brightly painted in true John Deere green and yellow, and, on either side the engine hood was a true John Deere logo. (I understood later that Dad got the decals for that logo from Smith and Cary, the John Deere dealer in town.) The steering wheel and seat were shiny black. The frame or skeleton of this tractor was not the light and strong tube steel found in store-bought pedal toys; it was that heavy pipe I saw Dad bending and welding up earlier in the shop. The hood was nice sheet metal work secured by rivets, not sheet metal screws. The steering wheel shaft was connected to the front fork with a nifty universal joint Dad had made. Instead of the typical chain drive connecting the pedals to the rear axle, this tractor had a V-belt drive—the significance of which we would soon learn. The pedals were mounted on a swinging bearing post controlled by a "gear shift lever"—when we pulled the lever back into a lock position, it pushed the pedals forward and put tension on the belt; the tractor was then "in gear"; if we pushed the lever forward it would release the belt tension and the tractor was "out of gear." And, there was a hitch on the back.

Well, we started riding that tractor round and round in the house—from the living room into the kitchen, out into the hall and back around to the living room, happily bumping over all the thresholds. I don't know about Eldon but I was soon aware I was relearning a life lesson I had learned earlier on the trike—WHEELED VEHICLES HAVE A REAR END YOU NEED TO ALLOW FOR WHEN TURNING CORNERS! Earlier on the trike my rear axle had made notches in the baseboard at both ends of the hall. Mom was not happy about that. Now my tractor's rear axle—higher because of larger rear wheels and more deadly due to greater total weight of vehicle and boy—was making new notches bigger and higher up on the same baseboard. Mom was even more unhappy. That tractor was forthwith BANISHED to outdoors! No matter how cold, it would be for outdoor use only! (By the way, those notches in the hall baseboard are still there.)

We mostly rode the tractor on the ground level front porch and out the sidewalk to the barn. We did sometimes get onto grass or hard packed dirt, but with that V-belt drive it pedaled too hard for much of anything other than level concrete or hard barn floor. Dad was aware of the friction issue with that V-belt. He showed us how to tinker with the tension adjustment mechanism, and soon I had learned a life lesson about V-belts—you have to strike a balance between low tension for easy running and high enough tension to avoid slipping under heavy load (such as boy-size heaves on the pedals). Eldon and I, and even little Shirley, noticed and talked excitedly about the easy, easy pedaling of our Suter cousins' store-bought tractor—it was much lighter and, most amazing, had a CHAIN drive! We became a bunch of little experts on issues of weight for pedal toys and the relative merits of chain versus belt drives. We wanted a chain drive but we knew well that our tractor was special anyway.

There was another life lesson coming at us with this tractor. We caught on immediately that the pedals drove only the right rear wheel. Consequently the tractor pedaled very hard when turning right and ever so easily when turning left. And generally, the tractor tended to veer to the left, especially when you put a boy-size heave on the pedals. I began wishing out loud to Dad that the pedals would power both rear wheels. Maybe I would then have enough control and traction to pedal up some of the hills and banks around there. You know how it is, a true boy (any age) is always wanting to see how steep a hill he can make his tractor climb—right? Dad didn't dismiss me with a grumpy "Be satisfied with what you have!" Rather, he explained that, without something called a "differential," if you make the pedals power both rear wheels, the tractor will be very difficult to steer and generally it will pedal much, much harder.

Well, believe it or not, one day there sat the tractor with TWO V-belts running from the pedals to the rear axle. Dad had gone to a lot of trouble to convert to a two-wheel drive system. I was on the tractor in an instant, and, *Woah here, this thing pedals HARD! And hey, when I try to steer the thing, it feels like it's glued to the ground!* So that's what Dad was talking about! Why didn't he make one belt drive both wheels? That could have been done and there wouldn't be so much friction with just one belt. Then I caught on—there was a reason for two belts. With the twin belt system, you could switch back and forth between one or two-wheel drive by simply dropping the belt off one of the rear pulleys. That way you could run most of the time in on-wheel drive for easier pedaling, but switch to two-wheel drive when more traction was needed.

And there was more —along with the twin belt drive Dad also converted that little red wagon—that wagon of ill repute that earlier found its way to Aunt Martha's hen house—into a trailer to pull behind the tractor. *Hot diggity dog!* Now I would see if two-wheel drive would allow me to pull that trailer up the hill at the west side of the house! I saw immediately I had plenty of traction, but now the question was whether I had enough boy power to use the traction. The friction of the two V-belts, the combined weight of the tractor and trailer, and the intractable steering—*Well, OK, OK, just forget two-wheel drive! But wow, it was fun experimenting!* So, we didn't use the two-wheel drive or trailer much, but we had learned A LOT and it was especially fun working as an "equal" partner with Dad on this experiment.

I have included those many details about that tractor both because they were such a big chunk of my boyhood and because they show something important about Dad. Thanks to my own adult experience with shop projects I now know that the amount of thought, time and energy required to produce that tractor (and those other toys) was prodigious! That was time and energy away from his busy farm work. Mom told me shortly before she died that Dad and his brothers had almost zero play time as children. They were ALWAYS working—hard work like planting potatoes, hoeing potatoes and corn and what not, picking strawberries, digging thistles, weeding the garden, etc. So, with our toys Dad was clearly working on unfinished business from his own childhood. The younger kids knew nothing of this side of Dad—by the time they came along, he was preoccupied with the more urgent matters of "making ends meet."

To underscore this—there was the time Eldon and I were working with some kites and it wasn't going well. Suddenly Dad showed up, on the run, and worked with us a while trying to get the tails right. Then he said he had to get back to work, and hurried off, running back to the field where he was working.

BICYCLES

Sometime after this I found Dad again in the shop puttering around. My curiosity quickly ratcheted up to keen interest as I took in two bicycle wheels lying over there and realized Dad was heaving and grunting over a bicycle frame. I had just learned to ride a bicycle on Leroy Kiser's bike a few weeks earlier when

Dad was helping Leroy's dad clean out his chicken house. Now, Dad had brought home a blue 24-inch girl's bike that had been run over. He soon had it straightened out and reassembled and *Whoopee*, Eldon and I, and soon Sister Shirley, were riding all over the farm. And, well, that bike forced us into some more life lessons—you have to take turns!

The next morning Eldon jumped out of bed early; he was going to ride that bike. I didn't want to get up so early, but I certainly didn't want him getting in a lot more riding time than me. So I dragged myself out of bed and followed him outside. The cold wet grass on my bare feet made me even more grumpy. I told him he shouldn't be riding the bike so early because the grass was still wet from the dew and that wouldn't be good for the tires. He stuck his nose up at my "superior understandings" and rode off. Mom's call to a nice warm breakfast defused the situation.

That "little blue bike," as we called it became the first occasion for me to discover that, in the minds of some folks at least, I had a vision impairment. I was really getting the hang of the bike and discovering how easy it was to go fast; you know—that nice breeze in your ears. I came barreling in through the lot and skidded to a stop right alongside where Mom and Dad and some of the other kids were standing at the backyard gate. My thinking was something like, *Wow, look how I can ride this thing!* but Dad's thinking was quite different; he scolded, "Sonny, you're too reckless! You need to remember you can't see very well and mustn't ride so fast!" I was shocked and puzzled—I had seen everybody standing there perfectly well and knew I was in control despite the gravel-scattering stop. I kept on riding my own way and Dad must have soon concluded that I was seeing and handling the bike just fine; I never again heard a word of that sort, not even as I came into the tractor driving stage.

Then one day Eldon showed up riding into the lot on a brand new bright red 26-inch boy's bike—AND IT HAD TANKS! He said he found it in the buggy shed. I wasn't sure we were supposed to have the thing but he said, "No, Dad means for us to have it." If Dad had been planning to make some grand presentation, we happily enough spoiled that. Did he mean for us to "just find it" in the buggy shed? We never knew.

Later Uncle Paul (then living across the road in the Lewis Wenger house) told me, "I saw that bike before you boys did. It was first stored here at my place, and, yeah, I saw your Daddy riding it and doing wheelies with it." Dad must have ordered that bike and had it delivered to Uncle Paul's place where he then "checked it out." After that Eldon and I were two boys on their bikes all over the place, and gradually, on the country roads around there, too. And Shirley got in her riding time, too.

ANIMALS HAVE FEELINGS

Soon after getting those bikes, Eldon and I undertook a mission to get rid of some starlings. We knew that robins and cardinals and bluebirds and the like were good birds and we should protect them. But starlings—they were bad birds and should be gotten rid of, you know, like you get rid of mice. We knew of a nest of starlings in a fence post in the back pasture. We rode our bikes back there intending to do the world a service by cleaning out that nest. We got out a baby bird and put it down on one of those flat limestone rocks in the grass. The bird began squawking. We rolled the front wheel of the blue bike over the bird. He just squawked louder. We tried the front wheel of the red bike which was heavier. He just kept squawking. This business was suddenly getting unpleasant. We bounced the wheel of the red bike on the bird, rolling it back and forth over him. That didn't faze him either; he just kept hollering. It was clear now that little birdie didn't want to get dead. We were desperate. He was surely injured so we couldn't just give up and put him back in the nest. We had to get him out of his misery. But how? Then Eldon found a rock he could handle. I turned away as he finished the job. We were both miserable. We rode away from there—nevermind the birdies still in the nest—each in our own thoughts.

To this day, that episode with the starlings grips me as a profound moment. As an innocent child I had discovered a certain reality in the way we humans are hardwired—namely, we can't cause pain or take a life without very unpleasant inner qualms. If we are angry or if we have certain rationalizations such as the need to harm or kill in self-defense or for food, we may not feel these qualms, or at least we can live with them. In this incident I was neither angry nor pressed by threat or hunger, so I was fully exposed to the awfulness of what I had done—yes, we are hardwired to feel such actions as awful, yucky!

I got more acquainted with this internal yuckiness—I found that a kitty would put on a dramatic show if I put him down on a piece of discarded linoleum lying in the grass just out of reach of a barking dog. The linoleum was slick so the kitty had no traction. He would stretch out to full length running in place. I would laugh with amazed delight as I "studied his marvelous athletic prowess." When he finally reached the grass where he had some traction, he was ONE GONE CAT!! Then I caught on—that kitty wasn't happily demonstrating feline athleticism, he was a TERRIFIED CREATURE!! Yucky remorse closed in.

I had the same reaction when I dumped a kitty into a watering trough—*Wow, how that Kitty can swim!* Scratches on my arm, from wrist to elbow, inflicted as he scrambled out of there and AWAY, no doubt hastened the awareness, *Hey, dumping a cat into a watering trough is cruelty.*

And, I would go on to learn that teasing and picking on sibs and other kids beyond mutual fun was also, "not nice," and eventually, with Mom's firm pronouncement, "Daniel, it's wrong to pick on so-and-so like that," I saw it was actually MORALLY wrong!

There are more stories like these (which some of my sibs like to tell on me) but I'm going to spare the reader and, well yes, me too, anymore such details.

Well, wait a minute, there is one more story I should include here. Dad and the Suter cousins, Everett and Nelson, were using a horse, Ol' Tom, to operate the hay fork to lift big bunches of hay from the wagon up into the haymow in the barn. They finished a load and tied Ol' Tom to the board fence that ran between the shop and the barn and took the wagon out to the field to get another load. I was around age four. I was on the opposite side of the fence from Tom. I got to tossing gravels at him. Suddenly my interest was hooked—that big ol' heavy beast could actually move quickly in response to my teasing! Then I found a bigger rock and landed that right on his muzzle just below his eyes. This time he "moved" really quickly and DRAMATICAL-LY! He jerked his massive head back, reared TALL on his hind legs and broke the strap holding him to the fence; he wheeled and galloped off. Now I was in distress. The sound of that rock on Tom's nose was sickening—that had to hurt, and yes, (discover discover) causing pain to an animal was bad, very bad. Furthermore, what's Dad gonna do when he finds Tom GONE? Well, when the men came back and found Tom gone, Everett (I believe it was Everett) just went out and fetched him back and hitched him up to the fork and they just resumed their work—

no questions asked. But I was still left with that yuckiness inside. What wonders me now is that I had to rediscover so many times "it is bad to cause pain to a living creature." I suppose that was the process of developing a moral faculty but I would be happier with myself now if I had learned faster.

A couple months after writing the above several paragraphs I recall what must have been my very first encounter with those inner qualms about causing pain to animals. On a beastly hot day I discovered that the brand new concrete floor of the lower front porch was oh so cool and pleasant to lie and roll around on. I must have been age five or so. On my tummy with my near-sighted vision I took note of the tan and blueish-gray and white details in the concrete. Along came some ants. I expunged several with my finger. Then I began wondering something like, "Do ants have feelings? Might their mommy be crying when they don't come home?" I began exploring and experimenting with "crying" on behalf of the ants' mommy. I don't really think it was a very convincing cry, but Grandma did come to her kitchen door and asked, "Daniel, what's wrong?" Embarrassed, I mumbled something about, "…just pretending."

OLD LUMBER AND OLD WHEEL

That Wenger place was an ideal place for a couple of kids to learn the basics of woodworking. A lot of fairly nice, flat boards from old fences and weather boarding from old buildings lay around everywhere, and we could pretty well help ourselves. We made ramps and catwalks in the barn, a little work bench "upstairs" in the pig house. We were allowed to use the hammer, handsaw, hacksaw, screwdrivers, pliers and wrenches, wood and metal files, brace and bits (hand drill and bits), the vice grip pliers and shop vice, the old drill press in the shop, the grinder with the emery wheel, and even Dad's homemade wood lathe. We were NOT allowed to use the table saw. Old bolts and nuts and washers and screws and nails must have been carefully saved by somebody in the past just for a future couple of farm boys! About those nails—most of them were bent—folks in yesteryear didn't throw away a single nail just because it was bent; so, we learned to straighten and use them. Three projects keep coming up when Eldon and I start reminiscing—the barn, the treehouse, and the cart.

THE BARN

I suppose it's not all that unusual for a couple of farm boys with lots of scrap lumber lying around to get the idea they want to build a barn. It wasn't all that big but I'm still sort of proud of the engineering we pulled off. We were in the six to eight age range. Eldon somehow managed to "toenail" slender vertical pieces to the floor at the four corners. These seemed awfully flimsy to me—the posts were split in many places by the nails—but we did manage to make them support the old weather boards we nailed on for the walls. We overlapped those boards in true weather boarding fashion. We did the required framing to support the weather boards at the front and back door openings. We made the proper angled cuts in some more slender pieces to serve as rafters for gabled ends and toenailed them in place—more splitting but they somehow stayed in place. We cut some more boards at the correct angles and boarded up the gabled ends. We didn't have roofing shingles or tin so we used the weatherboarding system for the roof. It really did become a fairly solid little structure, maybe 36 by 20 by 24 inches tall. We were proud of our "rain-proof" barn. When it rained, one or the other of us liked to crawl inside and enjoy staying dry in a structure we had cobbled together. Even now I can relive the pleasure and satisfaction as I caught on to what I now know to be basic engineering principles for a rain-proof structure.

THE TREEHOUSE

In the back pasture were several sycamore trees. Sycamore branches spread wide and quite level to the ground—meaning sycamores are wonderful to play in. I liked to climb around in them, but not so high as Eldon. A treehouse came into our heads—starting, I'm sure, in Eldon's head. We hauled lumber back there in the little red wagon—so, this project came before Dad converted that wagon to a trailer for the pedal tractor. Eldon climbed up about 15 feet and began nailing cross pieces to various branches. My self-appointed job was to stay on the ground (with both feet!) and tie a rope to various pieces; Eldon would then pull it up and nail it into place. I climbed up early in the project to check out what he was doing but soon had both feet back on the ground—I can still feel those butterflies. When he finished I climbed up again and sat for a bit on the platform. That was it—a tree platform—not a treehouse! A platform with no walls or railings—I was soon back on the ground and never went up there again! I'm sure Eldon once told me he spent many hours lying up there dreaming of travel to faraway places, but he doesn't recall that now.

THE CART

One day Mom took Eldon and me across the fields to Aunt Mary's house. Aunt Mary had a hand cart that we had played with before and really liked. It looked like a very primitive version of that classic Garden Way cart you now see in gardening magazines, but instead of rubber pneumatic tires it had wrought-iron wheels. The wheels were about 28 inches in diameter; they had five spokes and a light-weight iron rim. Now, wonder of wonders, Aunt Mary was giving this cart to us. Mom let us climb in and ride while she pushed it home via the road to the back gate across from Lloyd Trissel's house. I liked this ride a lot but felt guilty about how hard Mom had to work pushing that thing all that way.

Eldon and I soon transformed that cart into a marvelous toy. We were ages eight and nine. In a community junk hole in the back pasture (more like a treasure hole for Eldon and me) we found another pair of wrought-iron wheels almost identical to those on the cart. We also found an old yard gate made from galvanized pipe and woven wire fencing. Boy o' boy, we now knew what we wanted to do! We took the push handle and rear stands off the cart and bolted on a tongue made from a piece of pine two-by-two, just like a trailer tongue. We cut a section of pipe from the yard gate to serve as an axle for the two new front wheels—wonder of wonders, it was exactly the right diameter for those wheels. We wanted to put the two wheels on the ends of that axle and attach the axle at its center to the front end of the tongue—to make a four-wheeled wagon or "cart," we called it. It was in an *Alice and Jerry* reading book at school where I had seen this way of mounting steerable front wheels on a little "child's size" wagon. This would work perfectly for our "boy size" cart. Eldon bought the idea so easily it became our idea.

We had easily drilled the needed holes in the cart bed and wooden tongue with Dad's brace and bit. Now, drilling the necessary holes in that front axle was a big problem—drilling holes in a round metal pipe was beyond our ingenuity. We knew Dad could do it, but would he? He was so busy; our project was just kid stuff—and it was an unheard of idea we were trying to pull off. But we asked him anyway. Wonder of wonders, he got out his brand new half-inch electric drill and several bits. He questioned us carefully as to just what we were trying to achieve and where we wanted the holes—seven in all. He went to work just as seriously as if it were his project! Our excitement ratcheted up to fever pitch (at least mine did) when we saw he was doing just what we wanted with no second guessing or comments about our silly ideas; he was blessing our project!

When we had that axle with its two wheels bolted to the tongue, Eldon made a handle bar which he bolted to the front axle—that was a hinged affair to be used just like the tongue or handle on the classic "Little Red Wagon." You would put the handle forward when you wanted to pull the cart from the front, and you would fold the handle back over the front of the cart when you wanted to ride and steer. That handle took a lot of fancy toenailing, and it seemed rather rickety to me, but Eldon got it done. He fastened an old farm implement seat onto the tongue where the driver could sit while steering. You're probably catching on—the driver didn't get up front and pull very often. Yes, most of the time somebody ended up pushing the rig from behind while the driver rode seated up front, proudly steering like a stagecoach driver.

Well, we were soon having a lot of fun with that four-wheeled cart. We would push/pull it to the top of some hill, maybe with the smaller kids riding the whole way. The driver would take his place on the seat, and somebody would push from behind to get it going downhill at a good clip. Then the pusher would do a sort of turning jump onto the back of the cart and ride backwards with his legs dangling from the back.

The Burkholder cousins came over and joined in the fun—much like a sledding party. At some point we must have

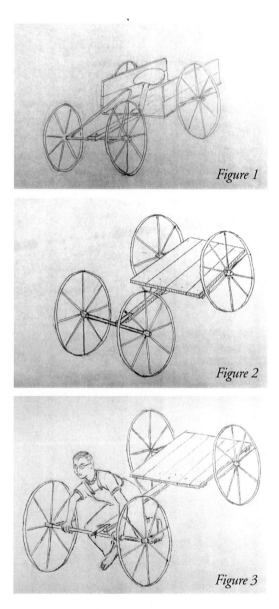

Figure 1

Figure 2

Figure 3

Eldon did these sketches to show our "wonderful four-wheeled cart." Figure 1 shows the way we first set up the cart. Note the big handle, the seat and the side panels. Figure 2 shows the stripped-down version we soon adopted. Figure 3 shows the way we would straddle the tongue and push and steer the cart.

decided to do a "grandest ride of all." We pushed the cart all the way to the top of the long hill back of the house. We started piling on. The cart had side and front panels at that time, so it was easy to pack a lot of kids onto that cart bed—smaller kids sitting on laps of bigger ones, etc. There were five Bowmans and, I think, four Burkholders. Eldon took his place on the driver's seat and took up the handlebar. Cousin Boyd and I were the pushers. That meant six kids packed into that cart bed. Boyd and I started pushing and immediately realized, "Hey here, this is a heavy load!" We heaved to and got the thing rolling. Soon it was going so fast we couldn't keep up even at a dead run. We just dropped back to watch and laugh. Eldon expertly guided the cart into the sweeping turn at the steepest part of the hill. It all looked so graceful and smooth. Then suddenly it was all confusion! The front wheels on their axle were going off by themselves, kids were flying and tumbling every which-a-way, and the cart bed flipped, I think, end over end, landing upside down. As Boyd and I ran down to the scene, kids were picking themselves up, brushing their clothing, rubbing this or that bump or scratch, and talking excitedly about "Whatever happened here!?" Some of the little kids were crying and whimpering a bit, but soon they were joining in the laughing and chattering about "our great crash!"

Then we noticed little Bernard, age three, was still crying and couldn't be consoled. We realized he was hurt for real and some of us took him down to Mom at the house. After a while we saw Mom and Dad with Little Bernard drive off in the '49 Ford. After another longer while we saw them come back and Little Bernard had a leather harness of some kind on his left shoulder—he had broken a collar bone.

Eldon and I regretted the accident and soon knew we were lucky that no one was hurt worse than Bernard, but we soon had

our engineering caps on figuring out what went wrong and what
to do about it. We could see plainly that the pine two-by-two we
had used for the tongue between the cart bed and the front axle
was a very soft wood, way too flimsy for the stress we had sub-
jected it to. When Eldon steered into that sweeping turn to the
right, the rim of the left front wheel dug into the sod, the right
front wheel came up and twisted that tongue off like a toothpick.
I don't think either of us thought for a minute of just discarding
the cart as too dangerous. We immediately scrounged around for
a more suitable something for the tongue—and quickly found it!

Dad always kept a well-stocked scrap iron pile outside his
shop. In that pile we found a piece of channel iron, about four
inches wide and exactly the right length for the cart tongue. It
was HEAVY but it would work. We would have to get Dad's
permission to use that valuable scrap, and we would have to pre-
vail on him to drill one more hole, this time through heavy iron.
Dad first protested, "That thing is massive overkill for what you
boys are trying to do!" He then said we could use it till he needed
it for something else. Then, wonder of wonders, he got out his
electric drill and drilled the hole for us. We were soon off and
running again! (Years later Dad did use that scrap of channel iron
for the tongue of a hay wagon he was building—meaning, that
that was sure enough a serious piece of iron we used.)

At this point we simplified the cart. We took the side panels off the bed to reduce weight. We discarded the handlebar and
driver's seat. Now the driver would simply straddle the tongue,
grab the front axle with his hands just inside the wheels and easily do his share of the pushing while steering. He had complete
freedom to walk or run or sit on the tongue. And there was plenty of room for another boy or two to push from behind.

We would come lumbering down the hill on the west side

of the house, make a sweeping turn across the front yard and get about a third of the way up the east side before having to push hard again. Those iron wheels cut up the sod in the front yard and I always wondered why Grandma never protested. I knew she cared about that front yard—I had many times seen her working and fussing over bare spots in the grass. But she never fussed about our rough riding!

We even took the cart bumpity-bumpin' down the lane and out onto the blacktopped road heading for the Burkholder cousins' place. As with the trike and wagon several years before, it was delightful how nicely the cart rolled along on the smooth pavement. That had to be an interesting scene for the neighbors—two barefoot farm boys trotting along with this crazy four-wheeled cart, one pushing and steering at the front axle, the other pushing from behind, a couple of smaller kids riding on the flat bed, the wrought-iron wheels sort of rumbling and crunching and skittering along on the hard surface. Some of the neighbors might have thought, "Hey, those are the kids that went by here several years ago on that trike and wagon! Look at what they're ridin' now! Wherever did they get that contraption?! Tell Martha Wenger to watch her hen house!" By the way, this expedition was with Mom's full knowledge and consent, and warnings about watching out for cars. The cart actually rolled along pretty nicely but we could see plainly how rubber tired bicycle-type wheels would be a huge improvement. And to reassure the reader, I'll add this yet: We did learn our lesson about keeping control of that thing when going down hills!

That four-wheeled cart was certainly a centerpiece for my years at the Wenger place. After we moved to the Carver place, I sort of outgrew the thing—I got too big to easily push and steer it. As I went into blindness, Eldon and Jim and Bernard morphed that cart into a variety of other wheeled contraptions before its wheels and other parts disappeared from our lives. It's too bad we never got photos of that crazy, wonderful four-wheeled cart.

GROWN BOYS AND LITTLE BOYS WITH FARM MACHINERY

Toward the end of the Wenger place years, the tractors plus related machinery such as trailers, wagons, disk plough and harrow, combine, bailer, hammer mill, etc., took center stage for me.

THE BLACK TRACTOR

When Dad married Daniel Wenger's youngest daughter, Oma, he took over operation of the Wenger farm. With the farm came an old homemade tractor—the "Black Tractor," as Eldon and I called it. That Black Tractor is rooted in my very earliest memories.

If you Google up terms like "homemade tractor" or "doodle bug," you'll discover a fascinating chapter of American farm history. By 1920 a lot of old, unused automobiles were sitting around farm buildings and in local junkyards. The financial hard times in 1920s agriculture followed by the 1930s depression and the shortages of World War II forced many farmers to get creative in their pursuit of mechanized farming. They began converting those old cars, most notably Model T and Model A Fords, into handy little farm tractors. The heyday for these homemade tractors was 1920 to 1950. I remember pictures and articles about these nifty creations in Dad's *Farm Journal* magazines; I remember pictures and diagrams of such tractors in another book Dad had lying around the house; I remember *Sears Roebuck* and *Montgomery Ward* catalogues selling kits for these conversions. A lot of farmers in those days had more than enough mechanical know-how to do these conversions without kits.

Well, that "Black Tractor" Dad inherited with the farm was one of these do-it-yourself conversions. There's some confusion among cousins and neighbors about who built it, but by piecing together my own childhood memories of what Dad said about the tractor with what Cousin Margaret Heatwole told me recently, it seems most likely that the Black Tractor was built by Uncle Will, Margaret's Dad, from Grandpa's old Dodge touring car—the car Grandpa bought in 1924 when he married Grandma Laura. Uncle Will probably converted that old car to a tractor sometime around 1932-35. Uncle Menno Suter also built one of these tractors from an old Chevy.

The setup of our Black Tractor was simple—a shortened automobile frame, an automotive front axle with wire spoked wheels and no fenders, a motor with a radiator and hood and (I believe) also a windshield, a steering wheel and seat. Just behind the seat was an over-sized rear truck axle and differential. That big fat differential housing was, I thought, a perfect place for a small boy to ride—right there behind Dad. (Yes, I was aware of that drive shaft down there and that I had to keep my feet away from it.) There were other places around the rear framing where Eldon and I could hang on. The rear axle was equipped with dual truck wheels, but I remember single wheels at times. Sometimes the rear wheels had chains—I really liked those chains!

I have vague recollections of the Black Tractor crawling over a plowed field pulling a spike-toothed harrow (hence those chains) but most of the time (in my memory) it was used with a trailer (also homemade) to haul feed and equipment AND SMALL BOYS about the farm—you guessed it, I liked that trailer, too!

Most clearly and vividly remembered was the buzz saw Dad rigged up on that Black Tractor. This was a circular saw, about 30 inches in diameter, mounted outboard of the right rear wheel. The shaft for the saw ran across the back of the tractor with a pulley that bore hard against the right rear tire. The idea was to drive the tractor to where you wanted to work, then jack up the right rear wheel and set the transmission and engine speed to run the wheel and saw blade at the desired speed. You would place your log on a movable table and push it past the spinning saw blade.

Dad sternly charged Eldon and me about staying at a designated safe distance to watch. I could see for myself that saw was a wicked thing and it kept me scared, but I was enthralled with the tractor wheel and saw blade spinning—opposite directions to each other.

Evidently, there was no way to put the saw blade in neutral because whenever Dad drove the tractor to a new location, the saw blade would spin. I remember one time running alongside (at a safe distance) to watch that saw blade—it spun backwards as the tractor went forward; that was a marvelous thing for this small boy.

Operation of this buzz saw was actually a two-man operation—you needed the second man to hold the cut-off chunk so it wouldn't pinch on the saw blade and fly to who knows where; also, you didn't want it to fall to the ground and maybe bounce into the saw blade. As I got bigger, maybe 10 or 11, and by then the buzz saw was mounted on the new Case tractor, my job was to be that second man. When I grabbed the end of the log to be cut off, my hands would be maybe 14 inches from that spinning blade, close enough to keep me tense and scared, but I was still enthralled with that saw machinery. I especially loved listening to the tractor's engine leaning into its load.

The Black Tractor was certainly handy about the farm but for really heavy work, Dad still used his horses—Ol' Tom and Bob. One day I was playing around on the Black Tractor, watching those horses straining and leaning really hard into their harness to pull a fully loaded manure spreader. The muscles on their haunches were really rippling and bulging! That manure spreader was clearly a HEAVY load! From those memories, young as I was, I can easily conclude today that that homemade tractor would not have been capable of handling that manure spreader.

THE CASE VAC TRACTOR

In 1945 (I was age four, Eldon three) the Case VAC tractor arrived on the Wenger farm, and it was "farewell," to the Black Tractor and the horses! Eldon and I were mesmerized when Dad drove that new tractor up the lane. Suddenly, right there before our eyes—and you could touch it—was the most wonderful toy, 'er, I mean tractor you could imagine! Eldon and I were ready on the spot to swarm all over that thing to check it out. Dad insisted, "No, we have to go eat lunch first, then you can come look at it." Well, after that hasty lunch, we were back out there and all around and all over that new toy, or rather tractor. It was a dazzling, bright orange, and the orange was accentuated by the shiny black of the big fat rear tires. The cleats, or treads, on those rear tires were marvelous! Those rear wheels towered over us! The little front wheels were cute—they were mounted on a single post such that the tops of the wheels leaned outward and the bottoms inward (to make easier steering). The whole tractor was so big and TALL—we (little boys) had to climb and climb to get up to the driver's seat. When we got up there we immediately found and staked out our places to ride as Dad drove here and there—we would stand on the nice, flat platform on either side of the seat and hold on to the big rear fenders. Much of our farm boy joy for the next 6 or 7 years centered around this tractor.

The Case VAC was actually a small tractor. It was a tricycle model, rated as two plow and 18 or 20 horsepower. It was equipped with power takeoff and a flat belt pulley.

We kids always suspected that, in his heart of hearts, Dad was a John Deere man—remember, he made our toy tractors emphatically GREEN AND YELLOW! So why did he get this Case tractor? Lloyd Trissel, Dad's lifelong best friend and farming partner, told me several years ago the answer to that question was very simple—"Credit!" He said the J. I. Case company offered farmers really good credit for purchasing farm tractors; no other company came close. This certainly was a brilliant marketing strategy as World War II was wrapping up. Harold Lahman, Dad's cousin, and Uncle Dwight Swartz, his brother-in-law, each got similar Cases. All of Dad's subsequent tractor purchases were Case.

Dad was a serious farmer and he was serious about mechanizing everything about the Wenger farm. Modern plumbing and this new tractor were the keys to it all. All sorts of tractor based equipment soon showed up—field mower, side delivery rake, bailer, combine, hammer mill, disk plow and spring-toothed harrow; previously horse-drawn equipment like the manure spreader and hay wagon were converted to tractor power. Equipment (built by Dad) for sheltering, feeding and watering turkeys on the open range were tractor based. The tractor was also put to operating the well pump when the windmill, or rather the winds, got lazy.

But, even with all this mechanization, this modern farming still required a lot of hard sweaty work—boy, could Dad ever sweat! And, there were moments of barked knuckles, broken equipment, and other kinds of exasperation. Dad's favorite strong word was "SUGAR," said with the same emphasis on the "sh" sound as that other commonly used sh-word. He could stomp a foot now and then. And, of course, there was stress and anxiety about crop failure, livestock, crop prices, and borrowed money. But, even in the midst of all this sweat and worry, it was clear to me then and it's clear to me now, Dad and Lloyd, and their other friends had as much FUN with their tractors and machinery as Eldon and I did with our toys—they were just grown-up boys with grown-up reasons for the things they did with their grown-up toys. That's the world where I came into adolescence—I reveled in that machinery and the fun the men were having with it.

BOYS DRIVING TRACTOR

Well, from the day that Case tractor showed up on the farm Dad would have Eldon or I sit on his lap and steer the tractor. What fun! What ultimate joy—except that Dad couldn't just let us quickly and easily learn the skill of steering a farm tractor. He was too much of a tease for that. He would put his foot on the right or left brake (the tractor had separate foot brakes for the two rear wheels); that would make the front end veer to the right or left despite our efforts to steer straight. Dad would holler, "No, no, Sonny, you gotta keep it on the lane!" When we finally got it back on track, he would hit the other brake and send the tractor off to the other side. We would hear, "Come on now, Sonny, you gotta keep it straight!" He would laugh and we would laugh too, sort of, it was so much fun, but it was frustrating, too. And of course, Dad was having fun playing with a braking system on his new toy that could individually break right or left drive wheels.

One day Dad was using the new tractor to harrow that

field behind the coal shed and outhouse. From the way he was leaning his body into the turn I could tell he was having fun swinging the tractor around that corner. He was probably using the right foot brake to make the tractor swing right around. Suddenly, right there in front of me, the front wheels quietly rolled off to one side and the front end just nosed into the ground; it was a jarring halt. The front post had just snapped off. Dad got off, looking exasperated and amused at the same time. He went into the house, I presume, to arrange for repairs. A new front post was installed, and the old front wheels were put on that.

Then, believe it or not, it happened again! Dad was driving the tractor home from somewhere; he was coming down the hill from Cook's Creek Church and starting to turn into our lane. Suddenly, the front wheel post broke off! This time the front wheels sort of rolled back under the tractor and were caught fast as the front end nosed into the pavement. I saw this scene soon after—that poor tractor was sitting on the road with its nose digging into the pavement; it looked so pathetic. This time the manufacturer sent a front post, which they promised would not break again; it never broke again.

Incidents like this made wonderful stories with which to bedazzle our cousins and school friends (and grown men had fun telling those stories, too.)

A most interesting tractor event happened when Dad decided to move one of the chicken houses from the back field up to the lot near the house and barn. This was a closed wooden structure about 20 by 20 feet with a slanted roof maybe 8 feet tall at the front. He jacked the building up and got two big timbers under it to serve as skids. Then he got three of his friends to bring their tractors to help pull that thing up to the new location. This was going to be a downhill pull for the first 150 feet or so, then up a significant grade for maybe twice that distance. On the appointed day Lloyd Trissel brought his McCormick Dearing Farmall tractor; Amos Rhodes brought his older McCormick Dearing tractor; Harold Lahman brought his new Case tractor; and of course Dad had his new Case tractor. They lined up all four tractors in front of the chicken house and hitched them to the skids with log chains. Eldon and I were practically dancing with excitement! On some signal, all four engines roared forth and the show began! Sure enough, the chicken house began to move! The noise of four completely different kinds of tractor engines under full load was wild! Harold's tractor started putting on a show of its own—it was bucking, jumping, jerking like a wild thing; the rear wheels were spinning, then taking hold, then breaking loose and spinning some more. Harold was bouncing and jiggling around on his seat, hanging on to the steering wheel. Amos' tractor jumped and bucked, too, but nothing like Harold's. Lloyd and Dad's tractors for the most part just crawled steadily along. They had to stop at least once to fix a broken chain.

When they crossed the low point, the soil changed from hard packed gravel to hard grassy sod. They were hoping to mount a running charge up the hill. But when the skids hit the grassy sod, everything ground to a halt. All four tractors just sat and spun their wheels. Then "BANG!"—Amos' tractor was suddenly crippled! The left rear tire was flat!

So what in the world happened? A large steel spoke in the left rear wheel of Amos' tractor had broken loose and punched through the rim into the inner tube. Well, well, the show was over—the chicken house was where it couldn't be used and Amos' tractor just sat there for days.

THE BULLDOZER

But then Eldon and I learned the show wasn't over after all. Dad arranged for Lester Frank to bring his bulldozer to finish pulling that chicken house up the hill and into place. Eldon and I couldn't wait—you know, a bulldozer was the strongest thing in the world and we were going to see it close up. Sure enough, late one afternoon a flatbed truck came up the lane bringing the bulldozer. The driver backed the bulldozer off, got back in the truck and drove off. We were told he would be back the next day to do the work—*we would be in school.* Well, OK, so Eldon and I did the next best thing. We walked round and round that bulldozer, touching and looking at everything. We inspected the tracks and wheels. We climbed up and sat on the operator's seat and pulled on the steering levers. We eyed the keys right there in the ignition—we already knew perfectly well how to start Dad's tractor, and…well…? I remember the scary thrill at the thought, but we didn't touch those keys. I expected at any minute to hear Dad call from the barn, "You boys get away from there!" Finally, he did just that, but by then we were satisfied—and it felt so good.

When we came home from school the next day that chicken house was sitting in its new place, all lined up like it had been there all along, and the bulldozer was gone. We had missed our show! I ran to Mom and asked her, "What did that bulldozer look like when it was working?" She sort of chuckled at me—she understood my disappointment. I could tell she was impressed herself with what that bulldozer could do.

She said, "Well, it just sort of sat there and then simply pulled that chicken house up the hill into place." Since she understood my disappointment, her report was a decent substitute for an eyewitness experience. (What a Mom!)

One day Dad and Lloyd were baling hay at Amos Rhodes' place. They were using Dad's tractor to pull that really heavy New Holland square baler. Lloyd was riding on the seat at the back of the baler. He noticed that whenever they came around the field to a certain very steep hill, Dad's tractor had BARE-LY enough traction to keep going. He started teasing Dad. He would jump off the seat, grab the back end of the baler, lean back and sock his heels into the ground. The tractor and baler would stop right there on the hill; the tractor would just spin its wheels until Lloyd let go. Dad's version of this story always ended with the bemused and pretend-disgusted comment, "Shoot, when Lloyd got that notion in his head, I couldn't do nothin' till he got over his foolishness." Once again, Dad and his friends were a bunch of grown-up boys having fun with their grown-up toys—and I loved it all!

Making hay was a social high point for our whole family. Dad, Lloyd, and Amos worked together with hay making. They did their mowing, raking, and baling during daylight hours. The baler was a big New Holland 76 square baler that left the bales lying in the field. They just left the bales lie there until evening hours. After supper, when it was not so hot, they would gather at the field with somebody's tractor and wagon. If we were lucky, Eldon and I would be assigned by turns to drive the tractor slowly through the field while Dad and Lloyd walked along either side of the wagon picking up the bales and tossing them onto the wagon. Amos, standing on the wagon or way up on the load, would stack and arrange the bales to make a solid, stable load.

How you stacked those bales on the wagon was critical—if you didn't do it right, that load would eventually slide off and there would be a bunch of cross, impatient men!

Eldon and I were quite young when first assigned this tractor driving job. Dad would put the tractor in low gear and set the hand throttle to a slow crawl so he and Lloyd could keep up with the loading, and so he could run up and intervene if we got in trouble or had to do a difficult turnaround. It was a proud day when we could do the clutch, gear shift and brakes by ourselves!

At the barn, the loaded wagon was maneuvered into place alongside a hay elevator, which Dad had cobbled together (another product of his creative ingenuity). One man on the wagon threw the bales onto the elevator and two or more men up in the mow arranged and stacked them properly. It was fun watching those bales going, one precisely spaced after another, up the elevator.

Yes, I said "precisely spaced." Recently Cousin Ruel Burkholder told me this story that shows why those bales should be precisely spaced: "When I was age sixteen I was on the wagon putting the bales onto the elevator. Uncle Millard was taking them off at the upper end. I was taking care to space the bales evenly as instructed. I must have failed to get one of the bales properly seated on the elevator chain, it slipped back against the next bale coming. That meant two bales were going up the elevator at the same time. I just stood and watched. When that first bale dropped off the elevator, Uncle Millard stooped to pick it up as usual. The second bale then came right down on his head, sending him and the two bales sprawling. I cracked up laughing and would bust out laughing all over again the rest of the evening. Uncle Millard got annoyed with me—'Now look here, boy…'"

It might be nine, ten, eleven, or even midnight till the day's hay hauling was finished. Everybody would be tired and

sweaty, but there was always one thing more—ICE CREAM!!
We would traipse into the house (nevermind the hay dust and
sweat) and sit up at the dining room table. Somebody would get
out round, pint-size boxes of Valley Gold ice cream. Every man
got a box, but we kids—somebody would cut the pint boxes in
half and give us kids each a half pint. Wonderful was the day
when we got big enough to do enough man-size work to qualify
for a whole pint! My favorite flavor was RASPBERRY, so cold
and smooth! Even when Dad's financial situation got tight later,
he saw to this ice cream.

On hay hauling nights Mom always had to deal with a
clamor from the younger kids, "Can we stay up for ice cream!?"
Depending on how late it was likely going to be that night and
on the relative ages of the kids, some got to stay up for ice cream
and some got herded off to bed—oh the woes of being among the
younger kids...or so I thought back then. After writing this paragraph I checked with several of the younger sibs, and, to my great
surprise, they have almost no memories of this ice cream ritual
after hay hauling; they seem to have no sense of missing out on
great fun. So, back then I had been unnecessarily carrying a burden of guilt (just a little burden, not too much) on their behalf.

THE TURKEY CATCHERS

In the last years at the Wenger place and continuing at the
Carver place, Dad raised turkeys. We would get them as baby
poults and raise them to 16 weeks of age, 18-20 pounds per bird,
or even 40 pounds for the big bronze toms. When they were
ready for market, trucks with a crew of turkey catchers would
show up. These guys would wade out into the flock, grab turkeys
right and left by their legs, carry them upside down several at a
time, and stuff them into crates (we called them coops). These

crates were then stacked on the truck, 6 or 10 birds in each crate. They were then hauled off to the processing plant to be made into turkey dinners. To say it accurately, this turkey catching was shitty work. Turkeys, when they are being thus rounded up, poop a lot—over everything and everybody. They also flap around a lot, and, according to one of my younger brothers, sometimes clubbed the catcher in his sensitive spot.

To my 10-12-year-old mind, these turkey catchers were a study in something I couldn't quite fathom or get into words. Their faces seemed resigned to a meaningless, dull existence. Their complexion was a gaunt ashen gray, and always, always a cigarette dangling from the corner of a downturned mouth. Their coveralls were DIRTY! They dragged about with a joyless, minimally co-operating gait. I began to see significance in the contrasting gait and body movements of Dad, Lloyd Trissel and their Mennonite farmer friends—they moved with energy and purpose, even joy in what they were doing. Their faces showed keen interest and in-volvement in their work. Not so with these turkey catchers! I was beginning to comprehend the idea of "work ethic" though I didn't know the words. Did I understand sullen lethargy? I do now.

Now, fast forward to 1977-81, I was attending Eastern Mennonite Seminary in Harrisonburg. At that time Mennonites and other conservative Christians in the Valley were up in arms over news that the Adolf Coors Brewery from Golden, Colorado, was planning to build a beer packaging plant in Elkton, 20 or so miles east of Harrisonburg. Coors' intent was to expand its mar-ket into northeastern United States. Many Valley residents were excited about the prospects for new high-paying jobs, but many devout believers were vehemently opposed. One day I found myself in the seminary lounge listening in as some Mennonite students were declaiming about Coors. Suddenly some Methodist students were coming down hard on the Mennonites—"The real reason you Mennonites don't want Coors to come into the Valley is you are afraid those high-paying jobs will break up your two-class social order where you Mennonites are the owner class and the rest of us are the worker class. We need Coors here in the Valley precisely to break up your two-class social system." Let me tell you, it was an astounding shock to discover we Mennonites were viewed as having that kind of privilege and power!

Within several days of that conversation in the seminary lounge I happened to be listening to a local call-in radio show. The callers were sounding off about the Coors invasion of our Valley. Then a course, gravelly smoker's voice came on the air saying, "We need Coors to come here to get the wages in this Valley up to living levels. I was a turkey catcher all my life and I don't want none of my kids to be no turkey catcher!" Boy, talk about light bulbs coming on in one's head!

OK, fast forward some more, another 10 years or so. Our oldest daughter, Laura, is teaching first grade at a very rural county public school. She had already explained to Ferne and me that some of her more dysfunctional students come from a near-by community termed by school officials as a "rural slum." I had caught on from family names mentioned in Laura's talk that this "rural slum" is where those turkey catchers years ago came from. One day Dick, a very dysfunctional student from that rural slum who should have been in third grade by now, was more grumpy than usual. Laura asked, "Dick, what's wrong?" Dick replied, "Well, you see, I sleep behind the big armchair in the living room. Last night the pile of books I stack up to keep out the light and everybody's noise kept tumbling down and waking me up." So, do we have here "a day in the life of an impoverished child," maybe a grandson of one of my turkey catchers?

For several years Laura followed Dick's progress through the school system—he was clearly on a path to trouble with the police, the courts, and jail.

I think of these turkey catchers often. They represent a life style my folks and community eschew—"For heaven's sake, don't let our kids comingle with their kids!" But, take note—my dad and his peers and also we today "need" those turkey catchers and people like them in our communities in order to maintain our standard of living. We need to have people around who have been MADE to be willing to accept poverty wages so we can afford to pay for their "needed" services without lowering our own standard of living! We look down our noses at them, but we need them around! Is this not the same bind we put today's undocumented immigrants in—we want their cheap labor, but we won't grant them the respect and rights due neighbors and fellow citizens? What's this—we need folks around who are content with their poverty and second-class citizenship so we can have our comfortable life style? This is too depressing—let's get back to my farm boy year.

THE TWO GREAT SUMMERS OF THRESHING

The summers of 1952 and 1953 were twin pinnacles in my farm boy life. To this day in my mind these are "The First Great Summer of Threshing" and "The Second Great Summer of Threshing."

The First Great Summer was occasioned by the death of Granddaddy Bowman in May that year. The Bowman uncles and cousins my age came together at Granddaddy's farm over several days and weeks to take care of his wheat harvest. The weather was hot. On threshing days Uncle Roy brought cases of Pepsi (soft drinks were a wonderful novelty to us boys back then) and cousin Byrl dispensed these bottles parsimoniously, seeing that we didn't overindulge. Dad's little Case VAC tractor (20 horsepower or so) was put on the belt to run the threshing machine and it worked so hard and long in all that heat it burned the paint and charred the metal where the exhaust pipe came up through the engine hood. I variously rode the binder behind the tractor to operate the cradle pedal, stacked sheaves of wheat on the wagon as the men pitched them up to us boys with their forks, drove the tractor and wagon while the men loaded, or, best of all, I sat on top the threshing machine to operate the blower. I was generally working around and operating lots of machinery with all kinds of wonderful wheels and belts and pulleys and chains and cranks and conveyers—fascinating equipment! But this equipment also sobered me—it could cripple and maim and kill. I saw I was starting into manhood; I was making a real contribution to farm production; the men seemed to acknowledge this. I was happy!

During the Second Great Summer of 1953, I did all this again, but this time we were harvesting Dad's wheat on our new home place. They set up the threshing machine on the main floor of our bank barn with its blower pipe sticking out the back door. By this time I was pretty much the official "blower boy." I sat on top the threshing machine—which was throbbing with wonderful noise and power—to control the big blower pipe that discharged the straw from the machine.

That blower pipe, maybe 10 inches in diameter, was really neat. With cranks and ropes I could telescope the pipe straight out and back in from, say, 8 feet to 16 feet or more. I could raise and lower the far end like a giraffe's head, or swing it left and right. On the far end of the pipe was a louvered nozzle in the form of a hood like those on our snow blowers today—I could pull it back and make the straw shoot practically straight ahead to who knows where, or I could roll the louvers all the way forward and shoot the straw straight down. I could also rotate the hood left and right.

The point of all this was to direct the straw here and there to form a nice rounded straw stack. Much of the time Dad and other men were on the stack doing the final stacking. They would signal with big arm gestures where they wanted me to direct the straw. I had to keep cleaning the dust from my glasses in order to see those gestures (but I know now that problem was more than just dust on my glasses). More than once I doused the stackers with a straw shower—straight down over them (they wore their shirt tails OUTSIDE their pants for just such possibilities).

One time when no one was on the stack I wanted to see how far around I could rotate that hood out there on the end of the pipe. I hauled back on the rope and, sure enough, the hood twisted around and pointed straight up—*Wow, whoopee! Look at that!* The straw was shooting straight up, and I wasn't seeing any coming back down anywhere around. *Where was it disappearing to? The moon? Surely the men in the fields and neighbors for miles around are seeing a gigantic plume of straw and dust—I better cut out my foolishness and get back to work.* I turned the hood back down and resumed building the straw stack. No one said a word, then or later. I'm quite sure that didn't mean the men were somewhere just watching with amused toleration—"Look at Daniel up there, learning to handle his machine"—but that's exactly what I was doing.

Soon after that threshing, we drove out the lane in our family car and turned up the road past the barn. One of my sibs commented, "Man, threshing is dusty! Look at all that straw and dust up there on the barn roof." Silently I thought, *Oh, so that's why I didn't see any straw coming back down when I turned that blower nozzle straight up—I was blowing it back up over the barn roof!* Over the next weeks I heard several times, "Look, that straw is still up there on the barn roof! How long is it gonna take for the rain to wash it all off?" I just kept being quiet.

TROUBLE COMING

About that problem with dust on my glasses when I was operating the thresher blower—actually, I was constantly cleaning my glasses (with my shirt tail) that whole summer—in the field, in the barn, or wherever. When I cleaned the dust off the lenses, things would clear up a lot, but not completely. I began wondering vaguely what was going on. Those black specks and the black curtain in my field of vision, which had appeared earlier that spring at school, were getting more bothersome. Poor lighting, as in darker corners of farm buildings was also getting more bothersome. Well, anyway...I finished up that Second Great Summer of Threshing and headed back to school for sixth grade.

In Chapter 4 I go back to my early years and chronicle my grade school days, grades 1 through 5. Then I will pick up the story at sixth grade when everything changed.

3
CHRISTMAS AT GRANDDADDY LUTHER'S HOUSE

Those Christmas get-togethers at Granddaddy Luther Bowman's house were among the highlights of my early years. Each year, maybe around Thanksgiving or even before, someone would write the names of all the cousins, aunts and uncles, and grandparents on slips of paper and put them all in a box. Over the next several weeks, as the various families came to visit Granddaddys, each person, large and small, would reach into the box and pull out a slip of paper. You were supposed to get a gift for the person named on that slip. This meant one gift per person, thus keeping costs down for each family. No Santa Claus talk in this Mennonite clan.

A big part of this Christmas fun was the wondering "who got my name," whispering about who got what for whom, and, as we older ones caught on, announcing loudly what we wanted, hoping the right person would get the hint. Evidently parents sometimes conspired with other parents to get these hints to the right places. Wrapping the gifts in all that colorful wrapping paper, making those ribbons curl up all nice and fluffy, and making the name cards was part of the fun.

On the Christmas evening of this story, the various families came trooping out of the wintery night into Granddaddy's house bearing presents, the older kids making sure the younger ones didn't drop things. The dropleaf table in the living room and the floor under it were soon piled high with presents of all sizes and shapes, all wrapped in red and green and white and gold wrapping paper. Ribbons of every color and curl were everywhere in the pile with name tags dangling every which way.

The living room lighting, from a typical old farmhouse style ceiling fixture, was poor; it made patterns of light and shadow which, to my child's imagination, added to the mystery and wonder of that pile of presents.

Finally, the time came to hand out the gifts. The kids sat on the floor, body to body, wall to wall. Adults sat or stood wherever they could wedge themselves in around the room. The doorways were full of adult faces looking over each other's shoulders. Uncle Linden and cousin David (Foch), with funny grins on their faces, began handing out presents, this way and that, in a hurry. They tossed some presents over the kids' heads to adults who could not be reached. Gifts dropped into the laps of kids around me here and there. "Hey Joe, wher' you at?!? Oh, back there!"—another package goes sailing over my head to Uncle Joe. "Lelia? Ah, there you are! Hand this over to her." You never heard such laughin' and hollerin' and paper rippin' racket! Suddenly a present, a big one, was poked at me! I immediately added my paper rippin' racket to the bedlam! "An Erector Set!" I had told Mom what I wanted, and somebody got the word!

Well, I'm afraid it is true, as we are told every year, those Happy Holidays include times of sadness and bitterness for some folks. I know of two such incidents in our family. That same Christmas when I got the Erector Set was a tough one for Eldon. When we drew names that year, Eldon, believe it or not, pulled out his own name. He began dancing around—"Daddy can I keep it, can I keep it?! I wanna keep it!" Dad hesitated, then relented. Eldon was ecstatic—he would be choosing his own Christmas gift. Sometime in the following weeks, Eldon was supposed to turn on the water for the cows at the watering trough near the barn. He then forgot to turn it off. Dad later found a horrendous icy mess around the trough and the reservoir drained DRY! Dad was NOT HAPPY! He said something about punishment to "teach you not to be forgetting things." He told Eldon to choose between a whipping or having that Christmas gift to himself limited to just some article of clothing instead of a fun toy. Eldon was not fond of Dad's whippings; he chose the dull Christmas gift. So, when I got the wonderful Erector Set he got a cap, the kind with a bill and pull-down ear flaps.

The next morning, I was playing with that Erector Set downstairs on Grandma Wenger's nice hardwood floor in front of that very sunny window—the sun really made those Erector Set parts bright and sparkling, the wheels ever so red! It was sunny but quite cold outside. Somebody had given us a football that Christmas. Eldon would go outside with the football and his cap with the flaps pulled down. He would kick the football around a while, then come in, stand and look at my Erector Set. He would go back out and kick the ball some more, come back in and watch me having my fun! I remember the look on his face and him pulling those flaps down snuggly over his ears, shivering and sniffing from the cold; his nose was red. I really identified with his forlorn situation; it dampened my delight in the Erector Set. I was young and not prone to critique Dad's doings. I believe I thought the offense was serious, but I most certainly thought it didn't deserve all this! This scenario was just too much, too heavy, too sad.

Jim came to know Christmas disappointment, too. Some Christmases earlier, Eldon and I had each gotten a model airplane—balsa wood, rubber band powered. A Christmas or so after that, we each got one of those wind-up bulldozers, the kind made with brightly painted sheet metal with rubber tracks—somebody was clearly taking the trouble to find out what we wanted. The precedents were set for little Jim. Jim got his heart set on one of those bulldozers. I think he played the "hinting game" properly, but somebody didn't get the word. He got a small set of Tinker Toys! He was disappointed, outraged, inconsolable—"Tinker Toys are for babies!" I'm thinking now none of us took his disappointment seriously enough. Many years later, after one of our many Bowman9 get-togethers (my sibs and I call ourselves the Bowman9) where we rehearsed old times, "Younger brother" Bernard got Jim a bulldozer—not one of those 1950s models but a nice contemporary toy. Jim appreciated the gesture.

So, when we are basking in joy and happiness, right next to us is someone caught in sadness and misery. Always?

Well, the Luther Bowman family finally got too big to continue those big Christmas get-togethers. Something was lost, but things had to change. Each family branch had to become its own family tree.

4

GRADE SCHOOL—
HAPPY YEARS, MOSTLY

One day, presumably coming up on school age, Mom and I were sitting in a dimly-lit doctor's office. Mom and the doctor talked a while. Then the doctor put his face close to mine and started trying to shine a tiny but very bright light straight into my eyes. I squirmed around to get away from the thing. The doctor kept insisting I sit still and keep looking straight at that light! That was impossible! I kept squirming; he kept holding my head and stabbing that light straight into the center of my eye. Then he and Mom talked some more. Sometime after that, glasses appeared on my face; they had a pinkish tan plastic frame.

Then one day I was told I was going to school. I was presented with a brand new bright green lunchbox with a big thermos jug, and a neat book bag. In the book bag were a tablet of lined paper, a pencil, and a box of crayons—*Ooh, look at those pretty colors!* Amazingly, all that stuff was mine; I didn't have to share it with anyone!

The next morning, they decked me out in nice new clothes. Dad took me down to the end of the lane and just stood there with me. A heavy gray fog closed in, obscuring everything beyond 75 feet or so. We stood there some more. Suddenly, out of the fog emerged a big yellow thing and came to a noisy stop right in front of me—too close for comfort. As it stopped, a big black hole opened up in the side of the yellow thing right there in front of me—like it was FOR ME! Dad urged me, "Go ahead, Sonny, climb on." As my eyes accommodated, the black hole morphed into a door with a little flight of steps going "way up" to a level floor where a tall man sat bolt upright holding on to a steering wheel. He was looking down at me with a wide, toothy, friendly smile. "Come on up here, Daniel," he said and directed me with my big lunchbox and big book bag to a seat right behind him. I would learn later that driver was Mr. Eshleman. The bus traveled over hill and dale along a road familiar to me to a schoolhouse we passed every Sunday on our way to church. The kids started piling off—my, they were noisy—so I started to follow. Mr. Eshleman grabbed me firmly by the arm and sat me back down. "You don't get off here," he said. "You stay right here with me." The yellow bus then traversed more hills and dales, but these were unfamiliar roads, to a schoolhouse I never saw before. This was the Dale Enterprise School on Route 33 about 5 miles west of Harrisonburg. This time when the kids piled off, Mr. Eshleman indicated I should follow.

Somehow I ended up in a front row seat in Miss Cox's first, second, third, and fourth grade classroom. Those school desks—wow! I hadn't seen anything like those before. They were screwed to the floor in rows, had curved cast-iron legs and a flat wooden top with a shelf underneath for books—and this one was MINE, all mine. My seat and back were attached to the next desk behind me—meaning, as I soon learned—if I wiggled too much I would get poked in the back by the kid behind me.

(I recently learned on the Internet those classic school desks were invented and patented in 1889 by Anna Breadin. Through my grade school years I liked those desks.)

Miss Cox was pointing out to us first graders that she had

copied each of our names in big CURSIVE script on the black-board. She began going to each first grader showing us how to copy what was on the blackboard onto our lined tablet paper. She wedged her big self into my desk beside me. She had no big friendly smile, but with a kind, no nonsense patience, she showed me how to write my name IN CURSIVE on my lined paper, just like what was on the black board. *Hey, I can do this. This school stuff is gonna be fun!*

Later that first day I had to pee, but I had no idea where to go or what to do. So, well, I did what any other intelligent first grader would do—I wet my pants. I don't recall anyone seeming to notice, not even Miss Cox, but it was awful. When I got home it was sure enough noticed. Phone calls were apparently made. The next morning Dad said, "Now Sonny, first thing when you get off the bus at school, look for David Burkholder, he's gonna show you the boys' bathroom." David was a first cousin about five years older than me. When I got off the bus, sure enough, there was cousin David, and he was looking for me—like a kindly big brother. He took me around the side of the building and showed me the boys' facilities—a low ceilinged dingy base-ment room with a commode and a trough(!)—I was to pee in that trough! There may have been a wash bowl also. If you don't know, let me assure you, when you are a little kid, finding some-one like David at an appointed place at the appointed time and knowing where to pee—things like that go a LONG WAY to-ward righting a scary world! As far as I was aware, my first grade world got along OK after that.

Some of the "big girls" (third and fourth graders, I believe) took an interest in me. I was small and they were fascinated with my thick glasses. They practically took them off my face, saying, like so many little mothers, "Don't worry, we'll be careful and give them right back." After ooing and ahhing and laughing at what they saw, they would hand them back or even put them back on my face with a maternal sounding, "There…"

These same girls got me to seesaw with them. At that time an old board fence ran along the west side of the school building. We would put a loose scrap board through the fence so we could seesaw on one of the fence rails. It was easy to adjust the board back and forth to balance our very different weights. There was no handle; you had to lean forward and hang on to the board with your hands. If you bumped your end down on the ground hard enough, the person on the other end would fly upward—they were responsible to hang on. It was even more fun to put the board across a lower fence rail, then seesaw standing up on the board while holding on to the top fence rail with your hands. This way you could really bang your end down and make the other guy/gal fly way up—mishaps were few since we would hold on to that top fence rail for dear life. At one point I noticed the board just lying there across the fence rail with nobody on it; the end on my side was very short and up in the air; I realized (with a little crooked grin, I think) the long end over there would really fly upward if I stomped on this short end. I stomped. That other end flew up alright—one of the girls standing over there was suddenly staggering around, moaning, and holding her groin with both hands. The other girls surrounded her trying to console her with words like, "Come on now, Mary (name is changed), it'll be all right after a while." If somebody recognizes herself here—SORRY ABOUT THAT!

But things evidently weren't getting along so well after all. One day I was sitting at my desk in the front row, drawing or coloring or whatever first graders do when they're only half attentive. Suddenly Miss Cox was telling me something, urgently.

Oh, she wants me to get out my reading book. I guiltily shoved my papers away and got out my reading book. The kids around me snickered and Miss Cox was not satisfied. She said it again. *Oh, she means my arithmetic book.* So, I put the reading book away and got out my arithmetic book. Again, everybody snickered, and Miss Cox still was not happy. I tried a third time, and still no satisfaction. I was completely stumped, bewildered, and everybody was laughing. Suddenly this second grader named Bill Good got up from his desk in the back of the room, came forward and sat down beside me in my desk and said, "She wants you to blow your nose." *Oh, well, OK, that's easy enough.* I got out my hanky and complied. Miss Cox smiled. The other kids were happy, too. All was well again. (So, what kind of social poise or audacity must it take for a second-grade boy to intervene like that on behalf of a bewildered first grader, completely unbidden by the teacher?!)

Sometime after that I was pulled out of school—I never even got my first report card. Years later Mom told me what happened. Word came home from the teacher about my difficulties. Mom took me back to the eye doctor who had prescribed those first glasses. She said, "That eye doctor made me mad. He said, 'Daniel ain't fit to go to school.'" Mom and Dad then took me to Dr. William P. McGuire in Winchester, Virginia. Dr. McGuire gave me another prescription for glasses and told Mom and Dad, "Daniel IS TOO fit to not go to school! Get him back in school." So, I started first grade again the next school year. Those new glasses certainly worked; my hearing by then was probably better, too; and, surely I was more mature by then—in any case, from then on, my grade school education ran pretty much on track until I lost vision in the sixth grade.

Actually, Mom must have fretted a good bit about my vision during those preschool years. Several years ago, one of my piano tuning customers informed me, "My mother-in-law, Elizabeth Rhodes Good, took care of you when you were a newborn baby. She could see your eyes weren't right." Mom, like most women in our community, had all her babies at home; they always had a younger woman, often a relative, come and do the housework and help with the care of the baby for 2 weeks or so. Elizabeth was Mom's cousin and helped Mom when I arrived. I'm guessing she and Mom's sisters (who also lived in the house at the time) were all abuzz about "Little Daniel's eyes." I do recall my own observations as an eight- or ten-year-old looking at my baby pictures—*My eyes don't seem very awake.* I certainly wasn't a bright-eyed baby. And, I recall from somewhere in those preschool years Mom holding me on her lap trying to make me count how many fingers she was holding up; she was checking my vision. Dr. McGuire's glasses certainly set me up for fairly normal vision, a nearsighted 20/70 or so in one eye till age 12.

Back in school (September 1948) I began getting the hang of things. Playground activities were always interesting even when I wasn't directly involved. One day I noticed a cloud of dust at the pitcher's mound on the ball field west of the schoolhouse. Two big boys were wrestling and raising a lot of dust. This went on for a long time. Finally they quit, got up and dusted themselves off. When the dust cleared a bit, I saw the one "big boy" dusting himself off and adjusting his jacket was Mr. Eshleman, the school principal. He was out of breath but seemed happy as he strode back into the building to resume whatever principals do all day long. About 5 or 6 years ago I was talking about Dale Enterprise school days with Dwight Rohrer, one of my piano tuning customers. He said, "In seventh grade I was big for my age. One day Harold Eshleman and I spent a whole recess wrestling all over the ball field. I couldn't pin him and he couldn't pin me." So, that's what I had witnessed.

Another time a game of "burny ball" was going on. Burny ball is like tag except you throw a ball (one of those two-inch air-filled rubber balls) to tag the other guy instead of touching him. The point was to throw the ball hard—hopefully hard enough to really sting the other guy's rear end. This game made you run hard, continuously, all over the playground. If you got hit with the ball, you not only became "It," you had to run however far to retrieve the ball. Since the ball could get you from a distance you had to run hard or duck around any nearby corner to stay out of range. If "It" threw and missed his target, he had to run however far to chase down the ball—and that while everyone else stood openly laughing and jeering at his poor aim. When "It" got the ball the jeering suddenly stopped, and everybody ducked out of sight. I was watching these proceedings from the little front porch area. Suddenly Harold Arbogast came tearing at full gallop in the back door of the schoolhouse, through the hall, out the front door, and around the corner to the left. A split second later, wonder of wonders, here came Mr. Eshleman running through the schoolhouse also at full tilt—with that ball! As Mr. Eshleman came out the front door and as Harold was about to disappear around the west corner, I saw a wicked "Gotcha" grin come on Mr. Eshleman's face as his long right arm came up and back and threw hard, just like a baseball pitcher. He didn't miss! Suddenly Harold was jumping up and down with both hands on his behind howling like it really stung back there! (I would soon understand Harold Arbogast was quite the playground clown.)

I said above I was getting the hang of things. Well, early that fall I had an unforgettable experience with being "forced into slave labor." Robert Lowry, a second cousin, was beginning third grade that same year. Robert had broken a leg and was on crutches. Mom told me he was recovering and would be at school when I got there. At recess I went out back and, sure enough, there was Robert on his crutches—but there were also those CABINS!

Those cabins at Dale Enterprise School were a marvel of playground enterprise. At the back of the school property was a board fence intended to keep kids on one side and cows on the other side. Scattered on the ground all along this fence were all kinds of things that could be used to build lean-to structures against the fence; we called them "cabins." First you collected some boards, probably old fence boards maybe seven or eight feet long. You leaned them against the fence, one end on a top fence rail and the other end on the ground. Then you gathered "straw"—whatever that "straw" was, I don't know. We kids called it "broom sage," and some adult alumni still think it really was broom sage. Each fall before school resumed, somebody mowed the playground "grass" and just left the clippings lie. These clippings, maybe four to ten inches long, more like straw and less like grass, were clean and dust free. It was wonderful stuff to gather, pile up, and tumble around in. And it was wonderful insulation for these cabins.

So, you put a layer of this straw on top those boards and laid pieces of tar paper over that straw. Then you laid on some more boards to hold everything in place. Next you used short boards and scraps of burlap cloth from old feed sacks to close in the triangular side openings. You lined the interior with straw, making it all nice and cozy. Some of the bigger cabins divided the interior into smaller "rooms" with burlap curtains. At any one time there might be several cabins lined up along that fence in various stages of construction or demolition. The girls had at least one cabin of their own.

Predictably, a playground social order emerged centered around these cabins. There were bosses, pecking orders, cliques, secrets and rules; there was social ranking within cabins and among cabins. There was cooperation to solve problems and there was competition for power and standing. And, there were "slaves."

That was the world I walked into that day. I went toward Robert expecting to be greeted and, I suppose, welcomed into whatever was going on. Up closer I saw he was red faced and out of breath from the exertion of limping about on those crutches. Or was the exertion from the hard work of being boss of that cabin? He pointed a crutch at me and some other little kids, including Eldon. "Gather straw, you slaves!" he ordered. We were to gather the straw into bundles and others would take it into the cabin. At first, I thought, "Hey, OK, this sounds like fun—making that cabin nice and cozy," but after a while Robert's bossing began getting a bit too real. He was really hopping about, an unbuttoned jacket flapping around him, gesticulating with crutch or fists, shouting, "Gather straw, slaves, hurry up! Bring it over here! Gather straw!" I saw we were reenacting the story of the Israelite slaves in Egypt that Dad had told us about many times. *So, this is the way it is to be a slave!* I also realized my earlier notion that crutches might be fun was very wrong—Robert was courageously doing what he had to do on those crutches, and it did not seem fun. Suddenly for some reason he had to get back to the cabin—quickly! He went, variously running, limping, and hopping long jumps with his crutches, coat tails flying, looking anxious—so, maybe he wasn't the boss after all; maybe he was a slave driver under orders from a boss, and in some kind of trouble?

After that the important action seemed to move inside the cabin. I ran over to crawl in, eager to see what we had built with all that work. Somebody yanked a burlap door flap across my face and hissed, "No, you can't come in here! You're a slave and slaves aren't allowed in here!"

I was socially immature in those days and you would think I went away crying. Not so! I remember my feelings perfectly well and I know now what I would have said had I the words to say it: "Oh?! Now wait a minute here! If I can't share in the goodies of this project WE ALL worked at, if I can't benefit from the labor of my own hands, play or no play, you get no more labor out of me!" I immediately revoked my admiration for those big boys and sluffed off any sense of obligation to obey any orders from them! Maybe this "shrugging off the yoke" was made easier because I saw the Israelite slaves as the good guys who were eventually vindicated. I just walked away from there figuring I would go find something worthwhile to do. (I wish I could say I handled other disappointments that well.)

I don't know when that "Cabin Era" began at Dale Enterprise but I know it ended suddenly—literally overnight. One day when I was in fourth or fifth grade we came to school and the cabins and all the boards and burlap and tar paper were GONE! The grass clippings were gone, too. The place was so clean and sterile it was boring. A story circulated among some of the kids that one of the cabins "went coed," so, the authorities acted decisively. At a school reunion in 2015 another reason for shutting down the cabins was given: two boys came up missing after recess. They were discovered out back trying to put out a fire at one of the cabins. Mr. Eshleman and a bunch of kids rushed out and managed to put out the fire. A big hole was left in the fence with charred fence rails on either side of the gap. Naughty cigarettes were suspected.

Everyone who went through Miss Cox's classroom at Dale Enterprise remembers the annual Fall outing back to Mole Hill. Mole Hill is an interesting geological formation in easy walking distance of the schoolhouse. I always heard it is the remaining core of an ancient volcano where lava pushed up but never actually erupted. Local wags like to refer to it is a "volcanic burp." The surrounding soil eventually eroded away leaving this pronounced round hill rising from the middle of otherwise flat farming country. Eldon tells me when flying over the area in a small airplane, you can see that Mole Hill is actually one of a series of pimple like hills running north and south in the middle of the valley floor. (After writing the above, I find that current geological science says that Mole Hill was an active volcano—a mere 47 million years ago.)

Well, anyway, every year on a nice Fall day Miss Cox would march us all, two by two, west along Route 33 (we called ourselves "Cox's Army") and down a side road to the northwest flank of Mole Hill to play in the autumn leaves. We would run and tumble in the leaves; we would pile them up and dive in and burrow out of sight. We would look for unusual leaf and rock specimens.

On one of these outings Miss Cox told us each to select four or five of the prettiest leaves we could find and take them along back to the schoolhouse. Then, over the next several days, we used crayons to color the back side of each leaf—red, green, yellow, brown, orange, and even some black spots, following the actual color patterns on the leaf. We even used the yellow-green crayon to color the stem and veins of the leaf. Miss Cox would then place the leaf, crayoned side down, on white cloth (cotton, I assume). She laid wax paper over the leaf and ironed it with a hot iron. The bright crayon colors transferred immediately to the white cloth making a perfect print of an autumn leaf—only the colors on this autumn leaf were the full bright colors you see in a child's crayon box.

At some point I caught on—these white cloth sheets with crayoned leaf prints were going to be curtains for the classroom windows. To make a border for each curtain one of the bigger girls used a yard stick and pencil to mark off three one-inch wide bands spaced one inch apart across the bottom of the curtain. We then colored those bands red, yellow, and green (we must have used up a lot of crayons on that cloth). The leaf prints were arranged across the curtain above this striped border. The upper part of the curtain remained pure white. These were café curtains with a separate valance at the top—and I think that valance also had matching red, yellow and green bands. The effect was breathtaking!! They made the whole room bright and cheerful!

Those curtains combined with the children's crayon artwork, which Miss Cox kept posting everywhere around the room, made a veritable feast of color for me. I never tired, even through my fifth grade rough and rowdy days, of walking in there to browse and just soak in all that color!

By the way, I never got tired of opening a crayon box just to gaze at the colors. Actually, I have come to believe that highly nearsighted people perceive color more vividly than normally sighted folks. See my comments on this in the Introduction to this book.

For the record, Miss Marie T. Cox lived to age 108! We kids must not have been too hard on her.

When we showed up for fourth grade in the Fall of 1951, things were all different at Dale Enterprise. The county school board had closed down Oakland Grove, a little one-room school on the other side of Mole Hill and transferred its 20 or so students, mostly conservative and Old Order Mennonites, and its single teacher, Miss Alice Keeler, also Mennonite, to the Dale Enterprise School. Now, all three classrooms were occupied—Miss Cox had the younger grades in the east room, Miss Keeler had the middle grades in the west room, and Mr. Eshleman had the upper grades in the back (south) room.

There was another, more significant difference. By this time (age 10 or so) I must have been at least somewhat aware there were public schools run by the larger community for everybody in the community, and there were church schools run by churches for their own kids. I was also increasingly aware of general distinctions between the secular and the sacred—some songs and activities were secular, belonging to the larger community, and some songs and activities were sacred, belonging to the church world. Regardless of how well I understood these things, I certainly was aware of a change moving from Miss Cox's room to Miss Keeler's room. Miss Cox's room, for my first three years, was run like public school. The only religious content was in patriotic songs, Christmas carols, Thanksgiving and Easter artwork, etc. I felt I was a part of a world larger than just Mennonite. Now in fourth grade Miss Keeler was sure enough running her classroom like a Mennonite church school, a quite conservative Mennonite school at that. She was starting the day with Bible reading and prayer, singing church songs, and having us memorize long New Testament passages. Her moral precepts and comments about "Christian living" were clearly what we today would call "sectarian." It wasn't that I disapproved of what she was saying—after all, this was the stuff of my religious training at home and at church. But something felt strange; this was supposed to be public school in the larger community—some of the kids here were not of our Mennonite persuasion.

One day Miss Keeler announced, "Tomorrow a man is coming to talk to you about guns. I'm letting you know I don't approve of this but since this is a public school, I can do nothing to stop him." She was talking from our Mennonite peace and non-resistance position, which was definitely a minority view. This turned out to be a lesson in gun safety with maybe some overtones of today's NRA style thinking. Mis Keeler's "warning" about this visitor shows she, too, felt the tension between this public school setting and her faith traditions. As I said, it's not as though I was fully conversant back then with the problems we today term "religion in public schools," but I certainly took notice of the issue. I do recall liking the atmosphere in Miss Cox's room better.

Upon writing that last paragraph, it dawns on me why I took notice of that "religion in public school" issue. It was at this time that Dad, at home, was drilling us kids on the Mennonite doctrine of "separation from the world." Starting in the 1920s, Virginia Mennonites began stressing in a new way what was, actually, an old Mennonite teaching—namely that Christians are supposed to "be separate from the world." This new stress on separation involved adoption of uniform dress standards (rigorously plain clothing), withdrawal of church members from corporate boards and community councils, prohibitions against participating in county fairs and other "worldly" amusements and entertainments, etc. Pressure on members to comply with these teachings at first was intense, but by my time things were starting to loosen up a bit. For Dad though, it was still urgently important that we kids understand that we must "be separate from the world." "We don't do everything our so-called Christian neighbors do." He paused, searching for wording, then said, "There are lots of people who say they are Christians, I'll just call them 'professing Christians,' who don't obey ALL the teachings of the Bible. They can be the nicest people, and seem totally sincere, but they don't do everything the Bible says." I understood him to mean "they aren't true Christians," but he didn't want to say it that bluntly.

About this time Eldon and I spied an announcement in the local paper for a "Tractor Dance" to be held that night at J. O. Stickley's, a prominent farm equipment dealer in Harrisonburg. This was going to involve a bunch of Farmall tractors—you know, TRACTORS, that favorite piece of farm equipment for any self-respecting farm boy! These big red tractors were going to be moving about in formation, in and out, round and round each other like a dance. Eldon and I clamored to go see this show. I figured it wouldn't happen. Wonder of wonders though, after supper Dad announced he was taking Eldon and me to that tractor dance! We got there late but found a place where we could stand and see everything very well. On the stage was a country music band starting the show. As I took in the scene, I got excited! I was hearing AND SEEING real live guitar music—for the first time! The lighting was just right, and the sound was just right! The string sounds of the guitar were positively seductive! The movements of that man's hands on the guitar strings were enthralling! His facial expression and body movements were COOL! Then the words to the music started—it was what our families called, "one of them ol' love songs." With that, it all collapsed. Dad pulled Eldon and me away—"Come on boys, we're not staying for this. This is just a bunch of worldly amusement that we don't participate in." Talk about a downer! On the way home Dad rehearsed his line about "professing Christians—they can be the nicest people and seem so sincere, but..." He went on, "I noticed a woman standing there—she seemed like a very nice person, but she gave me the awfullest look when she saw me pulling you boys away from that show."

Eldon says it was a clown out there, not on the main stage, which I didn't see, doing a drunkenness routine that made Dad pull us away. In any case, the build-up and let-down that night were for me a profound closing of a door—IN MY FACE! I felt this keenly because it happened just as I was becoming aware of the larger world out there beyond our Mennonite world—there were all kinds of fun and interesting things out there and I wanted to see and do them. I was elated on the way to that Tractor Dance because we were going to an event out in the larger community. Then that guitar music got added to the mix! Then the door slammed shut!

It was these kinds of teachings that created in me a consciousness of "we versus they"—we true believers versus those that just don't quite get it. That set me up to notice the religion in public school issue as I moved from Miss Cox's room to Miss Keeler's room. I did in fact go on to deeply appreciate my Mennonite heritage, but I never quite knuckled under to that strenuous expression of "be separated onto God" doctrine. As it turned out, my loss of vision two years later landed me in another school setting where I managed (not with forethought) to do a kind of end-run around that doctrine, but more on that later.

Well, back to fourth grade. In fourth grade my artwork turned decidedly toward things mechanical. I learned to use a ruler and compass to draw tractors, locomotives, threshing machines, water wheels, etc. More significantly, I began learning how to get three-dimensional perspective into a drawing on a two-dimensional page, how to do "vanishing points" on buildings and roads, etc. This knowledge of how three-dimensional figures are represented on a two-dimensional page proved critical later when I switched to Braille textbooks for math, science, and geometry. Braille textbooks often have raised line drawings of three-dimensional figures just like those in print books. I was to discover these were easy for me to use, but they are extremely difficult or impossible for people blind from birth to comprehend. Since they never experienced three-dimensional vision they just can't comprehend how those crazy angles in 3-D drawings on a 2-D page are supposed to convey the allusion of "depth" (three dimensions).

Certainly, one of my highlights in fourth grade was the discovery I could use the county bookmobile without supervision! The bookmobile was a van or maybe a school bus equipped as a little library on wheels. It showed up at surrounding county schools about once a month. We could check out books just like from a town library. Nobody objected to me checking out any number of books. I chose books with lots of pictures and minimal text. My prize find was a book explaining how engines and all kinds of mechanical devices work—lever and block and tackle systems, water wheels, windmills, steam engines, electric motors, generators, batteries, turbines, gas engines, diesel engines, jet and rocket engines, explanations of "horse power," etc. I must have checked that book out at least four times that year; the librarian would smile and comment when she saw it AGAIN in my stack of books. To this day those diagrams and cut-away drawings supply the visual imagery when I think about all kinds of mechanical contraptions.

That book was also an occasion for a "moment of truth" with Mom. At some point I realized Mom probably didn't understand how all these engines and mechanical things work— *Wow, in such matters at least,* I thought, *I now know more than Mom!* Standing in the living room I looked up at her and said, rather impudently I suppose, "I know more than you do." Suddenly Mom was more alive than usual and seemed a foot taller! "Come here, Daniel," she ordered. She didn't grab me; she took control verbally. "You don't sass me like that." She started to smack me on the mouth, paused and said, "Make a snoot." (She wanted me to pucker up my lips so she could carefully (!) smack me on the mouth without hitting my glasses or bloodying my lips.) I turned away. "No, Daniel, come here. Now, stand still and make a snoot." Talk about reluctant compliance—I stood still and made a snoot. Either I relaxed it too soon, or Mom half missed her smack. Anyway, she was not satisfied. "Daniel, look up here! I said, 'Make a snoot!'" "Make a snoot," she ordered again. "Look here and make a snoot!" Well, I finally did and held it and she landed her smack. This was not a hard slap across the face; it was a symbolic, careful little smack, well aimed and effective. I got her point. What a Mom!

An incident occurred in Miss Keeler's fourth grade that I still turn over in my mind even today. A Puerto Rican family showed up at Dale Enterprise School. There were three kids—a boy named Juan (name changed), and two younger sisters. They looked neat and dressed nicer than any school kids I ever saw. Miss Keeler got their mother, Mrs. Perez (name changed), to come play her accordion (and tap her foot) for us. I liked the music, especially the bass (this is one more musical instrument that hooked me for life). Mrs. Perez's swaying body movements as she pumped that accordion were as fascinating as the music.

One day on the playground some of us got some kind of circle game going. The Perez kids came up wanting to join in. They had no clue how to participate, and the language barrier made it impossible for them to ask how or for us to explain how.

The girls just walked off, but Juan threw himself into the middle of our circle. He was laughing and we sort of laughed at first, but he was ruining our game. We pushed him aside and tried to resume the game. Well, goodness, goodness, the game wouldn't start up again even though he was pushed out of the way! We could see that Juan was disappointed and how could we have fun when he was pushed to the sideline all unhappy?! The fun was gone and wouldn't come back. The game was done! What was needed was a new, bigger game that would include us all, but, being just a bunch of ordinary country school kids, none of us had the leadership resources to make such a thing happen. We were all a bit sad. I distinctly recall thinking something like, *Those Perez kids seem neat. I just wish we could find a way to play together.* Those kids weren't at Dale Enterprise long; I never knew where they went.

Whenever I think about the "immigrant problems" these days I often think of the Perez kids. We white Anglo Saxon Americans often complain about "all those immigrants" spoiling our cultural fun. Intuitively I can see if we ever find a way to ship all those immigrants back home and build a wall to keep them there, when we sigh with relief and turn back to our game, we will find the fun is gone and won't come back. What we need is somebody or someway to come up with a new, much bigger "Culture Americana Game" that includes us all. Who will that be?

Another guest to Miss Keeler's classroom talked to us about roadside litter and city trash and garbage disposal. I thought it was a "sissy" subject, but he went on to explain how virtually everything we humans do—farming, industry, our daily living—produces undesirable byproducts that mess up our world. Our cars produce exhaust; I don't know if he said, or if I just caught on, our own bodies produce "exhaust," too. He said that, as future citizens, we must plan how to dispose of all this stuff. With man-to-man adult candor he confessed to us kids that he was pessimistic about solving these problems. Today we have barges traveling up and down the east coast looking for a place to dispose of New York City's garbage, China refusing to take anymore of our recyclables, those industrial slag heaps and hazardous waste ponds, nuclear waste, and lately I've heard experts wondering how they're going to get rid of massive amounts of toxic brine from big water desalinization systems. Are we, presumably the most intelligent species on earth, going to be the one who most befouls our own habitat? Often when I hear this kind of talk, I think of that soft-spoken, pleasant man in fourth grade warning us about all this.

Fifth grade—well, in fifth grade I was increasingly aware of myself—it was like I was coming into my own, discovering I could take initiative in pursuing my own interests. While I was still quite content to stay in at recess to pursue projects of my own, I was also becoming more outgoing, more ready to join in playground rough and tumble. I was becoming social, rowdy, rambunctious, and ornery. Fortunately for me, the fifth, sixth and seventh grade teacher was Mr. Eshleman. He commanded my respect.

Mr. Eshleman was a great teacher! He was very present wherever he was present—he stood tall, moved about easily and quickly. His voice was big and strong—it got and held your attention. His face was expressive—usually it was the face of a friendly teacher who seemed to enjoy having you around; occasionally it was the face of a sober judge before whom you got very serious. The time or two I stood before his bar I was scared silly, but in the end, I felt he handled me fairly enough.

He was often out on the playground. During baseball games he would play catcher for both teams—that meant crouching behind home plate with that face mask and catcher's mitt for long stretches. He tried to get runners "out" from either team with equal enthusiasm.

One day Mr. Eshleman spent a lot of time coaching some of us how to ride bicycles in formation. A lot of kids road bicycles to school. We liked to ride each other's bikes around a dirt track along the fence that ran alongside the highway. Mr. Eshleman got the idea of riding three bicycles in tight side-by-side formation. Staying abreast on a straight stretch was doable with practice. The real challenge was staying abreast around that tight hairpin turn at the far end of the track! The guy in the middle was supposed to maintain constant speed through the turn. The outside rider had to speed up A LOT but it was hard to quickly speed up that much. The inside rider had to slow down A LOT but then he could hardly keep his balance. Sometimes Mr. Eshleman rode one of the bikes. I don't recall any three-bike formation getting around that turn intact, but I think several two bike pairs made it. It was from watching all this, plus what I learned earlier from the pedal tractor Dad made for us, that I came to understand and appreciate the role of the differential in the drive axle of cars, trucks, tractors, etc.

Mr. Eshleman's classroom was unusually well equipped for extracurricular reading and all sorts of arts and crafts. In the back left corner was a large magazine rack full of magazines like *Flying, Popular Science*, and *Boy's Life* (was there a Girl's Life— I don't know). There were all sorts of plans for woodworking projects, etc. The *World Book Encyclopedia* was back there too— with all those bright pictures of Aztec and Inca Indian cultures and North American Indian wigwams and teepees; pictures of old cars, sailing ships, ocean liners, submarines; photos and diagrams of old and modern AIRPLANES, etc. Back in that corner were also big, beautiful pictures of birds—was there an Audubon bird book in that collection? In the back right corner were shelves with little cans of paint—all kinds of BRIGHT COLORS (Eldon thinks most of those were Pactra paints ideally suited for decorating models), many kinds and shapes of paint brushes, lots of solvents, stains, and paint cleaners, lots of sandpaper. Somewhere in that mix were supplies for plaster of Paris projects. You could pour plaster into rubber molds to make figurines which you then hand painted. You could pour plaster into a pan or box to make a solid flat slab or block, which you then hand carved into some object (carving plaster of Paris is really fun) and then you hand painted that. There were supplies for papier-mâché projects. Best of all, along the right wall was a long work bench loaded with honest-to-goodness woodworking equipment—a big jig saw, a wood lathe (maybe 30 inches long), a little stand to which you could attach a quarter-inch electric drill thus making a small drill press, a miter box with a back saw, an assortment of hand saws, coping saws, many sharp and well-cared-for wood chisels suitable for lathe work and/or hand carving. And, down in the furnace room, in a big bin, was lots of scrap lumber—"Just help yourself if you can think of a use for it!" It's my understanding that all that woodworking equipment and those supplies were out of Mr. Eshleman's own pocket—he was clearly serious about industrial arts.

As I emerged into this fifth-grade world, it gradually dawned on me I was welcome to use all those supplies, tools, and machines to my heart's content—it was OK both at home and at school! Finally, I didn't have to put up with, "Now Sonny, you can look but don't touch…" I was soon immersed in many woodworking projects, some easy and some over my head, and thus began my lifelong pursuit of woodworking. In those days we had a half hour for morning recess, an hour for lunch, and fifteen minutes for afternoon recess; in addition, thanks to bus schedules, I had a half hour before and a half hour after school of free time—that was a total of two and three quarter hours daily of unstructured time on the school ground! I used it well for these various art and wood projects! But, as I said above, the social part of me was coming out too and, by the end of fifth grade, that cut into my unstructured time for industrial arts— more on that later.

Mr. Eshleman on religion was unforgettable. It's my understanding that he, along with Chester K. Lehman were the most progressive Mennonite pastors in the Virginia Mennonite world at that time. His religious teaching seemed more generous and less sectarian than Miss Keeler's, but it was still definitely Mennonite Christianity in a very public school. One day he was holding forth on the vanity and foolishness of wearing neckties. Neckties and bow ties were frowned upon or even forbidden among various Virginia Mennonites at that time. Suddenly Bill Good, his nephew, piped up from the back, left corner of the room, "Oh, come on, Uncle Harold, what's so bad about wearing a little bow tie? Lots of Christians wear ties." Mr. Eshleman's big strong voice trailed off into an unintelligible stammer, "Well, I-I guess…" He did not discipline or scold Bill for thus contradicting him.

It's his teachings from the Book of Revelation that Mr. Eshleman's students talk about to this day. Seemingly in contradiction to his otherwise more progressive theology, Mr. Eshleman was a premillennialist, and he could and did present the graphic content of Revelation GRAPHICALLY! His students reacted both positively and negatively. At Dale Enterprise School reunions to this day I regularly hear comments like these: "Mr. Eshleman's teachings from Revelation were the beginning of my Christian faith. I'm now a member of a conservative Presbyterian Church in Tennessee. I'm forever grateful." Or, "When he would start talking about Revelation, I would go down and sit in the girls' bathroom until he was finished." Or, "He scared the tar out of me and my friend. We begged our parents to transfer us to another school, and they did." At the last reunion in 2015, one alumnus was so appreciative of Mr. Eshleman's teachings on Revelation he wanted to know where to find a printed copy. At a reunion sometime in the 1990s Bernard Martin summed up the feeling of many: "Mr. Eshleman put the fear of God in all of us." At the same reunion, or maybe the next, Mr. Eshleman, now an old man using a walker, took the mic and said in his deep, strong voice with real feeling, "I want you all to know you are good people." It seemed clear to me he was reaching out to former students he had perhaps over-intimidated.

It was late in the day, almost time to go home. Everybody was quiet and lazy. Eldon and I rarely crossed paths at school, but for whatever reason on this day he was sitting in the desk behind me. I was busily minding my own fifth grader's business. Out of the blue, Mr. Eshleman suddenly said in his big, strong voice, "Daniel, blow your nose!" What!! I didn't know I had a problem. I usually thought of Mr. Eshleman's big voice as something good but why did he have to talk so loud now?! I checked my pockets for a handkerchief and was dismayed to find none. Talk about embarrassment! I'm sure I turned red as forty beets!

Then Bill Good called across the room from the diagonal far corner, "Here Daniel, I have a handkerchief you can use." (This was the same Bill Good, now in seventh grade, that bailed me out of trouble back in first grade.) *Whew-wee!!* I got up, walked across the front of the room behind Mr. Eshleman, in full view of everybody, then back the left side of the room past the work bench with all that woodworking equipment to Bill's desk—what a long walk! Bill gave me a clean handkerchief or perhaps some paper hankies—in any case I recall they smelled clean and fresh. I performed the required task though there was clearly no need for it, then walked the long, long way back to my desk, in front of everybody. I just let my red face hang out. I remember thinking, *I see now why, when people get embarrassed, they sometimes say they just want to fall into a hole.* I was embarrassed, but I surely was appreciating Bill's resourcefulness. Once again, what kind of sensitivity and audacity and social poise must it take for a seventh grader to intervene like that, unbidden by the teacher, on behalf of a fifth grader in a predicament?!

Fast forward about a year for the rest of this story. I was now practically blind, and I was home for Thanksgiving vacation from the School for the Blind. Eldon and I were discovering it was fun to figure out how to work together as a blind/sighted team doing some chores around the barn. (Yeah right, heretofore I was glad enough for any excuse to get out of farm chores, but now I was eager to find ways to be involved without vision.) We had put a bucket of calf feed on a pole between us; I found it was easy to follow anywhere that way. Suddenly he turned and said, "Do you remember that day when Mr. Eshleman made you blow your nose?"

"Well, y-ye-e-ess."

"Well," says he, "that was me sniffling that day."

His confession was so out of the blue, so candid, my astonishment was so great, and the story was so funny I never once felt inclined to bang him on the head. Now, back to the final weeks of fifth grade.

With the arrival of Spring in 1953, my world began changing—a lot. Much of the time up through fourth grade I had been sort of a loner on the playground, but not always an unhappy loner. Lots of times I stayed in at recess (if the teacher didn't shoo me out) to draw and color, or to browse through various books, magazines, Encyclopedia articles, etc., or to use that woodworking equipment in Mr. Eshleman's room. But in fifth grade I began to change. I discovered that I could get the admiration of the big boys, the "in crowd," by sheer rowdiness and rough housing. I was becoming less of a loner, more sociable. I wonder if maybe my male hormones were starting to trickle in, though my voice didn't actually change for another year or so.

This rowdiness came to full flower that Spring in a game we call "Fish." Any number of players would line up behind a base line on either end of a playing field. A person who was "It" would stand in the middle. When "It" yelled "Fish!" the players on the two ends would run across to the other end, trying to avoid being tagged or tackled by "It." If you were tagged or tackled, you had to join "It" in the middle and help catch more players who then also had to join the middle. As the number of players in the middle increased, it became harder and harder for the remaining players to thread their way across to the other side without being tagged. If any player got caught trying to sneak off his base before "It" yelled "Fish!" he had to join the middle. I caught on that I could trick players into leaving their bases too soon by yelling, "Ish," or "Dish," etc., making them think I had yelled, "Fish!"

The game sounds childishly simple but it got really rough. There were lots of flying tackles and football style pile-ups. I was scrawny and small for my age, but I enjoyed those tackles. One time my glasses went a flyin' and I had no idea where to start looking for them. Jim Burkholder, one of the big guys I really admired, picked them up from the weedy grass eight or ten feet away and brought them over to me. From the way he handed them to me, sort of shoulder to shoulder, I realized he was admiring my spunkiness. This went on recess after recess. When let out for recess, we would run pellmell down to the playing field. The last person there was "It" to start the game.

Mr. Eshleman finally put a stop to this game when I got a really bloody knee from banging it down on a rock in one of those flying tackles—the hole in my knee looked to be to the bone—Mr. Eshleman thought we had gotten just too rough.

In the weeks before this rough play I had begun to notice another change coming into my world—little black specks in my field of vision whenever I looked at the blue sky. At first, I thought they were distant birds flying across the sky, but why always in that same pattern? Then I realized I was seeing the same pattern of specks moving across the light-colored wall above the blackboard in Mr. Eshleman's classroom, so I knew these specks were coming from something going on inside my left eye (my good eye). Then I realized that the apparent drifting motion of the specks was actually the result of my gaze drifting around the visual world; if I concentrated on focusing on one exact spot, the specks did not move. Then one of the specks seemed to sprout little wings out each side. Toward the end of fifth grade, which was the very time of that rough "Fish" game, a black curtain started coming up from the bottom of the field of vision. It would disappear when I looked down, as in reading a book, and reappear when I looked up. I could still function normally in visual matters, but I was starting to worry about what was going on. I told Mom about all this. She was puzzled but, like me, had no clue we should be high-tailing it to an eye doctor.

That's the way my vision was when I finished fifth grade and headed into the Summer of 1953, and on to sixth grade when everything changed.

But before ending this chapter, one can't talk about school days at Dale Enterprise School without telling about the end-of-school-year picnic. On the last or next-to-last day of school one of the parents would show up with a one-and-a-half or 2-ton flatbed truck equipped with tall cattle racks. Once or several times it was Ruel Martin with his big Studebaker truck. They would set a little ladder at the back and we kids would all climb on. They would close the tail gate and we would head west on Route 33. This open truck ride was a large part of the fun—there was no seating—we mostly stood around the edges holding onto the racks, the taller kids reaching over or between the shorter ones for a hand hold on the racks. Some of us liked to stand or walk around in the middle of the truck bed showing off—"I don't need no hand hold…!" But then if you hold on to the rack at the right place, you could get close to a girl, so, we (or at least I) resumed holding on to the rack.

We would go to places like Hone Quarry, Ed's Park, or City Park. We kids, teachers, and parents all played horseshoes, baseball, or just lazed around.

Wow, look at those adults running around and yelling like us kids… Great day, those grownups hit that ball so high I can't see it!… Hey, this is fun to just run around exploring the place! And there's all that picnic food and Mom and Dad aren't here to tell me what and how much not to eat.

Hot dogs—to this day those hot dogs roasted by Frank Rhodes are my standard for a good hot dog. Cheese slices, watermelons, popsicles. Those popsicles meant dry ice to play with—just drop a piece of it down someone's collar and watch him get excited!

Evidently, before my time, some of the fun at those picnics was more rowdy. One alumnus, now a retired author of several books, told me this: At one of those school picnics a certain boy (a respected and now retired church leader in Virginia Mennonite circles) set off a firecracker under her skirt. It blew her dress to shreds. Her friends helped her find safety pins and fasten her dress together enough to be halfway presentable the rest of the day.

5

TRANSITION—FROM SIXTH GRADE SEEING TO SIXTH GRADE BLIND

In 1953-54 all kinds of events piled down on my family and me. I transitioned from a happy, carefree childhood into crazy adolescence. I lost vision and switched from print to Braille. My first ventures into man-sized responsibilities with farm machinery, which were garnering some recognition from Dad and others, were shut down; now I would be uncertain and dependent for a while. For my education I switched from a public school with mostly Mennonite kids to a boarding school where I had to sort through and explain and defend and modify my Mennonite religious heritage pretty much all by myself. Dad's efforts to start up a new dairy on a new farm were nearly derailed by my hospital bills, the collapse of one end of the barn, and Mom's nearly fatal illness and major hospital bills. So, to tell this story, this chapter will sound cluttered and disorganized. That's just the way the year was for us.

SIXTH GRADE AT MT. CLINTON SCHOOL

In September 1953, Eldon, Shirley, Jim, Bernard, and I entered Mt. Clinton School. Our family had finally transferred from the Dale Enterprise School to Mt. Clinton after our move to the new farm (we called it the Carver Place) the year before. Eldon, Shirley and I immediately noticed a different atmosphere

—these kids didn't have that cliquishness that we knew at Dale Enterprise. Also, boys and girls could play together without silly comments from other kids. We began making new friends and acquaintances.

Eldon and I were in sixth grade with Mr. Swank as teacher. The windows in that room faced north, meaning the lighting in the room was less than I really needed, but, well, school life just went on.

SIXTH GRADERS DISCUSSING CHURCH AFFILIATION

One day, in connection with some social studies class, Mr. Swank got us kids talking about what church denomination we belonged to. Maybe he was trying to promote a little religious tolerance—I don't really know. I was hearing kids around the room say, "I'm Baptist," "I go to that Cook's Creek Presbyterian Church up the road," "I'm Methodist," "I go to this here Church of God right down the road here," etc. I perked up my ears—*Hey, these kids are talking about their different religious traditions calmly, even with a little excitement and pride. This is neat!* I leaned forward, started to raise my hand to announce my faith tradition.

Eldon, sitting right behind me, saw me revving up; he grabbed my arm and shook me—"Don't tell them we're Mennonite," he hissed.

I hesitated, puzzled over his words a bit, decided I didn't agree with that policy, raised my hand and announced with the same pride I heard in the other kids, "I'm Mennonite." It felt good.

Thus it was that Eldon and I had our first encounter with the problem of ethnic Mennonite identity in the public schools, a well-known problem for children of other ethnic traditions too—he was embarrassed, I was proud. On that day we started down two different roads regarding what to do about our Mennonite heritage—he became our family agnostic, I became a seminary trained theologian.

MORE ROUGH PLAY, THE TROUBLE ESCALATES

In the course of making new acquaintances and friends I discovered that the big boys here at Mt. Clinton, the hot shots, were much like those at Dale Enterprise—I could get their attention and admiration with a lot of rough and tumble play. A game developed where we smaller boys would ride piggyback on the big boys. We would charge into each other, trying to knock the other rider off. If you knocked both rider and horse over, that was even better. During one recess, the last in the day, about five weeks into the school year, I hit the ground several times really hard. The jarring was a little much but I still regarded it as fun. Going back to the classroom after recess I discovered the black curtain, which I had noticed at the end of fifth grade, was coming still further up into my field of vision. As I entered the classroom the dimness seemed to bother me more. I went to my desk in the left front corner of the room and started into the assigned work, which was to copy some lines Mr. Swank had written on the blackboard.

THE EVENT

Hey, I can't read that writing up there. I walk over to the blackboard to get a closer look (like I've been doing since first grade). *Good grief, I can't read this stuff!* I get closer and peer harder, trying to focus right on the words. I can plainly see white chalk writing on the blackboard. I can even tell that it is neat and precise handwriting but I can't read one letter! The harder I try to focus on an exact spot, the more a black something gets right in the way and blocks my view. I go back to my desk. I get out one book, then another, trying to find something I can read. I can't read one letter no matter what size or type of print. This is crazy! I can see to walk around OK. I can see Mr. Swank sitting over there at his desk, but I can't see to read! I close the book. I put it in my desk. I just sit, my hands on my desk. How does a body arrange one's self to just sit at one's school desk and do nothing? I fidget, then sit, just sit.

"Daniel," Mr. Swank says, sounding like he might scold if I don't have a good answer, "why aren't you doing your work?"

I explain, "For some reason I can't see to read. I can see to get around but I can't read—I don't know why."

(There was no school nurse in those days to help hit the panic button.) Mr. Swank thinks a minute, then says, "Well, just stay there at your desk. School is almost over and you can take the bus home."

At home I tell Mom what's happening. She tells Dad. Dad hurriedly calls my eye doctor, Dr. McGuire at Winchester, two-and-a-half hours away. Dr. McGuire gets urgent—I am to be at his office tomorrow morning at 7:30 sharp. OK, now something is happening, we have a plan. I stretch out on that old sofa just inside the kitchen door. My vision is getting even crazier and distorted now. There are rainbow colors when I look at windows and ceiling lights.

It's at this point Eldon and I got into that crazy argument about my share of our chores. (See "A Look Ahead" at the beginning of the book.) He did go on out that evening and did my chores along with his—and, by the way, he did all those chores ever after that, too. When he went out, the truth finished settling over me that I was sure enough in trouble, real trouble. But there was a plan; so, for the time being, my job was to just wait till the next step—the trip to Winchester in the morning. Eldon tells me (as I'm writing this) that the rest of that evening I just curled up on that sofa with my face to the wall, not wanting attention from anybody. He says the gravity of the situation settled over him, too. I do recall that several times that evening he touched my shoulder tentatively, as though he was checking on me; I just shrugged him off.

THE OPERATION

The next morning Dr. McGuire immediately determined the problem to be a massive detached retina in my left eye (my good eye; my right eye had always been practically useless). He asked if I had recently had any blows to my head. Neither Dad nor I could think of any such thing. (It was months later when I connected "blows to the head" to the rowdy horseplay on the playground that last afternoon at school.) He wanted to do surgery right away, but he explained we had to get the blood inside the eyeball cleared up first. I was to go home and stay in bed for a week. I was to lie only on my back or left side, getting up only to go to the bathroom. Then I was to come back down to Winchester, prepared for two weeks in the hospital; he would then do the surgery.

Well, I went home and did the one week layin' around thing. I think I had a radio—from which country music started creeping into my soul. Mom surprised and delighted me. She seemed to easily morph into a comfortable, practical nurse— none of that emotional "Oh you poor thing" stuff. She quickly solved the problem of a urinal with a one-quart canning jar.

Then I went back down to Winchester Memorial Hospital to, as it turned out, begin the next chapter in my life. The two weeks in the hospital was a little chapter of its own. Shock number 1: *What, that gown is all I'll be wearin' around here—with no shorts?!*

The anesthesia they used on me was ether—you don't want it! They put this mask on my face and, next thing I knew, I was suffocating. The only breath I could get was more of this awful smellin' stuff. My brain started buzzing with searing heat as an ugly red brick wall went streaking past right in my face. As I panicked and went under, the nurse held my head close to her tummy—that was reassuring.

Then I was waking up flat on my back with my head between two sandbags and my eyes completely bandaged, but I could now breathe. I had to throw up. Hands held me down and, a voice said, "Just let it come up where you are, we'll clean you up." Shock number 2: *I'm supposed to stay on my back and puke all over myself like a baby!* That nausea went into dry heaves; I was supposed to keep my head between those sandbags no matter what! The nurses did patiently clean me up, again and again; I began to sense kindness in their hands.

As the nausea from the ether cleared up and the pain in my eye subsided over the next day or so, it came time for me to get busy staying flat on my back with my head between those two sandbags and my eyes bandaged for 10 days! This was a tough assignment for a twelve-year-old farm boy who had recently discovered the joy of handling farm machinery and the fun of rowdy horseplay.

Dad came in the day after the surgery with a combination radio record player and a stack of 45 RPM records. That record player was marvelous; when it finished a stack of records, it would raise the stack and play them all over again, indefinitely if that was what you wanted. At first I was too sick to care, but, as the sickness cleared up, the radio and records served well to fill my time—with that equipment I discovered George Beverly Shay, the Mill Creek Quartet, the Jordanaires, the Chuck Wagon Gang, Billie Graham, Paul Harvey, soap operas, radio comedy, various radio personalities like Red Skelton, and music other than "safe sacred" music.

I soon discovered that if I had to be fed with a spoon while flat on my back like a baby and have all my body parts handled by others, I preferred young, presumably pretty nurses, not old grouchy ones, nor male orderlies.

One young, "pretty" nurse, hearing all that religious music on my records, engaged me in some religious discussions. At one point she asked, "Are you saved?"

I told her, "No, but I'm thinking about it."

My voice had not changed yet but things were changing in me and I had plenty of time to notice.

Mom and Dad came every other day bringing various "get well" cards and gifts, including a bunch of "get well candy." Now that I understand what sugar does to kids, I see why I virtually invented a new game—climbing the wall while lying flat in bed with your head between two sandbags. I cranked and cranked and cranked and CRANKED on a silly little music box that played "Oh my Darling, Clementine." I squealed away on a plastic flute—the nurses tried to quell that.

Dr. McGuire came and checked my eye every day or so. The first time he removed the bandages, all I could see was white misty curtains. The second time was much better but there were a lot of red dots. The third time—wow! I could see his bright red tie and face—and his big smile! He and I were happy! The fourth time Dr. McGuire removed those bandages things were all distorted and hazy again. He looked into my eye a long time with that lighted tool of his. Then he sighed deeply; what I could see of his face was not happy. I understood. *Things weren't going so good after all.* Some of those songs on those records about life's troubles sort of spoke to me.

I suppose the rest of that hospital stay was to finish recuperating from the surgery. They put glasses on me with just a pinhole to see through and began letting me get up and walk around the hall. I immediately discovered that instead of trying to look through that silly little pinhole, it was much easier to just peer under the glasses frame. What vision I had seemed to be in the lower third of the visual field anyway.

When I left the hospital, everything was different. When I went in two weeks earlier, it was sunny, and the leaves were green and still on the trees; when I came out, it was dreary, the branches were mostly bare, and the leaves were brown and on the ground, and a chilly wind was scattering them every which way. My vision? Well, it was all different. I discovered I was now seeing not much with my left eye but more with my right eye, which heretofore had been turned in and useless. (Eldon would soon inform me that my crossed eyes had reversed—the right eye was now straight, and the left eye was turned way in toward my nose.) I had mobility vision but no reading vision. My body, no, my whole being was different in ways I couldn't really understand; I was still a kid, but something more. Through that radio and those records, I was now aware of a wider world out there beyond the Mennonite world of my earlier childhood, and it was interesting.

When I got home—Mom and Dad had gotten a new big double bed and had it set up in the living room for me. I sat down on the edge and, "Whoopee, what kind of mattress is this?!" It was foam rubber, an unheard-of kind of mattress. I started checking it out by tentatively bouncing up and down—

"No, no, Sonny," Dad scolded. "Don't you be jumping around like that! The doctor wants you to stay quiet for a while," Dad sounded scared.

Quiet!? QUIET!? Well...we'll see. This very active farm boy had been virtually tied down for most of two weeks and fed a lot of candy! Now he's just been released and there's a lot more of that "get well sugar" waiting here at home. I consumed that candy and Eldon and I soon found that mattress to be a WONDERFUL WRESTLING MAT! Eldon says he sort of tried to keep me quiet but I would have nothing of it.

RECOVERY AND A BUNCH OF NEW BEGINNINGS

Over the next several weeks Dad came home with more 45 RPM records. The Ours family cousins gave me a little AM radio (which proved convenient for listening to country music elsewhere in the house so as not to trouble Mom's ears). Then Dad came home with another record player; this one was to play those wonderful 16-2/3 RPM records of Alexander Scorby reading the entire New Testament. I did listen to the entire New Testament, several times, I believe. That second record player could also play 78 RPM records, so more records showed up—maybe from Granddaddy Bowman's old collection.

In the following months my Wenger uncles and aunts and cousins went together and got me a really nice Erector Set, a big one. It had an electric motor and an assortment of pulleys and gear wheels, including a pair of beveled gears. That was a perfect gift for me at that time. But there were some wrinkles too—that set created a lot of big brother fussing about little brothers Jimmy and Bernard losing precious screws when they played with it.

I was getting many get well cards with money included; so, Dad took me to the Smith and Carry John Deere dealership where I bought one of those neat little scale model John Deere tractors with a manure scoop in front and a big corn wagon behind. This brought more big brother fretting about little brothers messing around with his toys. In fact, I became quite uncomfortable about my seeming privileged status in Jim and Bernard's eyes. So, with some of that same greeting card money, I bought them a John Deere tractor and wagon like mine—except there was no manure scoop on the tractor since I thought that was a little too complicated for them.

Uncle Howard gave me his old morse code key and a set of instructional records to learn morse code. Dad had heard that blind people can become ham radio operators, so he got me a National (brand) short wave receiver (which also had AM radio). He said we would get the transmitter later if I really got into ham radio.

ENTRÉ TO BOOKS

Then, somewhere in these weeks Dad signed me up for Talking Books! In the 1930s the Federally-funded Talking Book program out of the Library of Congress had begun putting books into recorded format for blind people. It has certainly been one of the most successful and popular "entitlement programs" for disabled people. Some folks in our Mennonite world at that time would not have wanted me to have such easy access to ALL those "worldly books." But Dad signed me up. It certainly was a significant game changer for me. Before Talking Books, my interest—and it was KEEN interest—was in PICTURES. Books with mostly reading and few pictures were hard work for me due to my nearsightedness. That plus my rowdy ornery adolescent disposition at the time had me headed, I believe, toward an anti-intellectual life style—you know, the kind of person long on opinions and short on data. With Talking Books I discovered the world of books. As for Emily Dickinson, books became my way of traveling the world— "There is no frigate like a book," she said.[2] College education eventually became desirable.

Talking Books impacted other family members, too, not always favorably—like the time I started reading *Mutiny on the Bounty*. Cuss words seemed to be in every sentence and the reader entered into them with such gusto Mom couldn't stand it. I tried using headphones but eventually I couldn't stand the profanity either and sent that book back. I still haven't read *Mutiny on the Bounty*—but I certainly have read lots of books, surely a lot more, A WHOLE LOT MORE than if I had not lost vision—thanks to that Talking Book program. But now I've gotten way ahead of my story.

THE FINAL VERDICT

A couple weeks after the surgery I went back to Dr. McGuire for a follow-up visit. He looked in my eye a long time. Then I was taken to the waiting room while the doctor talked to Dad. On the way to the car Dad was sober. I asked, "What did he say about my eye?" Dad replied, "The doctor says that eye won't be useful to you anymore." To this day I'm amazed at and appreciate Dad's choice of words here—he did not use heavy emotional wording like, "Well, Sonny, it looks like you're going to be blind the rest of your life." And by the way, Mom never got into emotional histrionics either. As I sit here now writing this, I'm a bit puzzled as to my fairly unemotional response to this bad news. Maybe I was distracted by all the special attention I was getting and so did not feel the full impact of this report. In any case, Dad went on to say, "But, Sonny, remember, you have a good mind." Over the next weeks and months, moments of disappointment did come when I would discover a new something I couldn't do because of loss of vision. Dad would repeat, "But Sonny, you do have a good mind." He said that many times.

Recently Kathie Weaver Kurtz sent me a copy of a letter written by her grandmother, Myra Lehman, telling a friend about my eye situation at this time. Myra was married to Chester K. Lehman, our pastor at Mt. Clinton Mennonite Church where we attended. Brother Chester and Myra were keenly interested in my situation. Kathie, their granddaughter, was age seven at that time. Myra was intelligent; her letter has all the details and medical terminology correct and shows community interest in my story.

Daniel Bowman was in church too for the first since his eye operation. The Dr. said last week when Millard had Daniel back for a checkup that he feels that the operation was not a success as far as shortening the eyeball or even the repairing of the detached retina was concerned. He said he feared it might be so as the eye was in such bad shape when he started working on it that it was almost beyond help but he did what he could and is very grieved that it hasn't helped the boy. As it now is Daniel has the use of only one eye and that is what was already his poorest eye. He can see enough to get around but not enough to read. We may yet hope and pray that somehow this eye which was always the weakest (and maybe unconsciously not used because the other was stronger) may now become strong enough to give him vision.

So now, for the next nine or ten months, late Fall of 1953 to August of 1954, I would be functioning with mobility vision and no reading vision. The remaining vision was mostly in the lower third of the visual field and would become increasingly faulty and frustrating. I withdrew from school at Mt. Clinton and spent the rest of that school year at home—at home, yes, but I was not inactive all that time! A lot of trouble was coming straight at our family; my mind would be occupied with more than just my failing vision.

Now that I couldn't read, a very early issue for Dad was my Bible reading. Dad was always concerned to promote the habit of Bible reading among his kids—at that time he was having us older kids read three chapters each night before going to bed. He had earlier gotten me that New Testament on records. But he also wanted Eldon to read three chapters a night to me before turning off the light. So, each night, under the covers in that cold bedroom, Eldon would plod through three chapters of the Old Testament (I don't think we ever got to the New Testament). He got quite annoyed at and eventually just glossed over those passages where all those unpronounceable names begat more unpronounceable names who did nothing but beget still more unpronounceable names. (It was the King James Bible.)

A first problem for Mom was me lying around whining, "I want something to do." This really got to Mom, but instead of lapsing into pity for her poor son who was losing his vision, she found him something to do—drying the dishes, every meal, all the time! We kids had been taking rotating turns doing the dishes; now it was my particular job to dry them after every meal. I protested enough to maintain my "male farm boy dignity," but secretly was kinda glad.

My sibs began taking their turns washing the dishes. I immediately started protesting any dirty dish that came my way; I would put it back saying, "That's not clean." Eventually, when I put the same dish back a second or third or fourth time—"It's still not clean"—things got downright quarrelsome.

Finally Eldon yelled, "Mom, make him quit putting these dishes back over here!"

Mom intervened decisively—"Look here, Daniel, you clearly can tell whether those dishes are clean or not. From now on YOU are going to wash these dishes!"

Again I protested enough to maintain my dignity but was glad—I had indeed concluded that I could wash the dishes better than my sibs. From then on I washed, they dried, and we were all happier.

To finish this story—when I was about to marry Ferne, Mom or my sisters informed her about my dish washing. So, to this day Ferne has seen to it that I haven't lost my skill in washing dishes. I like to joke, "Soon after we were married I caught on that Ferne was going to sleep with her dish washer, so I figured I'd better wash the dishes." (Now, the ladies in my life can just thank me for including that story.)

HARD TIMES CLOSING IN

Back in the Spring of 1953 Dad had gotten the new dairy operation up and running on the new farm. On top of those start-up expenses came my eye surgery that Fall. About that same time the end of the barn collapsed. The haymow on that end had been stuffed with hay from an abundant hay crop the previous summer; the big, old beams just gave way, the floor with its load of hay dropped, and the end of the barn pushed out and off its footers. There it stayed, looking really precarious and scary. Now where was Dad going to get the money to fix that? That problem was evidently processed for several months.

That winter the barnyard had to be cleaned out, and that gave me a job that made me feel a little more like a needed farm boy again, riding the manure spreader. Dad would fill the spreader with a new manure scoop on the front of his tractor, then hook the tractor to the spreader and take it out to the field. I would ride the spreader to throw the beaters and drag chain in and out of gear as needed. This was an old horse-drawn spreader Dad had converted to tractor use. The control levers were positioned for someone sitting on the spreader seat while driving horses, not by a farmer sitting way up ahead on a tractor seat. So, my job was to ride that seat and operate the levers on signal. Well, that seat was mighty precarious and bouncy; there was no real hand hold and the spreader bounced around a lot—it was fun and scary. Once a big rock, about 5 inches in diameter, was thrown, or rather, lightly lobbed forward by the beaters and whacked me right between the shoulder blades. That gave Dad and me pause, but we kept working—the job had to be done. While waiting for Dad to reload the spreader I would stand around in the barnyard, getting cold in the very cold January air but enjoying the warm sun. To this day, on any bright, sunny, cold January day, I sniff to check for the smell of barnyard manure.

Along about this time Eldon and I got the notion we wanted to bat an egg with a baseball bat—what would that look like. We knew better than to just get a good egg and smash it—that would be wasting a perfectly good egg. So we got an egg and hid it in a hollow on top of one of the barnyard posts; we would leave it there long enough to get rotten; then, well, then we wouldn't be wasting a good egg—right? We soon got tired of waiting, got the egg down and set up for our experiment. Since I couldn't see very well, Eldon would handle the bat and I would pitch. After several tries, Eldon hit that egg with a mighty swing! The sound was just a little "smack," but what a big beautiful yellow flash! We doubled over laughing like a couple of bratty kids. I don't think either of us ever realized what we would have smelled like if we had been patient enough to let that egg truly "ripen." We washed the eggy mess off our bat in the cow's watering trough—you can't leave evidence like that on your bat, you know.

That February Dad and I were doing some logging work up in the woods. The air was chilly but with the smell of Spring; the sun was bright, and patches of thawing snow were scattered around on the ground and in the pine trees. The colors in these memories are so vivid—the orange tractor with the big black tires amidst the green pine trees, white snow, tan pine needles, and darker brown soil. Dad put me on the opposite end of a big crosscut saw—man, I had to stretch to keep up with his long strokes. Then I was riding on back of the tractor, jumping off and on to hook and unhook the log chains to this or that log. Suddenly, while watching Dad pull around and up front so I could hook up the next log, even with my poor vision I noticed the left rear wheel of the tractor was wobbling—or, was I seeing wrong? No, that wheel was wobbling A LOT!

"Hey Dad," I called, "that left wheel is about to fall off!" Dad stopped the tractor, turned off the engine, got down, came around and was thunderstruck as he saw how near that wheel was to coming off the axle. I had saved the day, and it felt good being accepted as man to man with Dad. That tractor sat right there in the woods until Dad got other manpower and equipment to fix that wheel. It was later that I learned that logging work was for lumber to fix the barn.

We kids were aware that money was short these days. Groceries were skimpy—Mom sometimes got wheat from the barn granary, carefully cleaned it of any insects and mouse droppings, boiled it, and served it with milk and brown sugar for breakfast. Most of us liked it. Sometimes she made graham mush, which she served with milk and brown sugar, and which she also later fried. Occasionally she made corn meal mush with milk and brown sugar and fried the leftovers—we liked the cornmeal offerings better. There were no store-bought cereals these days. Simple brown gravy on bread was also a staple.

Once I was in the dining room where Mom was sweeping up the floor after breakfast and after the other kids were off to school. The light through the window from high bright March clouds was just right for me to see her fairly well. She was wearing a droopy old sweater, which, hanging open, accentuated her big, pregnant tummy. The dirt pile, which she had collected with her broom, was a clutter of toys, junk, an old shoe, paper scraps and ordinary dirt. The floor in this half of the room was still bare wood; the rest of the linoleum would be installed later. She was about to pick up the good stuff before sweeping up the dirt when Dad came in from the shop. He was wearing a raggedy old denim jacket, a dirty old hat and dirty old shoes. The two of them looked the poverty we kids knew at that time—I think both took notice of their appearance and were amused. He went straight over to Mom, took her in his arms with the dirt pile on the floor between them, and gave her a big, long kiss. He went on back to the bathroom; she resumed sweeping, her face beaming—she was happy. I was happy. I'll never forget that scene—

money was tight for they had just gotten the new dairy started on a new farm, the barn needed major repairs, plus the expense of my eye surgery—but they had each other and their own place!

A LITTLE THEOLOGICAL INQUIRY

One more scene stands out from these days. I was almost 13. From adult conversations I was picking up the idea that in Biblical descriptions of heaven, there is something like symbol and metaphor (though I didn't actually know those words). For example, I heard Dad saying, "We don't know what those streets of transparent gold and pearly gates REALLY are, but, of course, they will be wonderful." One day I asked Mom, "Is the fire of hell real fire?"

She was working at the kitchen stove. At my question she turned her right profile to me, her head slightly tilted as in careful thought, her tummy hugely pregnant. (This visual memory is distorted and wavy like my vision was at that time, but it is a real visual memory.) She replied slowly, thoughtfully, "Probably not. We were made to be with God forever, but if we turn away from Him, our regrets will be like fire burning."

My question to Mom seems incredible in view of my age; her answer seems even more incredible in view of our understandings of Scripture in those days. For the Mennonites I knew back then, there was nothing metaphorical or symbolic about hell. My sibs almost all think the whole story is simply not true. Several months before she died, I asked Mom if she remembered anything about my question. She was astounded and even shocked that I would have asked such a question and that I would think she ever didn't believe in real hell fire. "Of course it's real and I always thought so," she said.

How in the world did Mom and/or I come up with this

metaphorical understanding of hell so out of character with our particular religious culture at that time? I have gone over that memory many times since then, even trying to view it like a skeptic. I remain sure that I did ask that question and Mom, standing at the kitchen stove big and pregnant, did give that answer. This metaphorical idea that hell is a state of profound regret after turning one's back on God for whom we were made to be in communion—that is the very idea I put forth later to the kids at VSDB when we talked about such things.

Chester K. Lehman, our pastor at this time, was also a professor of Bible at EMC. It has often been said of him that he was ahead of his time. He was the lone voice on the college faculty holding out against premillennialism. To hold out against premillennialism, one would necessarily, it seems to me, be open to symbolism and metaphor in Biblical interpretation. My theory is that, if not from direct teaching by Brother Chester, then in the general atmosphere of his preaching and teaching, Mom picked up symbolic or metaphorical understandings that makes her answer to me credible. The fact that she later reverted back to more literal understandings matches what I remember of Dad's thinking during my college years—I was aware he definitely settled back into a more rigid literalism than I heard from him in earlier years. And Mom likely followed his path. Or, could it be that Mom's unusual answer is best explained as a mother's soft answer to a child?

A NEW BABY SISTER AND MOM'S ILLNESS

Soon after that discussion at the kitchen stove, Baby Emily was born. When I woke up that morning, Eldon was all excited. "We have a new baby," he said. "It must hurt to have a baby! Mom was hollerin' and hollerin'. And something must have gone wrong; they took her out of the house and took her to the hospital. She was moaning and moaning. There was a lot of commotion. They took her in McMullen's hearse."

All Mom's children were born at home, so going to the hospital was bad news to us kids. Funeral hearses were used in those days as ambulances, so the hearse per se was not bad news for us.

Eldon and I got up and went downstairs. There was a new baby, all wrapped up and lying in the easy chair, and Aunt Brownie was there looking awfully serious. She told us Mom was really sick; we kids gradually caught on she could die. Dad was nowhere around. Uncle Wade was doing the milking. The house was in general disarray. Aunt Brownie told Eldon he would have to see to all the chores. Shirley remembers waking up and running downstairs into the middle of the confusion. She almost sat on the new baby in that easy chair. Shirley also saw the placenta in a basin beside the bed and asked about it; it soon disappeared. Eldon and I saw that placenta later in a chamber pot in the bathroom; it soon disappeared from there, too. Shirley says Aunt Brownie took her aside and told her, "If you ever wanted to pray for your mother, now is the time."

Aunt Brownie got breakfast. Her white gravy instead of Mom's brown gravy drove home the reality of Mom's absence. Some of the little ones were all upset and crying, and couldn't eat. Aunt Brownie finally got the older kids out of the house and off to school. Somehow in all this confusion Baby Emily was placed with Aunt Margaret Suter who kept her for the next three months.

As adults we nine kids have collected our memories of these days along with information we found in the doctor's diary notes and have pieced together a fairly accurate, I believe, understanding of what happened to Mom that night. In his diary notes, Dr. Jacob Huffman recalled that with Mom's eighth baby, there had been a problem with postpartum bleeding. Our sisters recall that he had warned Mom and Dad not to have anymore children. True to her faith (and Dad's) she decided to "leave things in God's hands." At this ninth birthing the postpartum bleeding got completely out of hand and Mom nearly bled to death. In the hospital at one point, she was given up for dead and wheeled out of the operating room under a sheet. Then someone noticed a toe moving. They returned her to the operating room and did a complete hysterectomy, including many blood transfusions—sixteen pints in all. By the time they got the bleeding stopped, her brain had been with insufficient oxygen for entirely too long. The purple discoloration of death had appeared on her hands and feet.

Mom came out of the operating room completely paralyzed on one side, some uncontrolled movement on the other side, and, for several days, completely out of her mind. Four or five days later, she went into convulsions (seizures).

Dad had hired Norma Heatwole, a neat 20-year-old woman, to cook and keep house and look after us kids. The phone rang in the kitchen; Norma took the call and immediately became distracted and agitated. While looking around for her other shoes she told me Mom had gone into convulsions and that was very bad. She gave up on the shoes and ran out into heavy rain and mud, mud, and more mud, in her nice high-heeled shoes, down to the dairy barn to tell Dad. He took the milkers off the cows, left the cows in their stalls, hurried up to the house, called Uncle Wade to come finish the milking, and, looking distraught, dashed off to the hospital. Those convulsions/seizures were the result of the earlier brain anoxia.

Before this I had been aware that Mom might die; now,

seeing Norma so agitated and Dad so distraught, things looked more scary. It felt like, *Not only might Mom die, but, hey, who's in control of what's gonna happen to us kids? Dad sure isn't.* Norma must have done a good job keeping the world together for us kids. Otherwise, I believe, we kids would have known more emotional stress. Over the next several days and weeks our family life sort of settled around Norma in the house and Uncle Wade in the barn; Dad was in and out, mostly at the hospital. Eldon remembers we began hearing less that Mom might die and more that she will be bedridden for life—progress of sorts.

In those days children were not allowed to visit patients in the hospital. Dad and the nurses came up with a plan. A day was set; we kids looked forward to it with excitement. On the appointed day, Dad piled us eight kids (all but Baby Emily) into the '49 Ford and took us to a lounge on the first floor of the hospital. The nurses were going to bring Mom down to the lounge in a wheelchair. We kids waited; two-year-old Esther passed the time by standing on her head on a nearby sofa. After a while this wheelchair came into the room. In it slouched an old woman, all but her head covered with blankets. She was gaunt, emaciated, pathetic. Who was this? Dad or somebody indicated this was Mom and we should go over to her. She didn't reach or make any other move toward us. We came closer but were still unsure. Dad urged the little girls to go to her, but they held back. Dad then put some candy on the woman's knee; that broke the ice for the little ones. Others of us moved closer.

My vision at that time gave me distorted images; if the light was right and if I tilted my head forward and looked down I could see much better. As I stepped up to the wheelchair I just naturally looked down at the figure slouching there and reacted strongly! *Goodness, this old woman, ugly actually—I'm supposed to connect with her as my mom from here on?* The familiar Mennonite hairdo topped with the white covering, the pleasant face were GONE! *O-O-O-oh...* Then she smiled at me. My vision was just enough to see that gap between her two upper front teeth. That did it! I melted. *Ah, this IS Mom! Yes, I CAN connect with this frail old woman as my mom!* Before this I had not been consciously aware of that gap between Mom's upper front teeth, but now it was her trademark. This look at Mom's face was the next to last time I ever saw a human face with any degree of clarity.

Mom's case was remembered and discussed in the community for a long time. We kids later heard stories about the doctors' personal involvement with Mom's case. We heard that Dr. Huffman was on his knees in the operating room praying for Mom. He was quoted as saying, "I never saw a surgeon's hands working with such smooth skill." We heard that Dr. Deyerle, the surgeon, said, "It felt like another hand was on my hands," and after the surgery he said something like this to Dad: "I'm sorry I did this to you. You have nine children; now you have a 10th child," pointing to Mom—meaning her brain was without oxygen so long that she would be totally dependent or even in a vegetative state the rest of her life. Much later Dr. Deyerle saw her walking normally with Dad in the hospital; he said, "You were on the edge of your grave with both feet on a banana peel."

THE BARN REPAIR AND MORE EDUCATION IN BASIC CONSTRUCTION

Somehow, toward the end of March or early April, I believe while Mom was still in the hospital (she was in the hospital about five weeks), Dad managed to turn his attention back to the problem of repairing the barn. The whole end of the barn needed to be replaced, and the overall length of the structure would be extended about three feet. A construction crew was brought in to do the work. My vision was such that I could move about the area watching bits and pieces how the work was done. I didn't just watch, I soaked up the information like a sponge soaks up water. When the men weren't around, as at lunch breaks or in the evening after the day's work, I would move in to get a close-up look at how things were done. I learned how wooden forms are constructed to pour concrete footers (very strong to support A LOT of liquid weight), how sand, gravel, and cement are mixed in the right ratio by counting shovels-full to make the concrete. I saw how the first wooden plank, called the "plate" was bolted flat down on top the concrete footer with bolts that had been set in the concrete before it hardened, and how the rest of the wooden structure was erected atop that plate.

I saw how the upright beams were carefully aligned to the vertical, tied together with horizontal beams and made rigid with diagonal bracing. I wondered how those short diagonals could be adequate for the very tall verticals. I saw how the horizontal beams that would bear the weight of the floor were notched into the verticals, not just nailed in place. I saw how smaller vertical studs (two-by-fours) were set between the bigger verticals to provide for nailing up the weather boarding exterior. I caught on that the weather boarding was not just a "skin" to keep out the weather; that "exterior skin" provided tremendous rigidity against lateral forces, and that was why they didn't need longer diagonal bracing in the framing. Observing this barn project became for me a veritable education in basic theory and technique of construction. Years later I would draw on this education as I built forms for a concrete back porch and steps, formed up for two different patios, built two different lawn sheds, and participated in engineering decisions as we built our present home.

Something else was happening during this barn repair. I still had useable mobility vision at this time. To get my close-up look at things, I was quite ready to climb around on ladders, scaffolds, beams, joists, and any accessible framing. But Eldon was catching on to what all I couldn't see—he stayed right there with me, making sure of what I grabbed for or stepped onto. We spent quite a few evenings climbing around that unfinished barn, both for the joy of climbing and to see how things were put together. This is when Eldon began functioning as a wonderful brother alongside as I headed into blindness.

MOM COMES HOME AND SHIRLEY PROVES CAPABLE

Then, in April, it came time to get Mom home from the hospital. Mom had made a spectacular return from the edge of the grave, but she was still totally dependent on others for all personal care. There was a lot of drama and controversy among the nurses and family relatives about whether Mom was actually well enough to be discharged from the hospital. The decision about where she should go for further nursing care was almost taken out of Dad's hands, but the doctor who had responsibility for signing the discharge papers had seen Dad caring for Mom in the hospital. He told Dad, "I've watched you handling her, and I know you can do it very well at home. I'm signing the discharge papers." As the doctor walked off, he suddenly turned back to Dad and said, "Get her out of here, the sooner the better."

Shirley, age 10, prepared for Mom's homecoming by decorating every room in the house with lilacs that were in full bloom.

To keep things more quiet and restful for Mom, the three youngest children, Miriam, Elva, and Esther, were placed out for several weeks with Dad's two sisters, Aunt Lelia and Aunt Vada. Baby Emily was still living with Mom's sister, Aunt Margaret, where she had been placed the day she was born. We had a new housekeeper now, Annis Coakley. Dad personally saw to Mom's nursing care, including daily baths, exercises and, for a while, carrying her to and from the bathroom—all that in addition to his farm work.

After school was out in June, the three little girls were brought home—to Mom's delight. Shirley began clamoring to bring home Baby Emily, too. Dad apparently was afraid that would make too much work for the new housekeeper; Mom surely couldn't help. Shirley insisted that SHE would care for the baby. Dad drilled her hard—"That would mean you have to feed and bathe the baby and change all those dirty diapers no matter how tired you are or how much you want to go play, and once you start, there's no turning back. Are you really up to that?"

"Yes," she said, "yes, yes, yes!" Baby Emily came home and ten-year-old Shirley, big for her age, rose to the occasion like a trooper. She assumed the care of the baby, the three other little girls, and lots of the housework alongside Annis. By the time school resumed in September, Mom was beginning to help with some of the lighter work, including some of the care of the baby during the day. Shirley managed to return to school and also continued her household responsibilities by getting up early and working late. At this point I went off to school at VSDB in Staunton.

Shirley continues the story by telling me that when Annis left in October to get married, Dad began talking about keeping her out of school, maybe 2 or 3 days a week. Shirley was desperate to stay in school. Mom's recovery was continuing—the extent and rate of her recovery was absolutely amazing to all who knew her medical story. So, somehow with Mom's supervision and Shirley's hard work, our family life began coming back to mostly normal. I remember being proud back then of my sister Shirley and I'm proud of her today.

THE PEAR TREE

I want to go back to late April or early May, soon after Mom came home from the hospital. That was about the time each year when a scrubby little pear tree on the west side of the house came into full bloom. That tree clearly had struggled sometime in its past to survive—its trunk leaned to the side a good 45 degrees. I saw this tree blossom three times—1952 and 1953 when I could still see and now again in 1954 when my vision was poor. The 1954 occurrence would become one of those occasions that drove home what I was losing. I was then an ornery kid, not much prone to introspection, but something profound happened inside me each year when that tree bloomed.

Those blossoms were simply beautiful, so delicate and lovely. The petals were a pure white, lucid and vibrant, clearly alive. If I weren't afraid you'd laugh at me, I'd be telling you those petals had a soft glow of their own. The ground under the tree, hard packed with patches of scruffy grass, became carpeted with the same pure, soft, vibrant white. I would pick up petals from the ground, by the hand full, then one at a time, and just gaze at them for long moments. I would pick off a flower and peer into the area of the pistils and stamens where I knew the pear would form. Something of ultimate importance was in there. I wanted to see and understand its secret, how it worked. All this beauty reached far into me. It wanted to lead me somewhere or to something. I suppose you would call the feeling "deep yearning," for what, I didn't know. Obviously, I had no words for all this back then, but I did comprehend that the very mystery of life was in there somewhere.

And on early foggy mornings there was another kind of beauty here. Folds of soft gray fog would surround and envelope the pear tree, making it look like a beautiful sleepy ghost. The pure whiteness of the blossoms on the tree and of the carpet on the ground was subdued but still vibrant. This produced a sleepy, quiet beauty. It was appealingly beautiful! Maybe it was like they say a sleeping girl is appealingly beautiful?

Now that I am an old man, I can see that I was just starting into puberty and I was standing in a place where beauty and creativity and spirituality and sexuality all come together. I was standing in a sanctuary where the mystery of life was calling to me.

That was what I saw the two previous years, and now in 1954 I was looking forward to seeing it again. But, when I picked off a blossom or picked up some petals for a closer look—*Shoot, my vision is not working right! That big black blob keeps moving directly over the spot I want to see!* I remember well the disappointment. I dropped the petals. I just stood there a while. Then I walked off, sad; I knew what I was losing.

(For those who need to know—I have taken care in the above paragraphs to keep my growing love for painting word pictures from over describing what I actually experienced.)

During the rest of that summer I sort of moved back and forth across the line between seeing and not seeing. Or, more accurately, the line between what I could and could not see kept shifting. I was discovering that I could read some print that was a half-inch high, obviously because my right eye was improving with use. But I was also finding that shadows and poor lighting bothered me more. I would set up my Erector Set just inside the front door where I could get full afternoon sunlight.

HANDLING FARM MACHINERY—THE END

Mom began having me do some of the lawn mowing. We used an old-time reel mower that you pushed by hand (with a lot of grunting). In full sunshine I could see the color contrast between the short, newly cut grass and the tall, darker uncut grass; I just tracked the mower along that boundary line.

I was also using the garden tractor (a two-wheeled Bolens with cultivators on the back) in the large area of the garden that was still unplanted. Again, I just tracked the garden tractor along the line between the dry, uncultivated soil and the dark cultivated soil. It was easy when the light was good. I didn't try cultivating between the rows of peas and corn and other stuff. Boy, did I ever enjoy working with that garden tractor, and folks seemed to acknowledge I handled it well.

Dad evidently saw how I handled the lawn mower and garden tractor and decided to set me to some "real" tractor work—harrowing that big field up the hill and west of the barn. He took me out to the tractor (the 1945 Case VAC) and spring tooth harrow that were already sitting up there in the field. He had already made a pass or two around the field. He explained, "Now, Sonny, you don't want to be constantly looking back over your shoulder to see where the harrow is going, so here's what you do: you sight along the exhaust pipe and air cleaner of the tractor and keep them lined up with the edge between the just harrowed soil and the still unharrowed soil."

I was elated. *Wow, yes, of course, I can do this! I can easily see the color contrast between the harrowed and unharrowed soil and can guide the tractor accordingly!* Then Dad explained that the engine was missing badly but that it could still do the job if I just leave it in low gear. Then he walked back to the barn.

Well I was nearly breathless. I had been handling the tractor a lot before my eye surgery the previous October. One of my jobs was to use the tractor and trailer to take hay up to the calves in the woods. That involved backing the trailer up the barn bridge and through the open barn doors—a specific skill that had to be learned. Dad had explained that when backing a two-wheeled trailer, you turn the steering wheel opposite to where you want the trailer to go. I had mastered this skill and was backing that trailer straight up the barn bridge and into the barn in one smooth maneuver. I was mighty pleased with myself. Dad was noticing and commending me. "Sonny, you're handling that tractor just pretty good." The next skill to master was that of backing a four-wheeled wagon. Dad had just explained that when backing a wagon, you turn the steering wheel opposite to what you do when backing a trailer. It would be tricky. That was where my tractor driving had been shut down, or so I thought.

Now here I was, sitting on this tractor again, with a man-sized assignment. I wondered if Dad had any real notion how much I'm not seeing these days. I looked again at the contrast between the harrowed and unharrowed soil and could see that OK. I started out, throttle wide open. Despite the missing and spluttering engine, the tractor did keep going, but oh so slowly. After a while I decided to try second gear. I pushed in the clutch and—SLAM! The steering wheel butted into my tummy as if I had driven the tractor head on into a stone wall!

When I finally caught my breath, I figured out what happened. The harrow was dragging so hard behind the tractor, that, when I disengaged the clutch, the whole rig slammed to a stop as if I had hit a wall. I can see now, while writing this, those "spring teeth" on the harrow were indeed "sprung"; when the pulling of the tractor let off, those spring teeth jerked everything backward a bit. To make things worse, I had been hauling back on the steering wheel to better reach the clutch with my short leg; that helped throw me forward over the steering wheel when the tractor stopped so abruptly. I experimented a while with the clutch and found that, with A LOT of care, I could reduce but not altogether eliminate that stopping jolt; the load the tractor was pulling was just too much to handle smoothly. And of course, I discovered second gear wouldn't work. So, I just let the tractor crawl on in first gear—slowly.

Finally I was bored. I had to do something besides just keeping the tractor on the straight line and waiting and waiting till the next corner. I turned out into the field and made a big loop, coming back around to my straight edge and continuing on, business as usual. I made a second loop but then decided I'd better stop this foolishness. After all, the evidence for my "playing around" was right there in the harrow tracks for Dad and the neighbors to see. Some readers will understand, of course, that I wasn't just "playing around." I was tentatively handling and exploring my machine in order to master it—just like with the nozzle on the threshing machine's blower pipe.

When I finally got around the field and back to my starting point, two things went wrong. First, the sun had dried the newly harrowed soil to the point I couldn't distinguish it from the unharrowed ground—my reference point was gone. Second and more scary, clouds had just then come across the sun and my very necessary full sunlight was gone; I was just that quickly blind. There was light perception but that was useless here. I turned off the tractor.

I climbed down. I just stood there, hoping my eyes would accommodate to the dimmer light at least a little bit.

Finally, I could sort of make out the barn down the hill and, better yet, the little brick well house near the barn; now I knew where the opening was in the electric fence. I walked down to the barn, found Dad, told him what was going on, and volunteered that I should not be working that tractor anymore. He said quietly, "OK," and turned back to his work—did I hear a little catch in his voice? I walked on to the house. (I'm sitting here now wondering, "Did Dad deliberately pull a wire off one spark plug to keep me from getting too happy with that tractor?")

That was the last of my tractor driving days—right when I had my first chance to do heavy field work. That was the last of my "man-sized work" on the farm. I knew it and felt the loss.

A CLOSE CALL

About this time, I had another experience that drove home in a chilling way how poor my vision was getting, particularly in anything less than full sunlight. I had discovered that I could entertain Baby Emily by putting her in a cardboard box to which I had attached a pull string. I would pull that box with her in it around the house, letting it slide along the floor, going gently over the various thresholds. She liked that ride. One morning with her in my arms I decided to go get the box and give her another ride. I went out onto the porch and started to the far end where the box was kept, and where the lighting that time of day was poor. With no particular thought I stopped, turned around, went back into the house and laid Emily on the sofa just inside the door; I put something beside her so she wouldn't roll off. I then went back out onto the porch to get that box—and promptly fell into the stairwell of the stone steps going down to the cellar! Someone had left the trap door open that was supposed to be covering those steps, and I immediately fell in! When I had stopped and turned back to put Emily down, my toes had to have been at the very edge of that open trap door! I was pretty bloody but there were no broken bones and no stitches were needed. If Baby Emily had gone in that hole with me, she wouldn't have been so lucky. Dad often declared, before and since that incident, "There just have to be guardian angels out there looking after children, or no child could ever make it to adulthood." I'll leave the reader to ponder that.

FAREWELL TO COLORS, TOO

About this time one of the monthly farm magazines had a big, two-page spread of a diagram of a John Deere combine. This was a cut-away drawing clearly and in detail showing the inner workings of the machine. I very much wanted to study this. Once again, that big black blob, that evil thing(!) kept getting dead center over the exact spot I wanted to see. After getting frustrated about that, I realized I couldn't even enjoy the beautiful John Deere green and yellow—this was that high gloss printing that made colors more vivid and beautiful than real life. Then it closed in on me—I won't be able to enjoy colors anymore either! At the same time there were some full-page magazine pictures of nature—green forest, mountain ridges, blue skies, waterfalls, birds on nests—all in the same VIVID high gloss colors. I had the same reaction—so, it's farewell to colors. This time there were a few tears—not too many, but a few.

STARTING TO LOOK UP

Once in a while blindness paid a dividend or two. One Sunday noon we all filed into our places around the table for a Sunday dinner—that's right, a big farmhouse table all set full with Mennonite Sunday foods and desserts, with two parents and 9 kids arranged around the table. After Dad's prayer I reached for my water glass. My knuckles brushed into the icing of a big cake right there in front of my plate. I didn't like messy knuckles so I just licked off the icing—so what if that icing happened also to taste good? Eldon saw this and voiced suspicion, "You jis' tried that"—he wasn't about to let me "get away with something."

After a couple seconds, I assumed someone did the obvious, namely moved the cake out of the way; I reached for my glass again—I just wanted a drink! My knuckles brushed into the icing again; I just licked them off again. Now Eldon was convinced, "You knew that cake was there and just tried to get your fingers into that icing!" Exasperated, I now reached for the platter with both hands to move it back a bit so I could get my glass. The icing on that cake was LAVISH—it sagged over the edges of the platter and now got all over both my hands. Now Eldon went off, "Look at that! He did it again, a third time! AND WITH BOTH HANDS!" I never did get Eldon to understand or rather acknowledge the obvious—I was just trying to get a drink, and that last time I was trying to move the cake out of the way so I wouldn't get my fingers messy, and indeed, I didn't want to be messing up that nice cake! If in the process I got icing on my fingers, why should I waste it by wiping it off on my pants or under the table cloth? He wouldn't be convinced. What do you bet he was jealous? (Well, OK, that icing tasted good!)

In the midst of these events where my life with vision was ending, some new activities and experiences were emerging that would prove useful, even critical, in life without vision. The first big event was the Talking Books, mentioned previously. Another was the discovery that it was actually fun to figure out how to do so many things without vision. And, (I guess I was a bit of an exhibitionist) I started finding it fun to do little show and tell demonstrations of what I could and could not see and how I could do certain things without sight.

Perhaps a most important development was the emergence of a new skill, which some parents and community leaders in our Mennonite world of practical work ethics might at first have discouraged as a bad habit, a waste of time—I discovered the art of "daydreaming" as I called it then. By the end of that summer before going off to VSDB I had discovered that, while lounging around on the grass in the shade of the maple trees in the front yard, I could conjure up a very rich life of the mind—I could create and play with whole worlds of people, places, and things, all while just sitting there in the grass.

It is my understanding that the largest portion of the human brain is the visual cortex, and furthermore, when brain cells of one area of the brain are unused, they may be co-opted into service by another area of the brain. I don't really know what happened to my visual cortex as I lost vision, but it seems to me that, if my visual brain cells had been put into service by other areas of the brain, I would have had a ballooning of other skills and abilities. To my knowledge that did not happen. My personal theory is, therefore, that my visual cortex was kept intact and was put to the service of IMAGINATION, first in all that daydreaming and later in a growing capacity to visualize all kinds of objects and mechanical devices. To this day whenever I imagine or conceptualize anything and everything, I'm very conscious that I am thinking visually.

Since writing that last paragraph I have learned that some people who lose vision as adults, actually lose the ability to visualize anything or even remember visual scenes from their seeing days. They cannot generate, hold and manipulate a visual image. That was/is certainly NOT the case for me—I live in a visual world and it started with this daydreaming (fantasizing) in the front yard that first summer after the retinal detachment.

So, my time under the maple tree in the front yard was not simply an idle wiling away of time. I created a steam powered engine, actually a cross between a railroad locomotive and a steam farm tractor, which was used to pull long strings of covered wagons across the vast western prairies—that way you were rid of the encumbrance of rails and livestock. I created a little streamlined car that ran on rails up and down The Valley. So that I could operate it without vision, I enclosed the railway with chain-link fencing on the sides and on top; that way I could run at 100 miles per hour with no fear of animals or people getting on the track. Oh, yes, I knew this would be too expensive to be practical, but at that time in my daydreaming world, I didn't have to worry about financing. By the way, that car also had a "no name pretty girl" in it; she just sat there and admired and admired.

I flew about the countryside on an experimental hovercraft Eldon told me about from *Popular Mechanics*. With that I deliberately worked at visualizing the countryside, mountains and valleys, rivers and roads, and how the view changes as you fly higher and lower. For that particular fantasy, I drew on visual imagery acquired from atop the Washington Monument a few years earlier when I could still see. While thus imagining, fantasizing, and daydreaming, I was developing skills I would use later. In fact, that skill at visual conceptualizing became the foundation for my woodworking hobby years later—still today I sometimes work out details for how different parts will fit together on this or that project while standing around waiting for a taxicab.

Dad and Eldon were aware of my daydreaming there in the comfortable shade. On their various comings and goings to-and-fro they liked to sneak up on me with a blade of grass or hair and tickle my nose or neck. They would laugh with delight when I swatted at a supposed fly. Sometimes I could smell their approach and spoil their fun by grabbing a pants leg or cracking a shin. Eldon positively relished the times when he could trick me into thinking it was Dad doing the teasing. He would taunt, "Now just why do you laugh when you think Dad is picking on you and get mad when you think it's me?" It took quite a few years, but he did finally acknowledge that, of course, a given act of teasing will be experienced or received quite differently by the victim depending on who he thinks is perpetrating the deed, and that is NORMAL!

BACK TO SCHOOL

Now, summer was ending, and a new school year was beginning in September. The question was what to do about my continuing education? Mom and Dad decided to send me to VSDB (Virginia's School for the Deaf and the Blind) up at Staunton, Virginia, a state-run residential dormitory institution. As far as I knew, this decision was simple, obvious, logical, un-emotional—"Daniel is blind and that's where blind people are educated; therefore, that's where he goes in September." It's only in recent years, with my awareness of how many Conservative families react so negatively to government institutions and ser-vices, that I have wondered how hard that decision really was for Mom and Dad. Within the last year I learned that one of my uncles did urge Dad not to send me there—"That is a state-run institution; he should be kept at home in a safe Christian envi-ronment." Mom did tell me in her later years, "It seemed hard to leave you there all alone that first day," but the basic decision to send me there was still clearly a no-brainer in her mind.

In early August Mom, Dad and I went up to Staunton for our preliminary visit to VSDB. (Yes, believe it or not, Mom had recovered enough to come along, but she leaned heavily on Dad's arm like a very old woman. Neither Dad nor I were embarrassed about her appearance; we were proud of her accomplishment and happy to be seen with her.) When we got out of the car in the parking lot, we were greeted by a most unusual flight of steps that we had to negotiate to get up to the main building. The first steps were very broad from front to back, like five feet; each succeeding step got shorter and shorter till the top several were little mincy steps, maybe ten inches, then nine, then eight inches from front to back, not really big enough to get your whole foot on. There was no way you could get into a uniform stride where your foot would anticipate the next step as you go up.

We started up easily enough, Mom leaning on Dad's right arm while I grabbed Dad's left arm to use him as a sighted guide. Soon Mom and I were tripping and stumbling on each step; those steps seemed to be coming at us faster and faster. We both were hanging heavily on Dad's arms to keep from falling. Dad couldn't figure what to do; he just tried to move carefully and stabilize both of us. He was embarrassed but he also saw the funny of it all. We surely were quite the show for anyone watching. For the life of me I can't figure how a flight of steps like that showed up on a campus designed from the beginning for visually-impaired students. What a lousy first impression for VSDB! I learned later that this area of the campus was not frequented by blind students, that the blind kids had dubbed those steps, "the devil's doorstep," and that some kids liked to take unsuspecting new blind students around that way as a prank.

Fortunately for Mom and Dad and me, the second and third impressions, and all the other impressions that day were good. We found our way to the office of a very friendly Mrs. Marshall. She gave us a lot of information and explanations about the place. Dad took note of her explanation that the school's social life seemed to center around Saturday night dances and going to downtown movie theaters on Saturday and Sunday afternoons. He immediately explained that, due to our religious convictions, he and Mom would not want me going to dances and movie theaters. Mrs. Marshall indicated they would respect that. The issue of wearing neckties for dress occasions also came up and Dad again asked that I not be required to wear a necktie. Mrs. Marshal agreed to that also.

My attention really perked up when Mrs. Marshall described the playground; there was a large concrete courtyard where the kids spent a lot of time roller skating after school. She stressed that the totally blind kids skated as much as anyone else—they would line up behind a sighted kid, making a train anywhere from 2 to 10 or 15 kids, and they would fairly fly around that court. (The reader should understand that at VSDB when we referred to "sighted kids," we meant kids with some degree of useable vision. We were all legally blind; only a few of us were literally totally blind.) Mrs. Marshall insisted that a pair of roller skates be included with my other recommended gear. She gave us a list of recommended clothing and explained the laundry system. As we left, I was favorably impressed with what I could see of the campus—lots of sidewalks, bridges and balconies, green grass, darker green boxwood shrubs, very tall shade trees. I was eager to come back in September.

Well, sure enough, Dad soon got me a pair of roller skates—the kind that clamped onto your shoes and had steel, roller bearing wheels. I quickly learned to skate in our new dairy barn. Dad took me to town and purchased every single item on that list of recommended clothing, and now I was looking like a dandy compared to my sibs.

Richard Rhodes, our second cousin about Eldon's age, came over on his bicycle one afternoon about this time. Somehow the three of us got into a little impromptu quasi racing with our bicycles around a little oval area near the dairy barn. I knew I was behaving recklessly—my vision was too poor for this foolishness. Maybe my old rowdiness was out for one last sighted fling. Richard's shadowy form was ahead of me. At the turn I got my front wheel inside his rear wheel and practically muscled him aside and took the lead. Richard was a lot bigger and stronger than me, but I had taken the lead with that inside pass. That was a brief and foolish episode, but I've never forgotten the thrill of being clever. Actually, Richard may have simply had the good sense to relinquish the lead to keep one or both of us from getting hurt—but I still relish the thrill.

A BIG BANG TO CLOSE THE OLD AND START THE NEW

On the eve of leaving for VSDB we were at Grandma Bowman's place. Dad and some uncles were clearing debris from the roadside ditches on either side of Grandma's driveway. A big terracotta tile ran under the drive connecting the ditch on one side to the ditch on the other side. The men were down in the ditch on one side with their heads toward that tile. Uncle Roy was standing at the other side of the drive by the road seeming available for conversation. Someone had sent me a 4-by-6 notecard with the Braille alphabet embossed on it. I pulled it out and began showing him how the Braille code works. He got interested in my little show and tell and began putting my finger on one letter and then another, getting me to name the letter. Suddenly—BOOM!!!

I never before heard such a heavy boom!! It made me dizzy; I staggered around trying to regain my balance. Uncle Roy grabbed my elbow to steady me and I realized he was reeling, too. Then Dad was coming up out of the ditch on the other side of the drive and straight at Uncle Roy—"Look here, Roy," he growled, "if that tile is broken, you're gonna fix it all by yourself." Uncle Roy backed up, then turned to me and explained, "Daniel, I put a cherry bomb in the other end of that tile from where they were working and then got so interested in your Braille I forgot all about it, so it scared the daylights out of me, too." So, I suppose I can claim I entered the world of Braille with a BANG! Or, was I leaving the sighted world with a BANG?

VSDB, A NEW LIFE BEGINS

As I said earlier, Mom and Dad's decision to send me to VSDB most likely was a straight forward, logical and correct decision, but that decision DID set a thirteen-year-old farm boy on a journey into a new world where he would be forced to think a lot (and alone) about his distinctive culture and religious traditions. But no such man-sized thoughts were troubling me when Mom and Dad and I arrived on the third floor of Perry Hall at VSDB in September 1954. (Mom actually made it up all those steps—with a lot of help from Dad, of course, but that was great good news for those of us cheering on her recuperation.) A friendly housemother, Mrs. Halterman, showed us my room, my bed, my chair, and my locker. Dad fetched my things from the car and helped arrange them in my locker.

That locker—it was metal, gun metal gray. Never before did I have so much space, all my own, to store and organize my things. Inside the left door was space for tall things and clothing on hangers; inside the right door were shelves, top to bottom, deep front to back. Where I came from nobody had that kind of space all to themselves. My Erector Set and roller skates fitted in perfectly. There were beds, chairs, and lockers for three more boys in the room, but no desks or work tables. This was an awfully Spartan dorm room, but with that locker I felt like I could function. Also, afternoon sunshine through a large window and the smooth hardwood floor added some cheer—oh yes, I still loved hardwood flooring.

After getting my things put away, Dad relaxed and began surveying the scene and sizing things up; he seemed pleased. "Daniel," he said, "outside your window is a huge tree. You're on the third floor and even from here I can't begin to see the top!" He showed me that my room was at the end of the hall and just outside my door were some old wooden chairs and benches arranged around the end of the hallway; this made a kind of lounging area. Sunlight from a big window at the end of the hall made it possible for me to see that the walls were a ceramic tile colored institutional green. And I could see several kids lounging on the benches.

The housemother showed Dad and me where the bathroom and showers were, where to put my laundry, and then said that supper would be at 6:00; until then I could do as I pleased in my room and on the hall. She said the other boys would be checking in throughout the afternoon and they would show me around. Then Mom and Dad left. Mom got a little emotional saying goodbye, but, to my relief, not too teary.

Well, that afternoon got awfully long; those "other boys"

were slow in coming. It was immediately apparent those kids over there on those benches weren't the boys who would show me around. In the sunlight I could see that one couldn't hold his head still—his head rolled round and round like his neck was rubber (a neurological disorder, I learned later). Another could hardly talk for stuttering; I made a friendly overture, but he just wanted to be left alone. A third kept rocking side to side repeating over and over and OVER, "I wanna doe home and dit in duh wockin' chaair." Uneasiness was closing in on me. I sensed the boy with the stutter wasn't so sure about this place either.

Finally, around four o'clock a few guys trickled in. Then kids were all around, unpacking suitcases, turning on radios, and generally making a lot of pleasant confusion. Some were really friendly, easily making their acquaintance and introducing other friends. One, Jimmy Randel, picked up on my interest in skating and offered to get me started with skating on the court the next afternoon after school. I showed several guys my Erector Set. I immediately realized I would be sending that set home at the first opportunity—they had no idea how to thread a nut onto a screw nor how to use a screwdriver—they could not conceive how the parts could serve as components of a larger something. One guy picked up one of the bright red wheels and put it into his pocket to have and to hold as a pocket treasure just like Tom Sawyer. It took a little polite but insistent explaining to get it back.

Then it was suppertime. Somehow about twenty of us ended up in a line, two by two, the guys with poorer vision grabbing the arm of someone with better vision. The housemother shepherded us off the hall, into a gloomy stairwell. We went down to a landing and swung hard around, down another flight and swung around again. I was groping with my foot for the first and last step of each flight. This was my first time navigating anything like this with so little vision in such poor lighting. Before this I was moving about on familiar territory and my fragmentary vision was actually useful. I was now discovering how blind I really was. My partner, Henry Wood, was laughing at my exasperation and farm boy amazement at "so many stupid steps." "You'll get used to them," he said. We went out a door, down one step and up four steps onto a big concrete courtyard and, thankfully, into better light. Over there was another troop of twenty or so younger boys with their housemother from the other end of our hall. Both troops proceeded across the concrete court and into a dark tunnel that zigzagged between buildings. Those dark places once again made me feel BLINDER and I didn't like it. We went up one step onto a wooden bridge, down three steps onto a wooden deck, off to the right and down ten or twelve more steps onto a landing, a right angle to the right and down another two steps. By now I was tired of constantly stepping up when there were no more up steps and down when there were no more down steps. Henry, actually a neat kid, was helping me keep some sense of humor about it all. "Don't worry, you'll soon catch on," he kept saying. We made another 180-degree turn to the left, went down four steps and up one step into a steamy dining room full of uncertain smells.

I'll just jump ahead here and say, I did learn to navigate that route to the dining room easily and alone, dark or no dark. And, it wasn't long before I was taking those stairs in Perry Hall like all the other boys—almost always running (up or down), always at least two steps at a time, and, ALWAYS on the right or you were mud! Surely we had better quadriceps than anyone for miles around!

Well, this dining room and its furnishings were obviously very old and very used. (This was Montgomery Hall.) We stood at our chairs around the tables until everyone was in place. Then, wow, we sang a hymn! It was "Now the Day Is Over"—unaccompanied! And the basses and tenors did their parts very well! For this Mennonite kid in this strange world, that was a welcome touch. (And, for the entire seven years I was at VSDB, at the evening meal, we always sang a hymn before being seated. I liked that.) Then we scraped and banged our chairs and dove in!

The table manners of some of the guys around me—well, nevermind. Between guys shoving bowls at me and the housemother helping me get the hang of things, I did get something to eat—sort of. Something was put onto my plate and said to be "corned beef hash." With one taste that went immediately and permanently onto my inedible foods list, as did Spam a meal or two later. I was used to good Mennonite farm cooking. This institutional food, particularly the meats, was going to require some discriminating picking and choosing. More than once over the next several weeks I left the table hungry, but it seemed I could always make up for lost calories later when the food offerings were acceptable.

During the earlier hubbub back in Perry Hall getting lined up to march to the dining room, I had heard some laughing and joking about a "Richard Harris showing up clutching his can of Nestle's Quick as usual." During this first meal someone across the table and down a ways called to me, "Hey Daniel, Richard wants to know if you want some Nestle's Quick in your milk?" I didn't know what Nestle's Quick was, but Henry explained, "That'll make it like chocolate milk." I accepted, and it was GOOD! I learned later Richard didn't see much better than me; we were not yet directly acquainted, but he was already aware of me in the group and was making a friendly overture—it felt good. I was beginning to think I was going to like this place.

Then we were back in the dorm and getting ready for bed. I wasn't too sure about undressing and getting into my pajamas with that housemother constantly coming and going, but that seemed to be the way they did things. A night or two later I would be mortified to learn that we would be in the buff in that gang shower with the housemother supervising. I went to bed, things got quiet, but I slept fitfully. All night long I kept hearing "airplanes," they sounded like big bombers coming and going. I began to worry, *Maybe the Russians are coming* (the Cold War was a bit "hot" in those days).

In the morning I asked the guys, "Did y'all hear those airplanes last night?"

Henry piped up, "Those weren't airplanes, those were the trains coming and going from the train station. They make all that noise."

"Oh," I laughed, "I thought maybe the Russians were coming." We all laughed.

Now it was time for me to learn a new skill. At VSDB a cardinal rule was, ALWAYS after getting dressed in the morning and before breakfast you make your bed—military style, with the pleats at the foot end just so, and the pillow positioned just so! ! *OK, OK, lesson learned! Next lesson?*

After breakfast I was shown to the adjustment classroom. Students who had previously functioned sighted in the public schools but who were now coming into VSDB because of vision loss were placed in this "adjustment class." The student would study Braille and other blindness skills for a year or so and then transfer to whatever grade seemed appropriate.

The teacher, Mrs. Stubbs, was warm and friendly, soft spoken, and gentle. She was delighted to find I already could read the Braille alphabet, so she immediately produced a Braille slate—the device used to write Braille—and started me off with writing. (You can easily find pictures and explanations of Braille and the "Braille slate" by searching the Internet.)

When writing Braille with the traditional Braille slate, you punch the dots into the paper from the back side. That means you write from right to left and turn the letters backwards; then you turn the paper over and read from left to right and the letters all face the right way. This, of course, is confusing at first, but when you master the skill, you can write as fast as anyone with a pencil. I was excited and glad to be getting back to real schoolwork.

But, in this adjustment class I would continue to discover what I had seen the preceding afternoon while sitting in the hall outside my dorm room, namely, in any sizeable population of visually-impaired students, there will be many with multiple handicaps. For most of the kids sitting around me in this room, visual impairment seemed to be the least of their troubles.

Sitting three seats behind me was a big fellow, maybe 20 years old, with a wonderful, man-sized body and a deep bass voice, but who functioned maybe several notches above "zombie." I would come across him later on the playground in the company of smaller kids, including the boy with the stutter; they liked to ride piggyback on him, guiding him here and there like one would ride a docile horse. This seemed to be genuine fun for all, including the "horse." It was not unkind abuse of a mentally-impaired person.

On the other side of the room sat Jessica Cline, totally blind, age 18 or 20. (The names here are changed.) She was very small, about like an eight-year-old but had a strong, full voice almost like a mature woman. Because of health issues, she had almost no academic training. From somewhere she had learned a very bossy demeanor. She tried to order students around in the classroom. She tried to relate to the teacher as a peer, such as, "Yes, Mrs. Stubbs, you're right about that. Johnny should be made to sit still." One day when Mrs. Stubbs stepped out of the room for a moment, Jessica ordered, "George, you go over there and stand in that corner with your face to the wall." Of course, George didn't budge. "George," she repeated, "I said go stand in that corner." Mrs. Stubbs heard this and came back into the room. She had a hard time getting Jessica to understand, "Regardless of the infraction, it's not your responsibility to be correcting other students."

Sitting directly behind me was a thirteen-year-old girl who was barely functioning at a third-grade level. She talked with a breathy, sultry voice and generally seemed flighty and flirtatious. Behind her sat George Brown. One day in the first week or so when all was quiet in the classroom, suddenly the teacher, who heretofore spoke softly and seemed refined and even delicate, was coming on loud and stern and still louder, addressing George: "George Brown, if I catch you touching her again, you will stand up here in front of this room, and you will drop your pants, and you will drop your shorts, and you will lean across this desk, and I will take this ruler to your bare behind until you are blistered!! Do you understand that?" There was a mumbled submission. Well, in this classroom it was clear, order and decorum would be maintained on site, no easy handing off the problem to the principal! Don't be fooled by the soft-spoken sweetness of this teacher!

VSDB, ON THE ROAD TO EMC

One day in that first week I had a surprise visitor to that classroom. The morning sun coming through the window by my desk was at just the right angle for me to see what little I could still see. I held up my Braille book to peer at the dots on the page, those rows of little pimples on the beige page looked interesting. Suddenly Mrs. Stubbs was there draping an apron around my neck and over my hands—that's what the teachers did when they suspected students were reading Braille with their eyes rather than with their fingers. Don't forget, most of these kids had a little vision, and some would eventually end up functioning with large print rather than Braille, and yes, some did continue reading Braille with eyes or fingers, whichever worked best at the moment.

I opened my mouth to protest the apron. A big hand clapped down on my shoulder from behind and a friendly voice with a definite Mennonite accent said, "Daniel, I'm Laban Peachy. I teach psychology at EMC and I have brought several of my students here to VSDB for a field trip. Your aunts, Annie and Edna and Lena, who go to our church in Park View, have kept us informed about you. They asked me to be sure to check in on you. Could you show us how you work with that Braille?" I tossed the apron aside and happily demonstrated the Braille, reading and writing.

When Mr. Peachy and his students left, I explained to Mrs. Stubbs, in a rather adult manner, "I won't be using that apron because I was just seeing what the dots on the page look like in the sunlight. I wasn't reading it visually and can't do so." She accepted my explanation.

Years later when he was in his eighties and I was maybe in my sixties, Laban Peachy reminded me of that time he found me in that adjustment classroom at VSDB with the apron over my hands. He told me, "Back when you were losing your vision as a kid, your Mom's sisters, Annie, Edna, and Lena Wenger, kept the EMC college community and its associated Park View Church well informed about your situation." He went on, "When Annie packed our lunches for the field trip that morning in 1954 (she worked in the college cafeteria), she reminded me to look for you. I told her we were already planning to check in on you, but the reminder was welcome. In fact," he added, "the college community tracked your progress through VSDB the entire seven years you were there."

So, that's how it came about, seven years after Mr. Peachy found me in that adjustment classroom, an application form for admission to EMC showed up at VSDB. One evening in study hall during my senior year, my math teacher, Doc Bruce, suddenly announced, "Reverend (that's what he called me), put your books away, we gotta fill out this application for admission to EMC next fall." I was surprised. I hadn't initiated that application. Laban's explanation those many years later explained that. It also clarified why, during the college admissions interview in 1961, and through the whole enrollment process, Dad and Laban Peachy, who was by then the college registrar, seemed to be mostly going along with an already written script.

So, my Mennonite world had sure enough been looking out for me the whole time I was at VSDB. Now, back to 1954 at VSDB.

INTRODUCTION TO RACIAL PREJUDICE

In these first days in this new world something strange was coming at me almost every day—like my first encounter with racism. I was standing in a sunny spot in one of our dorm rooms (I gravitated to sunny places when I could). I was talking to Allen who had till now been very friendly and helpful. I was curious about another kid who had a distinctive accent. "Is Sammy colored?" I asked.

Suddenly Allen was revving up. "Huh, whudd you say? Are you calling Sammy a n-word?" he said, his voice rising to confrontation. He was coming at me, gathering himself together to beat me up.

Naive as I was—and I sure was naive about this stuff—I saw clearly that I had pushed a certain button, which it took a split second for him to realize, he was supposed to fight about. "Wait a minute," I said, fumbling for words, "what's so bad about thinking Sammy sounded like a colored person? Where do you think colored people learned their English anyway? They learned it from white people, so it's not an insult if I think Sammy sounds like a colored person." Where in the world I got that logic I'll never know. Obviously, a bonified racist would never have bought that argument, but Allen was a good-natured kid; he backed off, acknowledging my point.

In this incident I had discovered that just beneath the friendliness and affability all around me here on this campus lurked, or might lurk, intense racial prejudice and bigotry. For me it was about like stepping unexpectedly into a cow pile in an otherwise beautiful green farm pasture.

In my particular corner of the Mennonite world before this, I had learned about slavery in the South, Uncle Tom's Cabin, the Underground Railroad, the Civil War, and there was something called "KKK," etc., but I knew nothing of Jim Crow and racial segregation. In summer Bible school we once were given a picture of kids of all races standing around Jesus; we were supposed to color it. I colored these kids bright red, brown, yellow, black and white—I thought they looked neat that way. (Remember, I was partial to bright colors.) We had been singing, "...red, brown, yellow, black and white, they are precious in his sight..." One summer Sunday evening a group of black kids from an in-town

Mennonite Church gave a program at Mt. Clinton Church, I had heard my grandparents' generation talking about "darkies" and "picaninnies," how cute they were. I didn't see these kids as cute; I saw them as cool, especially one girl. She was about my age and had a pleasant face; I liked her curly hair. She had a calm, stately, self-possessed way of walking and moving about. I would have liked to get better acquainted, but…that's about the extent of my experience before VSDB with racial prejudice.

So, here in this new setting where I was to be getting the hang of living without vision, I was also going to be introduced to the realities of race relations in Virginia. By the time I graduated I would be familiar with the genteel racism of the Old South where the blacks (the household servants at least) "knew their place," and with the potentially violent attitudes of racial bigots. Since my graduation from VSDB in 1961 I have followed with interest the efforts of the State of Virginia to integrate its two schools for the deaf and blind—the school at Staunton for whites, the school at Hampton for blacks. Every time the state legislature took up the question of integrating these two facilities, I got a notice from a kind of blind network, "Write your representative to stop this integration thing." This opposition by blind alumni is, I believe, what stalled integration for a long time. The two schools were finally merged into one institution in 2009. So, I suppose the take-away from the incident where I questioned Allen about Sammy's accent is that you can't assume that blind people are racially colored blind.

At the end of that first year, Spring 1955, I was sufficiently acclimated to VSDB life to try this thing they called "going steady." My girl's birthday would be right at the end of the school year. I took my meager allowance and went downtown to the five and dime store and carefully picked out a perfect gift for her—two little plastic doll babies about three inches long. I found a just right box and some cotton; I nestled the babies side by side in the cotton, just so! They were so-o-o cute lying there in their cradle, side by side—one white baby and one black baby— so cute and adorable! Well, it turned out that legal blindness did not mean my girl and all the other girls in the dorm were color blind regarding race. It was the last day of the school year when I sent the gift over to her in the girls' dorm. I didn't hear about the stir among the girls till the next fall. Was I naive or what?

SIXTH GRADE AGAIN

As I grew more proficient in Braille, late Fall 1954, I began spending more time in the sixth grade classroom and less time in the adjustment class. As I got back into sixth grade it was like coming home—here at last are the normal kids, the social, friendly, goofy, full of fun kids, even some girls that merited careful attention! These kids were like the kids I left in sixth grade at Mt. Clinton School! These were my peers. The guys on my floor of the dorm were younger than me, and the kids in the adjustment class were—well, I already told you...

For one assignment Mrs. Hamrick, the teacher, was going to dictate some lines of text for us to copy in Braille or large print, whichever we were using. My Braille writing was still slow, so Juanita Turner spoke up, "I'll put another sheet in my slate and make an extra copy for Danny." It was hard work for her to punch those Braille dots into two sheets of paper; it about wore out her arm, but she got it done. When she had it ready, I walked over to her desk to get it. As I reached for the paper I paused, caught by what I was SEEING! This was sure enough another one of those situations where I could see what little I could still see. The powerful fluorescent lights overhead and the nearby window were putting just the right light over Juanita. I was looking down at just the right angle and Juanita was looking up at me. For several seconds I just gazed at her face; a thrill went through me. I was amazed how blonde she was (I would learn later she was an albino). I was caught and held by her open, just plain friendly face. That was a brief encounter, but the memory of Juanita's friendly face was for keeps. Hers was the last human face I ever saw.

SIXTH GRADE DISCUSSION OF CHURCH AND RELIGION—AGAIN!

Mrs. Hamrick was great; she had a friendly rapport with her students and would draw us into extended discussions. During one of my early visits to the classroom she got us talking about religion and our various denominational affiliations—just like Mr. Swank in sixth grade at Mt. Clinton had done the year before! Charlie Jones, an older student I liked instantly, spoke earnestly of his Pentecostal faith. He told how worshipers in his church would drop to the floor "when the pire [power] of God fell on them." Some kids weren't too sure about that kind of worship and scoffed at "those holy rollers," but Charley held his ground, "When the pire of God hits you, you can't help it," he said.

Jenny Maynard announced her Episcopalian faith. Bill Kid was Baptist. Others spoke up. When I said I was Mennonite, the room buzzed with comments like, "What did he say?" and, "I never heard that word before."

Jenny said, "Midianite? Oh, yes, Midianite, they're in the Bible."

I said, "No, not Midianite. Mennonite," and spelled and pronounced the word again and again.

Finally, they got it right, mostly, and wanted to know "So, what do Mennonites believe?"

I quickly ran through my little list of Mennonite beliefs— "We are Protestants but we don't smoke or drink, we don't dance or go to movies, the women wear a covering, we don't fight back, and, well, we don't go to war either."

Jenny pondered my pacifism a bit but then concluded decisively, "But my menfolk better fight to protect me if necessary."

Generally, those kids were as dubious about my Mennonite pacifism as they were about Charlie's Holy Rollers, but we all seemed genuinely interested in each other's stories.

The guys in the dorm had already discovered my "strange" religion. I was not made to wear a tie on Sunday mornings when they had to. They demanded to know why I was exempt. When conversations came around to war games, movies, dances, etc., again and still again I had to refer to my Mennonite beliefs. Little by little I came up with that list summarizing Mennonite beliefs I used in that sixth-grade discussion; it was to make it easier to answer questions.

Thus, it was quickly clear in the first weeks at VSDB my Mennonite identity was going to be right there beside me in everything I said and did. It's clear to me now, I learned in Mr. Swank's and Mrs. Hamrick's classrooms that it was OK to be religiously distinct, and it could actually be fun to discuss religion. Mrs. Hamrick, particularly, had shown us how to discuss religion with at least a modicum of respect most of the time, and I was also learning that those martyr stories from Mennonite and Anabaptist history were interesting to many kids.

Now that I was getting a handle on how to live with my Mennonite identity in this strange world so far from my Mennonite roots, and now that I had found my true peers in Mrs.

Hamrick's sixth grade classroom, I began to see that I just might enjoy life in this new world—even while the last of my vision was disappearing. I was now pretty much back on track academically in sixth grade. I had lost a year switching from print to Braille; that plus the second try in first grade meant I was now two years behind. But, heck, many of the kids at VSDB were behind a year or two for the same reasons, so I was at home.

Oh yes, about the skating—Jimmy Randel did keep his promise to get me started skating the next afternoon after school. (See next chapter.)

6

HIGH SCHOOL YEARS—
BLIND AND MENNONITE

From the day I arrived on the VSDB campus till the day I graduated, I really liked the buildings and grounds of the place. There were a lot of huge, well-tended shade trees interspersed with sunny areas. The grounds were kept clean and well-manicured. There were sidewalks and porches and balconies and bridges and a tunnel or two everywhere. One of the tunnels dated back to Civil War days; it was off-limits for us kids, but it sure fired our imaginations. Situated in the midst of some of the key buildings was a big concrete courtyard (Dad estimated it to be an acre under concrete). Some of the buildings were very old, dating back to 1839 when the place was established; some were modern for the day. The layout of the campus and of the older buildings was clearly the result of history and change over many years, not from following a carefully thought-out master plan. That made lots of interesting nooks and crannies to explore.

Among the trees were a lot of buckeye trees—how buckeye trees ended up here I never heard. Those buckeye nuts were the perfect size for throwing (I immediately recalled those acorn fights at the Bank Mennonite Church when our family visited there several times). Some of the kids saw my interest in these nuts and informed me emphatically, "There is a hard and fast rule here, no throwing buckeye nuts at anyone or anything for any reason!" I never threw one; I never heard of any incident involving buckeye nuts. I was also told they were poisonous—"Don't even think of trying to eat one!"

The dorm rooms for the blind boys were incredibly plain, even Spartan—just a bed, a chair, a metal locker for each boy, plus whatever cabinet or little stand the boys could rig up individually for their radios, record players, tape recorders, and even occasional illegal AM radio transmitters. But, wonder of wonders, a full-blown culture was there, largely centered around the last of the Golden Days of Radio. Boys would cluster around somebody's radio or tape recorder, sprawled on beds or on the floor, or on chairs dragged from across the room, or maybe they would just stand and lean in across the other guys to hear. I was immediately welcomed into these circles with lots of chatter explaining events in past episodes of radio shows and telling me what to expect in future episodes. I was quickly and completely immersed into this radio culture—shows like Jack Benny, Amos and Andy, Fibber Magee and Molly, The Green Hornet, The Shadow, Space Patrol, The Lone Ranger, Drag Net, Gun Smoke, Sergeant Preston, Ren Ten Ten, Lassie, Uncle Remus, The Cinnamon Bear, Red Skelton, Art Linkletter's People Are Funny and Children Say the Darndest Things; and wow, here's the familiar voices of Paul Harvey, Drew Pierson, and Billy Graham. Radio drama was clearly the ideal entertainment format for blind kids. We could "see" all sorts of things with our radio-primed imaginations! Mennonite scruples about "worldly amusements" on the radio got rolled way back! By the Fall of 1955, my second year on campus, most of these shows were co-opted by TV—the Golden Days of Radio were over. I didn't miss them much because, by then, I was immersed in piano and organ lessons.

Sometimes the center of those dorm room clusters was

someone with a guitar, or a violin, or an accordion, etc. Finally, I could get my hands on and/or listen to chatter about various musical instruments that my Mennonite heritage had been trying to keep out of reach. I'll never forget the day Hubert Adkins, sitting on a bed, demonstrated his ability to sustain a note on his violin indefinitely with no audible break when he reversed the bow. A bunch of us crowded in listening intently—unless you had vision enough to see what he was doing—you could not tell when he reversed that bow!

On an afternoon in the first several days, John Bogart and Lou Stokes introduced me to a really neat game they called "Chatter," clearly a spinoff from radio culture. It was ideal for blind kids, especially those inclined to be sedentary. A couple of kids just sit on the grass, or anywhere within ear shot of each other. One player begins creating a story, perhaps aping some radio drama, except the plot and characters were all improvised on the fly—the faster the better. Somebody starts telling a story, preferably by acting the part of a character. Whenever this first character encounters a second character, another player jumps in, taking over the role of that new character. You can have any number of player/characters, all improvised on the fly; nobody knows where the story is going to go. If your character gets put in a jam by another player, it's up to you to improvise a way for the story to move from there. If your character gets punched in the belly, you could respond with, "… but Big George had earlier embedded three little spikes in his belt buckle, which bloodied the assailant's knuckles…" Now the first player has to improvise the assailant's response to an injured hand. If you are the Lone Ranger trapped in a corner at the base of a cliff, you could improvise an earthquake opening up the wall to a little cave into which Lone Ranger quickly ducks. The shaking earth closes off the cave. Lone Ranger is saved from Outlaw Bill, but how are you going to get Lone Ranger out of that cave? You could improvise an aftershock two hours later that opens the cave again—well after Outlaw Bill is gone. A couple of blind kids with fertile imaginations and fast tongues made these "chatter stories" wild and fast! Sitting here now, it wonders me that I didn't think of an Anabaptist trick like this: Outlaw Bill has just robbed my character. I could have my character say, "Wait a minute, I see you're hungry. Take this bread along, and also this cheese and dried beef. And here's a jacket—it's too cold for you to be out there without a jacket." I wonder how my opponent would have made Outlaw Bill respond.

That chatter game was interesting, but I wanted to be more up and about the place, skating for one thing. But before going on with my skating, I want to say more about that radio culture in the boys' dorm.

Well back in the years before my time on campus, and off and on during the seven years I was there, some of the guys carried on a lively little sublegal AM radio broadcasting "industry." From somewhere they would get these little radio transmitters, which could be set to broadcast on AM frequencies. These things were small; they looked to me like glorified freestanding microphones. They tried, as I understood it, to keep the power output low enough to just cover the blind boys' dorm and the blind girls' dorm next door. A couple of the guys had or developed really good broadcast voices and performed like professional announcers and disk jockeys on commercial radio. In fact, at least one went on from these beginnings to become a well-known radio personality here in the Shenandoah Valley. Most of the programming was the disk jockey format, but they also did news, sports and weather information. While a record was playing the announcer would get his news, sports, or weather information by listening to regular commercial radio. Then, when the record was finished or at whatever desired time, he would announce this information as though he had gotten it from "regular" sources. I particularly liked the way they signed off the air at 10:00 p.m. official bedtime in the dorm. These teenage announcers would come up with wording to convey peaceful repose, quietly retiring for the night.

SKATING MY WHEELS OFF

Jimmy Randel did get me started skating the first afternoon after school. He showed me out to the big concrete court. (Dad estimated that court was maybe an acre under concrete.) I got my skates on—clamp-on skates with steel ball bearing wheels. Jimmy got in front of me; I grabbed his belt. I said, "Wait a minute, you don't have your skates on." He said, "No, I'm just gonna run. I like to run." So he ran and ran, and I skated and skated. When he was out of breath I asked again about his skates. He insisted, "No, I like to run; I need to lose weight anyway." (He was pudgy.) I never knew whether he really liked to run or was he a poor kid without skates who wanted to run to befriend me.

That first year the afternoons between end of classes and suppertime were long, so, I skated A LOT! I skated with others who could see a little, sometimes with one partner, sometimes in long strings with a sighted kid up front. Sometimes two, three, or five skaters would squat in a straight line with a sighted kid up front. A runner, without skates, would push from behind. Sometimes I opted to be the pusher—that way I could run full tilt until winded—I loved the heft of getting a heavy load rolling and leaning into the load coming out of a turn or on an upgrade. I was surprised at how quickly I got winded.

I also skated solo. By looking down I could see enough to

skate carefully in small areas, but it was too nerve-racking being that careful. Then I found the straight wall of Main Chapel
along one side of the courtyard. In full sunshine I could look
down at just the right angle and track along the line where the
red brick of the old chapel wall met the light tan concrete of
the courtyard. I soon desperately wanted to skate FAST—full
stride, leg flyin' FAST! The kids I skated with had too much
sense to put the pedal to the metal. That solo run along the chapel wall proved too short for real speed—and actually not safe
enough either—I did once broadside a car that pulled up onto
the courtyard just as I cleared the end of the building at a pretty
fast clip. (Yes, cars sometimes parked on that court—I wouldn't
have wanted to park my car there. Yes, they allowed cars to park
where visually-impaired kids were allowed/urged to skate!)

Being mechanically inclined I experimented and fine-
tuned my skates and also helped others with their skate problems. I replaced the wheels on my skates at least three times that
first year. (There was a store downtown that knew of us VSDB
kids and kept an inventory of skate wheels on hand.)

The frustration with not being able to skate full speed,
became the occasion for, I believe, the last episode of grieving
over my failing vision. Right when I became aware of the wild
joy of skating high wide and free on that huge concrete court,
which seemed to beckon to the wild blue yonder, my vision was
shutting down to zero. To make things worse, winter darkness
was crowding in, shortening skating time each afternoon, which
added to the gloom. I didn't crawl behind some bush and cry,
though I felt like it. From the vantage point of this writing, I can
see that I skated on into darkness, but that concrete courtyard
proved to have a literal window into my next joy—organ and
organ lessons! More on that later.

THE MENNONITE NECKTIE THING

Come Christmas that first year, the ladies of the Staunton Garden Club extended their annual invitation for the VSDB chorus to come do a Christmas concert after which they would serve us a holiday banquet! Mrs. Rogers, our chorus teacher stressed that this was an important annual event and we kids MUST mind our table manners and dress properly. For the boys that meant a suit, white shirt and tie. I knew instantly this tie business was going to be an issue because I stood on the front row and the VSDB teachers and officials fretted a lot about our public image. When I told Mrs. Rogers I wouldn't be able to wear a tie, I discovered she already knew about my "official exemption." At the concert I stood in the front row and sang as angelically as everybody else, maybe even more so because of the girl next to me. At the banquet I discovered those big lettuce leaf salads which I immediately hated as much as the other blind kids—they were impossible to eat with any kind of finesse. After the meal the ladies started handing each chorus member a little gift—small dime store trinkets and toys. When I opened my package, I couldn't believe what I found—a necktie!! Those dear ladies had taken note of that boy in the front row who sang his heart out and was too poor to afford a tie! Somebody had dashed downtown, bought a tie, wrapped it up, and brought it back in time to hand me this "very special gift!"

Neither Dad nor some Mennonite preacher was available to step up and explain, "Oh, sorry ladies, neckties are a worldly vanity that we Mennonites don't use." No VSDB official stepped up to say, "Oh, ladies, this tie is a nice gesture but this boy's religion means he can't accept it. But thanks anyway." I certainly didn't have time to gather my wits and explain all this. I was on my own. On my own I decided: Yes, a nice uniform appearance for chorus members is important. I'll go ahead and wear the tie for chorus programs and similar public events. I informed my family thus and heard no objection.

Sometime after that, one of the older boys, seeing my dearth of ties, gave me one of his extras. After that, Dad showed up in my room on some errand or other. I showed him the ties. Without a word he went downtown, bought a tie, came back and handed it to me, saying, "Don't wear those other ties, use this one." Later, when Eldon saw those ties, he could see clearly why Dad bought me that new tie—it was more in keeping with Mennonite quietude. Eventually my Mennonite scruple about neckties went away altogether, and that with nary a word from Mom and Dad.

For what it's worth, there was another time I was noted for "singing my heart out." Our chorus was singing for a local Lion's Club. Again, I was in the front row and singing oh so happily. After the program several men came along the front row shaking hands and expressing appreciation for our program. Several singled me out and shook my hand most emphatically and said with matching emphasis, "Son, don't ever, EVER, **EVER** lose that smile!" So what makes a boy sing so? Of course it was the girl next to me, the girl with the last face I ever saw, Juanita.

At some point in that first year, I got an unexpected insight into Dad's thinking. For the kids my age and younger, their parents were asked to leave allowance money with the housemothers. The housemothers would then parcel it out daily or weekly or however the parents instructed. This made an interesting scene daily—a bunch of boys clustering around the housemother's door for their spending money for the day. At one point some of the kids got to alleging (in true adult gossipy fashion) that the housemother was taking money from the envelopes of the more affluent boys and giving it to some who had none. I backed off from this talk as irresponsible gossip. Later, in the car on a trip home, I told Dad about this; I told it as though to say, "See how silly those guys can be." To my complete surprise, Dad turned to me and said emphatically, "Now look, Sonny, if that housemother knows of someone who doesn't have enough money and wants to use some of your money to help out, you let her do it."

ORGANS, PIANOS, BRAILLE MUSIC

Before I arrived at VSDB, my musical world centered around Mennonite style unaccompanied congregational singing. I liked that music, but by age 7 my musical heart had been captured by instrumental music. At home I was learning to play the reed organ using the shaped note system in our Mennonite hymnals. My true love, though, was the pipe organ that I had only heard on Grandpa Wenger's radio downstairs. It was while skating on that big concrete courtyard that I heard organ music coming from an open practice room window off the courtyard. It was Shirley Lyons practicing; she kindly explained through the screen that VSDB had an organ and organ lessons were available! By the end of my first year I was learning Braille music and taking piano lessons. I began organ lessons my second year— and most of my free time thereafter was structured by organ and piano practice, and also some time in the piano tuning shop. It's clear to me now this preoccupation with music is what provided a way for me to remain a Mennonite and still have some social standing during my time at VSDB. The social life there outside the classroom centered around dances and trips downtown to the movies and around the school wrestling program. I could not participate in those things. Music gave me the way to belong, to have standing and respect among my peers, and it likely kept me out of trouble. Ironically though, the type of music that played this role was instrumental music with a lot of emphasis on solo performance, and my Mennonite community back home frowned on such with varying degrees of displeasure. More on this later.

The organ I discovered through that open window was a Hammond electric organ, purchased by VSDB in 1946. It was located in a practice room just off the Perry Hall chapel. It was not a pipe organ but on it I could learn pipe organ music—and I did. Some of the older organ students were delighted to show me around the organ, to explain do's and don'ts in organ music, to talk about different kinds of organs, and to let me listen to their records of organ classics. As I became proficient in Braille music, I spent hours rummaging through a Braille music library on very dusty shelves picking out pieces I wanted to learn.

Braille music—ah yes, what a system of music notation! There is no such thing as lines and spaces, no seeing at a glance the rise and fall and flow of the music or the relation of the right hand to the left by observing the arrangement of the notation on the printed page. All the various Braille symbols are written straight across the page one after another. For example, a fourth octave C major chord to be played staccato with fingers one, two, and four is written: staccato symbol, fourth octave symbol, quarter note C, first finger symbol, third interval symbol, second finger symbol, fifth interval symbol, fourth finger symbol. That's eight spaces across the line—for just one simple quarter note chord. There is no such thing as sight reading; Braille music is a memorizing system.

As I've gotten older and very aware of how the brain works (partly because I've read a lot in brain science and partly because my brain doesn't work so well anymore), I've become conscious of and fascinated with the brain processes involved in learning a musical passage from Braille music. You first read one or several measures with, say, the left hand while playing and memorizing the music for the right hand. Then, while retaining that right-hand music in short-term memory, you read with the right hand and play with the left hand and commit that left-hand music to another section of short-term memory. Now you start integrating these two sets of notes into one musical idea while also getting the two hands to learn the moves to properly execute that idea. This is a lot of brain processing! As your hands master the moves to execute the musical idea, your comprehension of that idea improves and deepens. That whole package—the musical thought and the muscle memory for the hands to execute it—all that is what is finally committed to long-term memory. When the music is simple, or at least familiar, this Braille music process is quite doable. When the music is complicated and totally unfamiliar, I found/find it difficult to retain the music just learned for one hand while learning that for the other. Braille music is better than no music at all; it works for those who are motivated.

Around 1958, my sophomore year, a Baldwin electric organ was installed in Main Chapel. This had a standard pipe organ console—two full manuals, 32 pedals, a full selection of pipe organ-type stops, combination pistons and toe studs, separate swell pedals for each manual, and a crescendo pedal. The tone was much closer to authentic pipe organ sound. There were almost no other organ students at that time—I had that wonderful new organ virtually to myself! Some of the other students got to calling the chapel with the organ my second home—"Hey Danny, did you spend all afternoon in your second home today?" I didn't like their teasing; it had a certain jeering tone to it. But they were right. It was a good second home for me.

TEENAGE THEOLOGIAN

My teenage religious formation was driven by two major influences. The first was Dad's way of telling the Bible stories to us kids at home. The second was my time at VSDB—that put me on a very different faith journey from my peers back home.

My larger starting point was, of course, the world of Virginia Conference Mennonites. We were like many of the more sectarian Christian churches in one important respect—we all thought we were THE only TRUE Christians on the straight and narrow road to heaven and the other groups were on that other road, the broad one. The watch word for the Mennonites around me was, "separation from the world." I had heard so many warnings about "so-called Christians," "professing Christians"— "They can be the nicest people, but they are worldly, not separate from the world." From practically my first day at VSDB I was surprised to discover these "worldly Christians" couldn't and shouldn't be dismissed so casually. The housemother for our floor, Mrs. Halterman, was clearly a warmhearted Christian but of another denomination I had never heard of. I suppose my experiences in those two sixth grade classrooms helped prepare me to see that you can have interesting and serious conversations about religion with all kinds of people.

The first thing I noticed was what I now understand to be a fundamental difference in the way we hold and state our religious beliefs. I was raised in the "Believer's Church tradition"— The believer was supposed to study and KNOW THE BIBLE FOR HIMSELF; when discussing religious and spiritual matters, he stated his beliefs as his own convictions and understandings. In contrast to that, when conversations at VSDB came around to questions like, "What do you believe about the divinity of Jesus," many or even most of the kids would defer to an external

authority with some variant of, "Well, my minister says that…"
My usually unspoken response was, "Wait a minute, what your
minister thinks is beside the point, it's what YOU think that
counts." If I did push, "But what do YOU think," they would
get all fidgety and stammer to a halt. My "certain knowledge" of
religious matters was, of course, a set up for haughty dogmatism,
but, judging from the many neat conversations I had with fellow students and teachers, I must not have fallen too deeply into
that trap.

As already noted, Dad's well-told Bible stories were the
first step in my religious formation. His Anabaptist martyr stories were a solid second step. The most gripping of those Anabaptist stories was the book, *Not Regina*, by Christmas Carol
Kauffman (published in book form in 1954, but first serialized
in *Youth's Christian Companion and Words of Cheer*). Dad read
that to us kids just before I went off to VSDB. I was thus thoroughly steeped in my Anabaptist Mennonite heritage by the
time I arrived in that new world.

But then, in the VSDB library, I encountered a third influence on my faith—I found a Braille(!) copy of the book *A
Man Called Peter* by Catherine Marshal. I devoured that book!
Somehow, I also got some LP recordings of several of Peter Marshall's sermons. He was Scottish and Presbyterian and COULD
SPEAK! His thick Scottish brogue made his sermons, his story
telling, and his prayers, all the more compelling. He was a popular preacher at an upscale Presbyterian church in Washington,
D.C., and eventually became Chaplin for the U.S. Senate. I realized I was finding genuine Christian spirituality in places quite
other than anything I knew as a barefoot Mennonite farm boy.
Discovering familiar Christian truth in other than Mennonite
garb—well, I liked that. Actually, I was beginning to transcend

denominational walls—and that without just dumping my Mennonite heritage.

A fourth influence occurred in an unlikely place—those barren rooms in the boys' dorm. From the Federal Talking Book program, some of us guys got the books *The Robe* and *The Big Fisherman*, both by Lloyd C. Douglas, and the book *Ben-Hur: A Tale of the Christ* by Lew Wallace. These books were recorded in the days when Talking Books were on 12-inch LP records. Somebody would play the records, with the volume turned up so the rest of us sprawled around the room, could hear. We would listen after study hall till bedtime and often in the morning while we were getting dressed and making our beds before breakfast. The suspense was as dramatic as any of our favorite radio shows! These books were historical novels centering on the life of Jesus and other New Testament characters plus other fictional characters from the writer's imagination. Now and then someone would ask, "Is this what really happened?" or "Is this really in the Bible?" I could often explain which characters or quotes are actually in the Biblical record or in the case of fiction, how the fictional material helps us understand what really happened.

For teenage me personally, these historical novels made the New Testament breathe and come alive. Despite the considerable romantic embellishment in these books (which I was aware of), I began to get a grasp of the Judeo-Greco-Roman world in which the New Testament story is set. Indeed, the whole Bible story became believable in a new way. Maybe it was my intellect developing to the point where I could start thinking like a historian—I caught on that the Biblical story is actually set in real history.

A fifth shaping influence grew out of my piano and organ recital in my sophomore or junior year. By this time Mom and Dad and my whole family were coming to all my recitals. On this occasion a very friendly gentleman came to me in the crowd of well-wishers after the recital; he said he was a lay leader in a Methodist Church in Danville, Virginia. He was impressed with my performance and commented, I thought casually, that it would be neat if I could come do a concert at his church. A bit later Dad pulled me aside and said the same man had come to him and worked out plans for he and Mom to pick me up from VSDB and take me on south to Danville to do a full concert in his Methodist Church. The date and times for rehearsal and the concert, and plans for overnight lodging, were all set. I nearly flipped—I was going to do a solo concert (something my Mennonite heritage frowned on as worldly entertainment) in an uptown Methodist Church (a worldly church), and my mom and dad, in their full Mennonite garb, were going to take two whole days away from their farm work to help me do it!

Well, it all happened as planned. The unforgettable part was the way the minister's wife and my parents "discovered each other." Our lodging and meals were in the church parsonage and the minister's wife was our hostess. She was a really poised and gracious person and quickly got Mom and Dad comfortable and at ease. I listened with amazement as they soon were discussing and explaining their respective religious traditions. I saw Mom and Dad opening up to the preacher's wife as they discovered genuine faith and spirituality in the traditions of her Methodist world. Once again, I was discovering that you don't have to be "separate from the world" to be a good Christian. I was becoming sure of my insight on this. In my teenage way I could see that a tradition involving separation from the world and a tradition involving work and witness out in the world can each contribute significant witness to the Kingdom of God. On the way home I waited for the usual warnings about "worldly Christians that can be so nice." There was none. I liked all this—a lot!

WRESTLING, NOT FOR THIS MENNONITE

VSDB had a strong intramural wrestling program. We were recognized as a strong team in various athletic associations. We often heard it said wrestling was the one sport where blind people could compete on a par with sighted people. Much of the regular boys' phys. ed. time centered around wrestling— strengthening exercises and learning and drilling and drilling AND DRILLING the standard wrestling holds and maneuvers. My Mennonite faith forbade participation in organized sports, so, I never participated in formal wrestling matches with other schools. My regular exercise time, though, involved learning wrestling skills; that included wrestling and tumbling around with other guys not formally on the team. In these informal tussles you immediately knew where you fit in the pecking order. Jimmy Lowe and Ronnie Bolen were two guys I enjoyed "keeping in their place." Well, one Fall these two guys came back from summer vacation with their testosterone turned full on—they were MUSCULAR and BIGGER! Either one could now handily mop up the mat with me! Thereafter I found it expedient to be deferential and respectful!

Actually, I did wrestle in one formal match. The team desperately needed someone to fill in the 107-pound slot; the coaches began leaning on me hard to join the team and take the slot. I wrestled with my Mennonite conscience for a while, then consented to wrestle "this one match." So, I had to get my weight down from 110 to 107 pounds within the week. Basically, I starved it down. On the morning of the official weigh-in day I was still a little overweight. I was told not to drink any liquid, put on two sweat suits and lift weights a while in the hot weight room. That did get my weight in line, but good grief—is that a way to get energized for an athletic competition? I couldn't pin my opponent; he couldn't pin me either but scored more points so he was the winner.

I enjoyed that experience, but it wasn't really my cup of tea, at least not enough so to risk stirring up things with my Mennonite roots back home. But, back home I happily used my wrestling skills to keep my "little brothers," Jim and Bernard, in line. I knew full well the day would come when they would be mopping up the floor with me like Jimmy Lowe and Ronnie Bolen did. Meanwhile, it was, *Heck, I'm blind; that's a definite handicap. It's therefore fair enough to avail myself of whatever advantage I have. They'll have the ascendency soon enough. So I'll just enjoy the ascendency while I have it!* With that quirky logic I had fun teasing, taunting, and tussling. If the fracas was at night, I liked to maneuver the scuffle over to where I could switch off the ceiling light—I claimed things would be more equal if everyone were in the dark, but Jim and Bernard certainly didn't see it that way. Well, the day came—one Sunday morning getting dressed for church, Jim had his "nuff of my mouth"; he lunged at me and Bernard then piled on. The two of them couldn't get me down, but I could plainly see the handwriting on the wall— these little brothers were growing up! Finally, right when I was on the verge of giving up, they gave up. I do believe if they had held on ten seconds longer they would have had me. I forthwith closed that chapter of my "older brother rowdiness," it was now expedient to show deference and respect here, too! In his memoir Jim recounts an incident that perhaps indicates I overdid the horsing around, but if I had been a "nice big brother" he wouldn't have had his story—right? It's amazing what happens to boys when that testosterone kicks in! OK, I digressed, let's get back to VSDB.

ON THE OTHER SIDE OF MISSION OUTREACH

In my junior year I had the unusual experience of sitting on the receiving end of Mennonite mission outreach. EMC at that time was encouraging its students to participate in various forms of mission outreach—helping out in the Sunday schools of surrounding churches, teaching in vacation Bible schools, conducting street meetings and planting new churches, or singing and preaching at local jails or at other institutions. One of those "other institutions" turned out to be VSDB.

As already noted many times, the social life at VSDB centered around Saturday night dances and around Saturday and Sunday afternoon trips downtown to the movies, boys and girls together. This social life was intense and important. Suddenly it was announced, "This Sunday afternoon, and one Sunday afternoon of each month hereafter you will not be going downtown. Instead, you will attend a program in Main Chapel to be given by students from Eastern Mennonite College." This was going to be compulsory attendance at a religious service; the students were indignant! I squirmed inside, knowing what was coming. By then I had achieved a good measure of respect among the other kids despite my Mennonite ways, and indeed in some cases, because of those ways. In fact, since my first days on campus whenever I had to explain my ways, I tried to put a teenaged positive spin on things Mennonite. In some ways I was a bit successful, I thought. And, I had seen the students respond positively to guest preachers who were good public speakers (such as Dr. Louis J. Evans Sr. from First Presbyterian Church of Hollywood, California) but I knew the Gospel presented in EMC student style to this captive audience wouldn't fly. It would mess up my "public relations campaign."

The program consisted of 20 or 30 students singing several hymns Mennonite a cappella style, several testimonies along the line of "I'm so thankful Jesus saved me from my sins," a short talk, and another song or two. There was some effort to get the audience involved in singing, but it didn't go well—those kids were sullen.

In the dorm afterwards, some of the guys began reproaching me with a lot of indignant "You Mennonites" kind of talk. The program hadn't been all that long, but, as far as the guys were concerned, their afternoon downtown was shot. And, they resented having religion stuffed at them in captive audience format. One said to me pointedly, "We don't want your Mennonite religion around here." I was shocked as I caught on that he, and some others too, actually suspected I was in some way behind all this. The truth was I was quite embarrassed on their behalf. I never knew whether they believed my denial. The program might have been tolerated, maybe even enjoyed, had it been presented in one of the regular chapel times.

As the guys got over their grousing at me, one piped up, "Well, I'll say one thing for them Mennonites—their women are some kind o' good lookin'! Uumm um!" There was a chorus of assents. Remember, I pointed out earlier in the book that in a population like this where everyone is legally blind, there is still a lot of useable vision. This includes vision a plenty to appreciate pretty girls, especially when you're at the age where your hormones can readily fill in any blanks. The Mennonite cape dresses of the younger women at that time did accentuate the waistline and, therefore, the hips; the effect was to sabotage the intentions of the designers of the cape dress, even with a bunch of guys with poor vision.

Then, to my surprise and delight, some of the more musically inclined guys expressed appreciation for the Mennonite style a cappella singing.

A LITTLE POLITICKING

During the 1960 Kennedy-Nixon election my senior year, our government teacher took seriously the business of making us understand the structure and workings of our state and federal government systems. He also showed how political machines, dirty campaigning, name-calling and the like have been a part of the American political scene from the beginning. He emphasized critical listening to slogans and speeches. He talked about the humorous side—relatively harmless political pranks and jokes—including pranks by previous VSDB students. Several weeks before the election he took us, a class of eight or so, downtown (walking) to visit the Republican and Democratic headquarters. He had primed us with appropriate questions. We got to the Democratic headquarters first. They were friendly and talked freely with us. They gave us a bunch of pamphlets and bumper stickers. Then we went to the Republican headquarters. The place was closed! We were surprised, then annoyed. To "teach them a lesson," we pasted a Kennedy bumper sticker right across Nixon's face in the store front window. As we walked home we stuck Kennedy stickers over any Nixon stickers we saw on parked cars. Our teacher kept exclaiming, "You kids are gonna get me fired!" All the while though, as it seemed to me, he was enjoying and relishing these pranks as much as we were. Back on campus we found a Nixon sticker on a teacher's car (she was known to be quite conservative); we put a Kennedy bumper sticker on top of hers, too. As far as I knew there were no repercussions from all this, but I find it hard to believe literally no one knew who the culprits were.

A LITTLE MENNONITE HOSPITALITY

Near the end of my senior year I got an idea. My Mennoniteness had set me slightly off to the side of the VSDB social scene. I decided to arrange a class outing to my home, a traditional Mennonite farm, just a 45-minute drive from VSDB. This would be an evening of Mennonite farm hospitality. It would be my "Mennonite gift" to my VSDB friends, a neat "last positive spin on things Mennonite." My family enthusiastically agreed to this, including setting out a big picnic style supper. Two VSDB teachers, Mr. Hickman, our class sponsor, and Mrs. Kiracofe, my music teacher, agreed to provide the transportation with their own cars. The invitation was extended to my senior class plus 2 or 3 others who were practically seniors, maybe ten or eleven teenagers packed into two cars.

The outing went well, I thoroughly enjoyed playing the generous host, showing the kids around the farm, explaining farm life (some of it) as though I knew what I was talking about. Juanita, the girl whose face I last saw, stuck close to me through the evening; I liked that.

When it came time to eat, we all gathered in the living room. By now I was getting a little carried away with playing the hot shot host. When one of my sisters came in with a tray of big tumblers full of lemonade, I took the tray and proceeded to go around the room presenting the tray for each guest to take a glass. This went OK—at first. Now remember, I'm blind; most everyone else had enough vision to reach out and take a glass, and the one or two with no vision would have someone next to them who would help get the glass—so I thought. One of my best friends, Neal Ewers, also totally blind, decided to play smart blind man like me. He reached out to get his own glass—a blind man reaching for a glass of lemonade on a tray held by a blind man! You guessed it—a big tall glass of ice-cold lemonade tumbled straight down into his lap! And mind you, he was sitting on one of those 1950s sofas upholstered with solid water-proof plastic! The whole glass of ice-cold lemonade then pooled under his butt! I was mortified! Well, my sisters, ever the capable farm girls, hustled in with towels and cleaned up the mess as much as possible, but Neal, having no way to change clothes, patiently sat around the whole evening, and then sat patiently in the car for the ride back to school. Neal and I are still good friends.

THAT NECKTIE THING AGAIN!

On my graduation day in June 1961—that old necktie issue popped up one more time—I couldn't believe it! When commencement exercises were over, I joined Mom and Dad and my sibs at the back of the auditorium. I was surprised and delighted to find some other folks from my Mennonite world there waiting to congratulate me—Grandma Bowman (I was surprised to find her up and about thus), Aunt Annie's, Uncle Durward and Aunt Barbara with cousins Loretta and Florence, Uncle Paul, plus others. Everybody, including Mom and Dad, were clearly identifiable by their clothing as Mennonite. But I took note, there was none of that hushed voice stuff signifying "We Mennos don't quite belong in this worldly place." We were all comfortable there and I liked that!

Suddenly Dad was exclaiming, "Well, look who's here"— Mr. Joseph Healey, the VSDB superintendent during my first several years there but since retired, had just walked up. He started to greet Dad—the two of them had come to genuinely appreciate and respect each other. Without finishing his greeting to Dad, Mr. Healey reached over and grabbed my tie; he said with bemusement in his deep bass voice, "Hey boy, you aren't supposed to be wearing that!" I fumbled with the tie to put it back in place and started to laugh (too loudly) and to say something like, "…but the Mennonite world is changing." I stopped as I realized that Dad was embarrassed and mumbling something like, "That's not the way we raised him."

That tie—I had by now learned to tie a really good-looking knot and I was wearing a shirt with a nice collar; I thought I looked sharp and spiffy, and Mr. Healey had to go and yank it askew like that! So that Mennonite issue about neckties, which had come up at my first visit to the campus in 1954 sure enough bracketed the first and last of my days at VSDB. To this day I feel badly about how the Mennonite necktie issue spoiled Dad's last encounter with Mr. Healey, his old friend.

VSDB IN REVIEW

Reflecting back on my education at VSDB, it's clear to me those educators thought of more than just the usual academic subjects. They tried hard to equip us blind and visually-impaired kids with skills for independent living as adults in the sighted world. Typing—A LOT OF IT—was a required course for all of us every school year. And, *home ec* was also required—even for us boys. Home ec included cooking and food prep, dish washing and general kitchen procedures. The teacher dictated many recipes, which we were made to copy into Braille notebooks. (My sisters later, with smug glee, informed my soon-to-be bride, Ferne Lapp, of these reluctantly acquired kitchen skills and of the Braille recipe notebook.)

That home ec course included basic reproduction biology. For this, a "trained instructor" was brought in from the Red Cross. We were taught all about egg and sperm, about the nine months of pregnancy with its morning sickness and crazy food cravings. We boys had our "wet dreams" explained and were told about the girls' monthly cycle. About that monthly cycle, we boys were told we must be patient and just wait a few days when our girlfriend or wife is suddenly not very sweet and responsive. Believe it or not, we were told how, in an emergency, to deliver a baby, how to tie and cut the umbilical cord, and how to clean up the newborn. Using a life-sized doll baby, the instructor made us boys, one at a time, go through the steps of cleaning the newborn—make sure the airways are clear, clean the head (be careful of the soft spot), clean behind the ears, and gently clean the eyes. Despite our reluctance, she made us go through the steps of cleaning "the little crease or creases in the baby's little bottom."

Home ec for the girls included training in basic home nursing skills—changing bed linen with the patient in bed, handling a bedpan, and I'm scared to think what all else.

We also got a lot of counseling, in home ec and other settings, about genetics, how some forms of blindness are hereditary and others are not. We were urged to be well informed about these things when planning for families and children.

Vocational or trade skill classes were also offered—chair caning, woodworking, piano tuning and repair for the boys; sewing and clothing care for the girls, etc. By the time I graduated, I had soaked up the piano tuning instruction to the point where I was tuning and servicing virtually all the pianos on campus. On my high school diploma was an extra certificate for piano tuning, which I was told amounted to a two-year junior college education in piano technology. Probably the most important nonacademic training I received was orientation and mobility, that is training in the use of the long cane and in various techniques for getting about the seeing world independently. I began this training while still at VSDB, but the bulk of it was finished some years later when I was living in Richmond. That story will be told in a later chapter.

7

BULLIES AND CHILDHOOD
NONRESISTANCE, SORT OF

My first encounter with a bully was on the school bus early in first grade. Riding a school bus was still new and scary.

There are all these noisy kids around me, strange scenery going by the window, the bus is laboring up a hill on an unfamiliar narrow road, I'm hanging onto my lunch box and working hard to keep on calmly minding my own business. Bang! A hand from across the aisle grabs my arm and shakes me roughly. I look over—right into an unfriendly face with large, glowering eyes. "Eyes!" the face hissed. *Oh, I see,* I catch on. *My glasses make me look different. He's trying to get everybody to look at my eyes.*

That happened often on that bus in the first year. The term "eyes" became "pop eyes." When they changed the bus route, that bully disappeared, but another one came into my school bus world and stayed off and on till I finished fifth grade.

Jack Grainger was a year or two older than me and big for his age; I was small and scrawny for my age. I was also very nearsighted, and that made my glasses about a quarter-inch thick at the outer edge and, I was told, as thin as paper in the center. That, of course, made my eyes look funny. On top of that, I was very cross-eyed—the right eye turned in toward my nose and was essentially useless. Jack got to calling me "Cross-eyed jackass." I would try to sit away from him but as the bus emptied out, he would close in and start picking on me all over again. More than once he put a charley horse on my arm. Sometimes he would just stare at me and softly mouth, "Cross-eyed jackass!" My Mennonite heritage insisted that I could not fight back, but he was so much bigger and all over me that any such scruples never REALLY had a chance to become relevant. I began trying to outwit him with words. I would think up a clever epithet and save it for the right moment. Once I had one ready when somehow I ended up in the very back seat of the bus with only an empty seat between Jack and me. He turned and sneered, "Cross-eyed jackass." I shot back with my prepared epithet, "You're a blood-thirsty demon." He reached back across that empty seat and backhanded me across the mouth so fast that, despite the pain and the blood, I was actually amazed—how in the world COULD he reach that far that fast?! I managed to sputter, "See what I mean?!" I thought, but wasn't sure, maybe the sight of blood made him back off a bit, for a while at least.

After that I tried tossing my epithets at him as I jumped off the bus safely out of his reach. The sight of his frustration when he couldn't get his hands on me made me gloat inside. Of course he soon stationed himself on that right front seat just inside the door and again raised a charley horse as I jumped off. I was in tears—this one really hurt. As the bus pulled off, Eldon was upset, too; he was a year younger than me, but he said in a really kindly wise older brother sort of way, "Daniel, you need to just stay away from him." I replied, "I do try to sit well away from him but as the bus empties out, he moves in on me."

Every day, first thing after school Eldon and I would read the funnies in the local newspaper. One day in the comic strip, "Blondie," I came across the boss, Mr. Dithers, really ripping into Dagwood for some infraction. His string of words got my attention. Wow! I started to smile, then grin. I told Eldon, "There's what I'm gonna call Jack Grainger next time he bothers me!" I memorized those words and practiced saying them over and over; I wanted to make sure they flowed off my tongue when needed. Then came my chance…

It was now the end of my fifth grade, maybe the last day. I had taken the seat right behind the bus driver, thinking maybe here near the driver I'll be a little safer. I was in a good mood about something. Engrossed at the bus driver's copy of *Popular Mechanics,* I forgot all about Jack Grainger. Suddenly, bang! A heavy fist landed hard on my left shoulder, jarring me all over. I turned, and there was Jack Grainger, leaning forward with his face almost in mine. "Cross-eyed jackass," he greeted me. I let my practiced words fly, "You're a snaggle-toothed, lop-eared baboon!" Jack had a popsicle stick in his hand and gave it a little toss right at me. The end of that stick hit dead center on the glasses lense of my good eye, right on the part that was thin as paper. The glass shattered. Suddenly I had tiny little glass shards all over my eyelid, on my eyelashes, and on my cheek, but wonder of unbelievable wonders, not one fragment of glass in my eye proper. I was frozen in place; I was afraid to try brushing off those shards for fear of knocking some into my eye. The driver stopped the bus. He got up, said, "Here, Daniel," and turned me toward him; he pulled my hand down from my face, then carefully brushed the glass shards off my face. Without a word he returned to his seat and drove on, business as usual. I put my broken glasses in my shirt pocket.

The driver didn't say a word to Jack. He didn't say a further word to me. Jack didn't say a word to me, much less an apology. I didn't say a word to Jack—I figured he could see well enough what he had done and maybe now he would be sufficiently ashamed to amend his ways. The driver didn't report the incident to Jack's father, my father, nor to school authorities. My dad said nothing to Jack's father nor to school officials—a miss-application of traditional Mennonite teachings about nonresistance (in my opinion); he just ordered me another pair of glasses. I never saw Jack again; after that we were on different buses to different schools.

So what was going on here? Did the bus driver think I had it coming after calling Jack a snaggle-toothed, lop-eared baboon? But surely he heard Jack calling me a cross-eyed jackass again and many times again, loudly, for several years running. Actually, the school bus culture of that time and place didn't seem to call for the driver to monitor and intervene in student behavior (Eldon and I witnessed some other outrageous behavior on that bus that was never addressed by the driver). Did I really have it coming? I was sure enough a victim of bullying, which I did not initiate, but over the years since then I came to see that just maybe I wasn't all that helpless a victim. I was reduced to tears more than once, but I just didn't cave in; I was not crushed. I remember well my delight and relish when I found Mr. Dither's words to Dagwood—I had sure enough begun to get a kick out of besting Jack with words. Just maybe I had learned to do a little sneaky aggression of my own. I wonder if my male hormones were starting to trickle in—this was after all the beginning of that period in my youth when I got pretty rowdy and ornery. Maybe Jack saw me as an insufferable smart mouth that needed to be put in his place. In the end I became a little tickled with my handle—isn't a jackass a little donkey; isn't a donkey a spunky, sometimes ornery little critter? Just maybe I was sure enough a spunky, sometimes ornery little critter. I could have been worse.

Now, fast forward about 26 years. Ferne and I are living in Harrisburg, Pennsylvania. We have two little girls—Laura, age

6, and Diane, age 4. Diane was very nearsighted and wore large, thick glasses, much like mine. One day Laura and Diane were seeking adventure; they decided to ride all the way around the block on their trikes. They set out in high spirits. When they came back around, Diane was all upset and indignant. "There was a boy over there that came running out and calling me 'Eyes!'" I'll leave my reaction to your imagination. Back to my story…

Back on the school playground, grades one through five, I experienced the usual run of picking, teasing, taunting, pushing and shoving, struggling for position in the pecking order, and bullying. I heard the term "pop eyes" off and on. I caught on that sometimes I could take what I had learned on the receiving end, turn it around and dish it out to some kid further down in the pecking order. I was too scrawny for team sports, so much of the time I was a loner on the playground. Nevertheless, I did have some friends and good times, enough so that grade school at Dale Enterprise ends as a high point in my life—except for those school bus rides.

At VSDB, grades six through twelve, my Mennonite heritage regarding nonresistance and loving your enemy was tested. I passed my first test with flying colors. Soon after moving into the boys' dorm in September 1954, I met Alfred. He was a big boy, strong, a bit clumsy, and retarded (a term we used then but which is avoided today). He would casually punch anybody on the shoulder as he walked by. He was more of a nuisance than an all-out bully, but his arms were heavy and his blows did jar you. He did have a quirky sense of humor. One day in the gym locker room I heard him picking on Dicky, a feisty little fellow with a major stuttering problem. Dicky stuttered out, "You b-b-b-be-better st-st-stop that or I'll kno-kno-knock the h-h-hell right out of you!" Alfred thought a moment, then replied in his tongue-tied way, "W'll, then I be good boy." I just tried to avoid Alfred.

The following Spring when I was home for Easter break, I made a formal commitment to Jesus and the church—I was "born again." This was a genuine religious experience for me, but I was also aware there were some elements of "just doing what our family and church circles expected you to do at this age." Then, the following Sunday afternoon I returned to VSDB. Always when we came back on campus, we were supposed to check in at the infirmary. I headed that way, and "Oh, shoot, here comes Alfred." He was headed to the infirmary, too. Now that I was "born again," I knew I was supposed to "love my enemy"—that is, be nice to Alfred. I took his arm and we headed on toward the infirmary. I chatted with him as with an old friend. This was for real, I wasn't faking. To my amazement, Alfred became a loveable goofy sort of friend to me. After that I heard him several times announcing to anybody in general, in his tongue-tied way, "Nobody better mess with Dan Bowman, he's my fwend." I well remember reflecting on this—was Alfred's changed behavior a result of my "supernatural born again" experience, or was it simply what would happen if anybody, born again or not, treated a bully kindly? I kept these reflections to myself.

Along about eighth grade I handled things very poorly. The guys knew that according to my religion I was not supposed to fight back when picked on. They took note, though, that while I didn't hit back, I did get very angry. I would fling back verbal insults like, "You filthy dog!" They began testing me on this and were delighted to observe my inner conflict.

One day when I headed down the hall for class, somebody took a punch at me. I said my insult and kept going. Then another bystander took a punch, then another, and still another and another—all totally silent. To harass or pick on a totally blind guy without identifying yourself was considered grossly unfair in that world and I felt the insult keenly. The next day, at the same time and same place it happened again, only there must have been eight or ten guys, all lined up along the wall, throwing a punch at me, one at a time. Mostly these blows were hard pushes, designed more to insult than really hurt. I could tell some of the blows were from totally blind guys—they sort of glanced off my face. From a certain body odor I detected one of these silent assailants was a best friend—that really got to me. I realized those guys had deliberately set up a gauntlet for me to run; they were evenly spaced and silent. I was furious—*Where the hell was that house parent! Why should I have to be a tattle tale to get respect?* They had set up a test for me and I had totally failed it. I was miserable. I don't recall that it happened more than twice. (I now wonder why it didn't recur; had the guys found out what they wanted to know. Did they "see" for themselves what they were doing and back off? Or, had the house parent intervened?)

Then there was Bobby Braght. He could be so friendly and engaging but he was a consummate con artist. He would weasel me out of my allowance money—he called it "borrowing" but had no intention of paying it back. He also thrived on stealing—for Bobby, the sight of any new lock aroused the exciting prospect of a new conquest. Once my dad unexpectedly showed up in my dorm room and found Bobby picking the lock on the very wooden safe that Dad had built to protect me from the likes of him. Another time Dad found him tampering with my record player. Dad, true to his understandings of Mennonite nonresistance, wouldn't let me report such misdeeds to the house parent.

Bobby could be friendly, but he also could communicate more sneer and contempt than anyone I've ever known. One day as he got up from the lunch table and walked behind my chair on his way out, he reached around my head and thumbed my nose—pure contempt that was! Reflexively I shoved my elbow back to push him away and caught him solidly across the middle. There was no retaliation from him and I wondered that he would give up so easily. A few minutes later I was in the men's room, leaning over the sink to wash my hands, when the door opened behind me. A full forearm blow slammed down on my back and Bobby hissed, "That'll teach you," and he ran away. I realized then that I had completely winded him with my elbow back at the table; that was why he didn't jump all over me then.

Later, in the same men's room (downstairs in Battle Hall— that was the name of the building sure enough) my Mennonite patience ran out. After another insult from Bobby, I, with deliberate forethought, laid aside my Mennonite scruples and took a swing at him. I meant to hit him with all I had and settle this thing once for all. Well, my Mennonite scruples were still a bit active and made me pull that punch—and it's good they did! I missed Bobby and hit the wall, and that wall was one of those hard ceramic tile walls. Bobby hurried out and disappeared. To this day the first knuckle on my right hand, that is, the MP joint of the index finger, bears witness to my poor aim. The bone is partially crushed and the extensor tendon is dislocated over toward the middle finger. The pain was unreal! I went on to class, trying to hide my suffering, but I could not properly hold my Braille stylus to take notes. I was too embarrassed to go to the infirmary so I just suffered in silence for several days. Finally the pain let up and, to my amazement and relief, I could resume playing the piano and organ. If my Mennonite scruples had not pulled that punch slightly, the injury to my hand might well have ended my keyboard days.

For whatever it's worth, in some reading in psychological literature during my senior year there at VSDB, I came across a definition for "sociopath." That definition seemed in my teenaged mind to describe Bobby perfectly. Now as an adult I don't know that my teenage diagnosis was proper, but I'm afraid that, to this day, I haven't figured out how a pacifist Christian is supposed to deal with a sociopath—can it be that "loving your enemy" just won't change the brain cells of a sociopath?

There were incidents with two other VSDB kids involving some pushing and shoving, but they were smaller affairs and I'm too embarrassed to spend more time on this subject. Memories of incidents like these where I wasn't the one-sided victim keep me from too much righteous indignation about bullying. Happily, from my sophomore year on, my classmates and other friends seemed to genuinely respect me, even with my "peculiar" Mennonite nonresistance; those were three good years.

One memory that helps keep me a little bit humble about bullying is an incident when I was around age ten in summer vacation Bible school. I began making fun of a handicapped girl. She was profoundly mentally handicapped, responding to almost no verbal communication. She could walk unaided and sit in class and mess around with crayons, but that was about all. She drooled continuously. What got my attention and started my teasing was a very large birthmark on the whole left side of her face. It was dark reddish and purple—just like the pictures of "witches" in fairy story books. I began mocking her as a "witch" behind her back. Mom got wind of this and boy did she ever lay the moral law on me. She did not yell and scold; she just made me see plainly that this behavior was unkind, totally unacceptable, and totally beyond the pale of human decency. Sure enough, after that when I saw the girl, I had a different feeling inside—pity. Mom had taught me pity and compassion. I don't remember that I apologized; Mom and I both thought, I believe, since the girl was so out of touch, and since my behavior was behind her back, an apology seemed irrelevant.

Soon after that Bible school incident Mom laid the moral law on me again regarding excessive teasing of a younger brother, and it did change my thinking on such things. Jack Grainger's mother had died. Community talk had it that what was left of his home life was troubled. Jack maybe had no one like my mom to lay the moral law of human decency on him regarding his bullying. I now sometimes grieve for him. But that grieving certainly isn't the horrified hand wringing of a morally superior person.

SOME REFLECTIONS

As a farm boy I had not missed the lesson that in every litter of pigs there seemed to be a runt. I was skinny, wore thick glasses, was cross-eyed, had crooked teeth, and was hard of hearing—I was a runt. But I eventually understood that I was also scrappy and quite capable of dishing out my share of picking and not-nice teasing—in other words, I was not always the poor little victim. Yet I remember well that I also delighted in holding and playing with my baby brothers and sisters—sitting here now I can easily "re-feel" those kindly nurturing impulses. I suppose we are simultaneously bullies and lovingly sweet as children simply because we are on the way to becoming what we will be as adults. As an adult I have come to see that along with our loving and nurturing ways, we humans are violent and murderous—when you survey the human scene down through history, how can you conclude otherwise? Our dual nature along with the resulting conflicted inner being—all that is our lot. Biology tells us it originates in our genes. The religion of my roots talks about original sin, a fallenness that impacts all of nature. How do we cope with this? I was raised in the Mennonite world where we taught and tried to practice nonresistance, more commonly called pacifism by the larger community. I remain convinced that pacifism/nonviolence is the superior way. But, to be honest, I wonder sometimes if we aren't just beating our heads against a rock wall trying to practice nonresistance/pacifism against all that dysfunction and violence, which after all is our very nature. To maintain a sustained conviction on nonresistance I'm beginning to see that will require a tenacious belief in a robust theology regarding Almighty God's sovereign plan, a plan which dictates that, in the end, love and kindness, not selfishness and violence, will stand at the center of what the cosmos is all about, and those who live accordingly will be there too, and death won't intercept that.

Nowadays there are promising programs and groups for helping children, adults, communities, ethnic groups, and nations deal with violence and conflict. You can easily learn about and contact these groups with the Internet. For children's issues use search terms like "coping with bullies" and "peer mediation"; for adult issues search with terms like "restorative justice," "conflict resolution," or "conflict transformation." Those peer mediation programs that are appearing in our schools today would have been helpful for me back then, whether as victim or bully.

For serious academic studies on these things, I commend you to:

The Center for Justice and Peacebuilding
Eastern Mennonite University
1200 Park Road
Harrisonburg, Virginia 22802

8

A MUSIC JOURNEY IN A
MENNONITE WORLD

As I began thinking over how to write this chapter, I was also reading various sources on how Virginia Mennonite Conference leaders and EMC leaders shaped and built the world in which I began life. I became fascinated with how my music formation occurred in very definite interaction with Virginia Mennonite Conference history.

The world of music started for me with Dad sprawled on the living room floor with us kids scattered around, Mom puttering around with after supper kitchen chores. Often, before bedtime stories, Dad would start singing and urge us to join in. We kids would join in with varying degrees of interest and enthusiasm. We sang and did many hand motions with songs like these: "This Little Light of Mine;" "We are Climbing Jacob's Ladder;" "Do Lord, Oh Do Remember Me;" "Jesus Loves Me;" "Deep and Wide;" "Climb, Climb Up Sunshine Mountain;" "My Cup Is Full and Running Over;" "I Will Make You Fishers of Men;" "I Have the Joy, Joy, Joy Down in My Heart;" "Swing Low, Sweet Chariot;" "Jesus Loves the Little Children of the World;" "Dare to Be a Daniel;" "The Wise Man Built His House Upon the Rock;" "In a Little Basket" (about Baby Moses); "Everything's Alright in My Father's House."

About that last one—Eldon and I loved to lie on a chair with our legs straight up against the back and our heads hanging down over the front edge of the seat so we could see the room upside down; we would sing lustily, "Everything's Upside Down, in My Father's House."

One song deserves special mention—"When the World's on Fire." The words ran:

> *Oh my loving brother,*
> *When the world's on fire,*
> *Don't you want God's bosom*
> *To be your pillow?*
> *Hide me over, in the Rock of Ages,*
> *Rock of Ages, cleft for me.*

The rhythm was perfect for guitar accompaniment but there was no guitar in the house. But nevermind, we really got into the rhythm and had a lot of fun singing it. What a song for children? Oh yes, I was aware, per our community's beliefs, the world would end in fire and it was a little scary, but I mostly rested in confidence that at the end of the world, fire would be no problem for God's people.

One children's song, that my daughters and I like to this day, was about Baby Moses:

> *In a little basket, under skies so blue,*
> *Floating down the river where the rushes grew;*
> *While the angels watched him, Baby Moses slept.*
> *When the princess found him, Baby Moses wept.*
> *Chorus: God took care of the baby, and in his word we see,*
> *Still, that our Father in heaven careth for you and for me.*

Dad, in his own way, also taught us music theory by teaching us the Do-Re-Mi's! He would sing up the scale, a note at a time, having us imitate each note—"Do, Re, Mi, Fa, So, La, Ti, Do," and back down. Then he would drill us on different intervals, such as "do mi, do fa, do mi so mi do," etc. Our actual comprehension of pitch and intervals dawned a bit haphazardly, but nonetheless, some rudiments stuck. One time Dad had us singing the intervals "Do Mi So Do." Little Jim was missing the high "Do." Dad would say, "No, here," and he would sing that high "Do" again, louder. Jim would try again and miss again. Dad would sing that high "Do" again, louder and still louder. Finally, Jim caught on, sort of, and yelled "Do" at the top of his lungs, but obviously nowhere near correct musical pitch. He had confused "louder" with "higher." Dad and everybody laughed; Dad was pleased with Little Jim's effort—"Well, OK, that was better. It wasn't quite right yet, but that was a good try."

The music culture of the Mennonite churches of Virginia's Shenandoah Valley in the 1920s through the 1950s was the larger context for Dad's music training and indeed the soil for my music roots. From their beginnings, Mennonite congregational singing was simple, unaccompanied unison singing. But by my time, Joseph Funk's singing school tradition with its "shape note" system of musical notation had transformed most Mennonite congregational singing into good, solid four-part harmony. It was still a cappella singing, of course, but it was good, hardy church singing. I liked to listen to individual voices around me singing their alto, tenor, or bass line against the soprano's melody. I liked to sing, too. I remember well the annual New Year's Day event we called "The Old Folk's Singing" at Weavers Church where they sang and sang and sang those old songs from Funk's singing school book, *Harmonia Sacra.* Boy, those tenors sure enjoyed their high notes! It became a point of pride for me to discover that Joseph Funk's music publishing and singing school was "back there in Singers Glen" near my great-granddaddy Eli Bowman's little farm.

While music instruments were stringently kept out of our churches, they were appearing in Mennonite homes. By my time, as we visited different families, we would find harmonicas, reed organs, violins, guitars, auto harps, accordions, trumpets, pianos, etc. Church elders were unhappy with these instruments—they were poor stewardship; they were worldly distractions from Christian spirituality—and for a time through the 1920s and 1940s in the Virginia Mennonite Conference, music instruments were prohibited altogether. The same was true for record players and radios, and TV's when they came along later. Then the prohibition was lifted for lay folk, but not for the pastors until 1947.

Regardless of the then current official church policy, individual families through these years often did their own thing, either fervently eschewing instruments or owning and using them, sometimes defiantly. For example, my Uncle Will "submitted" to the church regulations and took Aunt Mary's reed organ, which she had brought into the marriage, out back and chopped it to pieces. On the other hand, Catherine Holsinger Miller told me her father, Henry Holsinger who was a deacon at Lindale Mennonite Church, "stood up to them, and said he's not getting rid of his piano." Instead, he systematically took Catherine to other churches where she could play for worship services. Nettie Pearl Suter, wife of minister John Early Suter, cried the day they came and took her reed organ away.[3] Our pastor, Chester K. Lehman, and his brother Daniel, both prominent leaders among Virginia

Mennonites, struggled with Virginia Conference negative attitudes toward music instruments. Chester and Daniel had come from Lancaster Conference in Pennsylvania to join the EMC faculty. Music instruments had been appreciated and used well in their boyhood home; it was hard to give them up when they came to Virginia. In 1947 Virginia Conference finally reversed itself and allowed pastors to own music instruments. Chester's daughter, Esther, told me when her dad returned from that Conference, he went straight downtown and came home with a nice, big Stieff piano! A daughter-in-law of Daniel recently told me, when Conference banned music instruments, Daniel took a reed organ he had gotten from his mother into the backyard and dismantled it, but he put his precious violin in the attic—a typical very hot and cold attic! I learned elsewhere, when Conference later lifted its ban, Daniel retrieved his violin from the attic with joy. All that is the cultural context for the entrée of music instruments into my life.

So, one day, sometime in 1948-49 I believe, a reed organ appeared in our living room. I never heard where Dad got that wonderful thing, nor why. Surely it was a significant event in the larger context of Mennonite grouchiness about music instruments.

Dad's music formation as a young man was complicated. His dad, Luther Bowman, had come from non-Mennonite background and never knuckled all the way under to then current Mennonite standards regarding dress and music instruments. He, Luther, played the accordion (I was told he wore out three) and there was a bugle around the house when we went to visit. There was also a wind-up Victrola and lots of 78 RPM records. Luther encouraged his two youngest sons, Wade and Linden, to play the violin/fiddle and guitar. But Dad, Luther's oldest son, seemed to pull away from that instrumental music toward Mennonite a cappella singing. My recollections include the sense that he sheltered us older kids from his dad's records and accordion and from Wade and Linden's music. This changed by the time my younger sibs came along—they recall listening with Mom and Dad to Wade and Linden play.

I suspect Dad's preference for Mennonite music was part of his intense effort as a second-generation Mennonite to be accepted into the Mennonite world. Harold Lahman, Dad's first cousin, told me Dad was a really good student in the late 1920s music classes at Eastern Mennonite School, which insisted on strictly a cappella music. In fact, it was Dad's clear explanations of music notation that saved the day for Harold when Harold was floundering badly in eighth grade music. (It was Harold who later formed that quartet that Dad sang with all his adult life.)

Now, after Dad had thoroughly immersed himself in Mennonite a cappella music, Mennonite attitudes toward instrumental music were starting to change. Our pastor, Brother Chester, had his piano, and here was that reed organ sitting in our living room.

This reed organ looked exactly like a full-sized upright piano, eighty-nine keys and a big high top. It had two little stop levers at each end of the keyboard. You operated the bellows by pumping the two outside piano-style pedals. Pressing the middle pedal would turn the bass and treble octave couplers on and off. It pumped and played easily.

Some community excitement arose about this organ. A teenaged neighbor girl came to see and play it. Her excited chatter and graceful hand movements (she was pretty!) expressed her approval. Then we were told that Brother Chester was coming to check it out! He came, sat down and pumped and played easily, and wonder of wonders, he would cross his left hand over the right at times. Even to my child's eyes he was clearly enthralled with that organ. His delight in that instrument and his ease of playing surely helped sanction instrumental music in my mind.

In no time Dad was playing that organ—he played hymns, all four parts, from our Mennonite hymnals—the 1902 *Church and Sunday School Hymnal* and *Life Songs No. 2*. He used the shape notes and Do-Re-Mi system. I would sit or play around on the floor behind him, watching his feet on the pedals and soaking in the music. My younger sibs know nothing of his playing; he quit playing altogether soon after Mom's illness in 1954.

Mom also messed around with the organ a bit, playing two parts for some hymns.

Before continuing with this story of the reed organ, I want to say more about the family and school context for my music formation. First of all, downstairs, Grandpa Wenger's radio was introducing me to music other than traditional Mennonite singing. I believe it was Uncle Menno Suter who gave that radio to Grandpa while radios were still only grudgingly allowed by Virginia Conference. I would listen to Galen Weekly singing hymns while accompanying himself on a reed organ in the studio at WSVA radio. I liked the sound of that reed organ. More significantly, it was on that radio that I got hooked on pipe organ music—by age 7. A local church with a pipe organ must have been broadcasting its worship service. What I heard had to have been low fidelity sound, but I got hooked on the pipe organ for life! And, for what it's worth, I also remember Dick Johnson, for Schewel's Furniture, coming on the air playing a little rinky-tink piano singing, "It's Schewel time, Schewel time, eight fifteen is Schewel time..."

One evening about this time, we went to visit Granddaddy Bowman's. As we went in, lying right there on the dining room table in easy reach, I spied two musical instruments—just like the pictures in the *Sears and Roebuck* catalog, a little one and a big one. *I just have to get my hands on those things. I have to move quickly before they stop me. I reach out a finger and pluck a string on the little one. Wow, that's a neat sound! Hurry, before they stop me—I pluck a string on the big one, and quick, another. Oh what a beautiful, full sound, and it keeps on ringing. Oh, I like the big one best. I wanna pluck another string, quick now—bump! Dad's hand lands on my arm pulling me back, "No, Sonny, you keep your hands off those. That's Uncle Wade's violin and that's Uncle Linden's guitar."*

Well, my musical soul was ensnared by another musical instrument; it was a brief sound and quite different from the pipe organ, but I was ensnared nonetheless. It would be a long time—not till my VSDB years—before I could listen to guitar and fiddle music live and up close.

Then came public school at Dale Enterprise where I was soon learning and thoroughly enjoying still other kinds of music. Our teacher for the first three grades, Miss Marie Cox, would open each day with singing—lots of singing! There was no accompaniment, but heck, who needed accompaniment. Miss Cox would just start a song and we would jump in, song after song after song. Sometimes we did use song books. I recall noticing that sometimes we sounded neat—like something I would later call "in tune." Other times we sounded pretty rough—but who cared, we were having fun! To paraphrase a line from my wife's Uncle Mose in another time and place, "Tune or no tune, we sang!" I wonder if modern educators would approve of all the time we spent singing.

We sang: "Jingle Bells;" "Home on the Range;" "Over the River and Through the Woods;" "Oh Susanna;" "Billie Boy;"

"Away Down South in Dixie;" "Swannee River;" "America the Beautiful;" "My Country 'tis of Thee;" "Star Spangled Banner;" "Old MacDonald;" "Froggy Went A'courtin';" "Eating Goober Peas;" "Up on the Housetop," "Reindeer Paws;" "Red River Valley;" "Down in the Valley;" "Clementine;" "Shortnin' Bread;" "John Brown Had a Little Indian;" "Skip to My Lou."

We did rounds energetically—"Row, Row, Row Your Boat;" "Are You Sleeping;" and best of all "Three Blind Mice."

In fourth grade under Miss Alice Keeler, and in fifth grade under Harold Eshleman we sang "Battle Hymn of the Republic;" "Tramp, Tramp, Tramp the Boys Are Marching;" "I'll Give to you a Paper of Pins;" "Old Dan Tucker;" "John Brown's Body;" "The Marine's Hymn;" "The Old Oaken Bucket;" "Ain't Gonna Study War No More;" "The Little Brown Church in the Wildwood;" "Cool, Clear Water;" "Tumbling Tumble Weed;" "My Grandfather's Clock;" "I've Been Working on the Railroad," etc.

In Miss Keeler's and Mr. Eshleman's rooms we sometimes sang church hymns such as "Fairest Lord Jesus" and "Onward Christian Soldiers." From somewhere I had caught on to the distinction between secular and sacred music though I did not know those terms. I knew this was a "public school" and singing church songs here seemed a bit odd. I liked and would continue to like our Mennonite church music, but I was also liking this secular music in public school; I was sort of aware of tension between the two.

My entrée into the world of blindness in 1953 (I was in sixth grade by then) opened the door to still other kinds of music. When I was in the hospital that Fall, Dad got me a bunch of 45 RPM records by George Beverly Shay, the Mill Creek Quartet, the Jordanaires, and the Chuck Wagon Gang, etc. To play these he brought a little record changer, which marvelously would play those records over and over indefinitely, at least indefinitely enough to drive the nurses crazy. That record player also had AM radio on which I discovered another interesting music instrument—the "Hammond organ." When I stayed out of school after the failed eye surgery, more 45 RPM records came. Then a second record player and a bunch of 78 RPM records showed up. The Wenger aunts and uncles gave me a little AM radio, on which I promptly got fond of country music—Mac Wiseman, Johnny and Jack, Earnest Tub, Don Reno and Red Smiley, Hank Snow, Hank Williams, Lee Moore, and best of all, Bill Monroe. I discovered and appreciated Blue Grass music before it had the name and was kosher. Mom would protest, "You shouldn't be listening to those ol' love songs." To reduce her stress, I took the radio to more remote regions of the house.

Recently, Boyd Burkholder, a first cousin from across the road, told me that as a child he was very jealous of my good luck—as a result of blindness I was allowed to have radios and record players! In his family, records and radios were strictly taboo. He said my records and radio came near making blindness worthwhile in his mind—if he were blind, he could have records and radios. So, I wasn't the only Mennonite kid in those days who was succumbing to the "Siren sounds" of music other than the sanctioned music of the Virginia Mennonite World of 1920-1950.

Now, back to that wonderful reed organ that appeared in our living room—I took to it immediately. Dad got me started by orienting me to the keyboard and quickly taught me the names of the white keys—C, D, E, F, G, A, B, C. He explained that when you start the "Do" on the C-key and play up and down the white keys, you get the familiar Do-Re-Mi scale he had taught us earlier. He showed me how the shapes on the notes in our hymnals indicated the Do-Re-Mi's. From that point I began playing the melody line for quite a number of hymns. Dad, and sometimes Mom, would occasionally stop by and give me pointers. I began adding some alto notes as well. Dad explained that you can start the "Do" on any key other than the C-key but you then had to use certain black keys. I didn't really comprehend this so he just had me remember by rote, "When you see one flat up there by the time signature, you start the 'Do' on the F-key and play the B-flat key for the note Fa; when you see one sharp up there by the time signature, you start the 'Do' on the G-key and play the F-sharp key for the note Ti." Sometime after the singing school mentioned below, I suddenly comprehended the significance of those "whole steps and half steps" and could then figure out which black keys to use when starting "Do" on any other key.

Sitting here now, I can see plainly that Dad had good training in basic music. He clearly enjoyed handing these rudiments on to me. He enjoyed that organ and he enjoyed showing me how to play it. To my knowledge none of my sibs got that kind of intro to music. Once, after I was at VSDB and had started formal piano lessons, Dad and I were driving somewhere in the car. Out of the blue he announced, tapping on the steering wheel for emphasis, "Middle C is called 'fourth octave C.'" It didn't sound like he was giving me further music instruction. Rather, he seemed to be ruminating on past music studies. Had some earlier music studies and aspirations been interrupted or even crushed by life circumstances? I believe so.

Finally came the pinnacle of my music world before I lost vision; this was one of the really, happy times of my early childhood. It was that two-week singing school conducted by Brother Chester at our church, Mt. Clinton Mennonite Church in the

Fall of 1951. (I am certain about that date from memory, not from written documents; I was age 10.)

For that two-week singing school, Brother Chester had prepared a little pamphlet that he gave each family. It was about the size of a 3-by-5 notecard, certainly not bigger than 4-by-6. It outlined the points or lessons that would be covered in each evening's class. Each lesson included the hymn numbers for songs in the *Church Hymnal* and *Life Songs* that would be used for that lesson. The feature of that booklet that I remember most vividly was "CHESTER K. LEHMAN" printed boldly in a different font from the surrounding print. I was enthralled with the idea that someone I knew had his name in PRINT! (And that was probably this farm boy's first hint that Chester K. Lehman was "Somebody.")

Brother Chester's enthusiasm was contagious. He taught us the Joseph Funk shape note system (which Dad had already started me on). He explained the various shapes for the "Do-Re-Mi's" by drawing them on the blackboard. He would make us sing various scales and intervals using those note names—"Do, Mi, So, Do, So, Mi, Do; Do, Fa, La, Do, etc." he would have us sing little songs like "Are You Sleeping," "Scotland's Burning," and "Row Row Row Your Boat" by singing the musical notes rather than the words. Then we would sing them in rounds. Finally, we would sing the words in rounds. The singing, especially the rounds, at times got quite rousing—it was really FUN!

Now, as an old man I often re-realize (if I may create a word) that those drills where we sang the music note names really did ingrain in us a good sense of musical intervals and harmonic relationships. When you sing a "Mi" when someone else is singing a "Do," you get a major third. When you sing a "So" against someone else singing a "Do" below that, you get a fifth. If you sing "Ti Do," you've moved a half step. Once you've learned the Do-Re-Mi system you really do gravitate toward the right pitch when you sing the note names. And this shape note system works so well on the keyboard you don't have to bother learning the lines and spaces; so, I didn't bother. Consequently, to this day I don't really understand the lines and spaces of print music; I switched to the Braille music system before music sophistication would have forced me to learn those lines and spaces.

When showing us how to beat time for the different time signatures, Brother Chester would draw the beat patterns on the blackboard. Wow, could he ever draw—he would do big, majestic, sweeping flourishes with the chalk and beautiful beat patterns, and many other musical symbols as well would appear on that blackboard! He would call for volunteers to come up front to practice leading a song.

Once Brother Chester must have seen an eager look on my face; he grabbed my arm and pulled me from the front bench to the center front floor.

Sure enough, here I am up front—this skinny 10-year-old with thick glasses and crossed-eyes. I boldly announce, "Number 630, Church Hymnal" ("In the Sweet By and By"). Brother Chester leans over me with his pitch pipe giving me the pitch. My wordless reaction—*Pitch? Heck, let's sing!* I launch forth and to my delight and relief, the people, both adults and kids, jump in with full voice, sweeping me along. They get me on pitch! *Wow, this song leading stuff is easy! Just follow the crowd—like singing along on Sunday mornings! This is fun!* Now Brother Chester comes back over beside me, takes a FIRM GRIP on my right arm and begins synchronizing my random beating to the music. I understand what he is trying to do but his firm controlling of my arm doesn't match the natural movements of my arm and body and so I am being pulled off balance. I finally pull away and Brother Chester steps back with a resigned chuckle and lets me do my thing. Now I recall a mannerism of Amos Rhodes, our Sunday morning song leader—I do that little sway, forward and to the right, glance up at the congregation and say, "Last." Sure enough, we all jump to the last verse. *(Wow, I had exercised a little "leadership" and they all followed me!)* I sit down, feeling pleased but also a little embarrassed about not beating the time correctly. (I did eventually catch on that the down beat was supposed to synchronize with the first note after that measure bar.)

I would come home from singing school and apply what I had learned to playing on the organ. Soon I was sight reading a lot of hymns, the soprano and alto lines. I could struggle through several with all four parts. One hymn I learned to play very well in all four parts was page 610 in the *Church Hymnal*, "Some Sweet Day," I was working on "Shall We Gather at the River" in all four parts when this chapter of my music life ended.

At this time, trouble was coming regarding my vision, but I didn't understand the signals. I remember paging through our hymnals looking for pages with songs that seemed playable. "Playable" for me meant not so many notes packed close together, not so many eighth notes and sixteenth note flags, and not so many flats and sharps in the music. My extreme nearsightedness made me see those pages as cluttered! Seeing all that detail was hard work.

That singing school at Mt. Clinton Mennonite Church in 1951 based on Joseph Funk's shape note system may well be the last of that type of training in a cappella singing in this area until recent years. It certainly was the high point of my Mennonite music heritage in my early years, and it was the platform from which I launched into instrumental music. I switched to Braille music at VSDB, and there, instrumental music finished the capture of my musical soul. It relegated my Mennonite a cappella heritage to second place—a solid second place, but definitely second place. I discovered classical music—instrumental classical music!

The teachers at VSDB quickly noticed my interests and abilities in music and got me started in piano and organ lessons. As I moved into this wonderful world of instrumental music, I was increasingly aware that I was pushing back against a vague but real musical straightjacket in my home culture. Musical instruments in the home were being tolerated by now, but solo up-front performances of any kind were still very bad because they were "just entertainment" and they would promote pride and individuality. We strongly emphasized humility—quiet, stay-out-of-the-limelight humility. But now, while I still liked our humble unaccompanied singing well enough, my boy's heart was running off after instrumental music, which included solo performances. I was increasingly anxious about getting crosswise in my native culture. Actually, I began to worry that Dad might terminate my piano and organ lessons altogether. Playing a little reed organ in one's private living room was one thing; playing up front for the public was something else. Well, VSDB came to the rescue.

VSDB frequently staged "demonstrations" for special guests and dignitaries. These were usually full-blown programs staged in the brand new gymnasium to present what blind people can do, how blind children are educated, how blind people perform daily living tasks, etc. Students would be trotted out to demonstrate reading and writing Braille, typing professional documents, cooking, sewing, gymnastic routines, Braille music and piano performance, writing checks (using special templates laid over the check), wrestling matches—anything where they could find a gifted student or two who could put on a good show. The purpose was "PUBLIC EDUCATION"—to correct widespread myths, prejudices, and simple ignorance about blindness. We kids were constantly urged, practically harangued, to present ourselves well in these performances. We were told, "You have a serious obligation to do your best because we are striving for public understanding and acceptance of blind people. That will make it easier for you to get a job later. And indeed, if you do well now, that will make it easier for blind people coming after you." And there was more—"Actually, you are obligated lifelong to do your best because public education about blindness never ends, and furthermore, that's how you repay your debt to the taxpayers for your education here at VSDB." This was like a "Blind Great Commission."

I was put forward to participate in these demonstrations many times. As I began internalizing the moral obligation to perform well, I began sensing a new understanding of "self," a different philosophy about deliberately putting oneself forward to be seen, to be thought well of. I couldn't have put it into words then, but I was dealing with two distinct philosophies of how I was supposed to view my "self." My native traditions insisted I was to be humble, never promote self-interests, and above all, avoid any kind of "showing off" or seeking after worldly glory. But the "Blind Great Commission" urged me to step forward and present myself well, even to entertain or "show off" (something necessary for good music).

The fifth grade teacher, Mrs. Sensabaugh, evidently worked hard at getting her students to be more assertive, more ready to step up and present an idea, more ready to join in whatever was going on. I'm guessing she was working with some of the children who were painfully shy and socially backward. She evidently tried to inject humor into her teaching. Her students loved to mimic her slow Bostonese drawl while quoting her thus: "He who tooteth not his own horn hath not his horn tooted." Over the years I've enjoyed a little mischief by quoting those lines to Mennonite friends—it sets their teeth on edge.

Dad and my whole family attended quite a number of those demonstrations and seemed to warm up to them. I tried to convey to Dad my sense of obligation to present myself well, to excel in music in the interest of public education about blindness. Wonder of wonders, Dad began to relax and buy into the idea; he began to bless and promote my music. It was probably made easier for him as he saw I wasn't just abandoning hymns and sacred music for "worldly, secular music." And, when our pastor, Chester Lehman, realized I was performing Bach, he too got excited and began pushing me forward at events around home.

As it turned out, musical influence at VSDB flowed both ways. It was a regular scene in those sparsely furnished boys' dorm rooms—a cluster of boys sprawled around on beds and a chair or two listening to someone's radio, guitar, tape recorder, or record player. When somebody started playing records, I would crowd into the group. I soaked in the symphonies, jazz quartettes, and what not. I especially liked listening to the guys' running commentary on the music and the different kinds of musical instruments; the best of this commentary was from Neal Ewers. This was Music Appreciation 201 greatly accelerated. Then to my surprise, some of the guys, especially some of the more musically talented like Neal, took note of my "Mennonite Hour" records. They liked that Mennonite a cappella four-part harmony sound and seemed to understand it was indeed a special musical tradition.

Now, fast forward to my senior year at VSDB—by then I was pretty well recognized by teachers and students as an accomplished pianist and organist. My Mennonite world back home was also recognizing and accepting my gifts. Most days I was getting in at least two hours of practice, and it was beginning to show good results. Then it came time to make college plans, where to and what major. When it fell out that I would be going to Eastern Mennonite College in Harrisonburg as a math major, my piano and organ teacher, Mrs. Louise Kiracofe, was really upset. She had been assuming I would major in music at a conservatory or at least go to a college where I could do a serious music minor. When she learned that EMC had not one piano anywhere on campus she was outraged! Unknown to me, she swung into action!

When I showed up for my next piano lesson, she greeted me thus: "Danny, when I learned that Mennonite College has no piano where you can keep your music alive, I couldn't bear the thought. You can't just drop your music. So, I put in a long-distance call to Curtis Institute in Philadelphia and told them all about you. Curtis Institute is a prestigious music school funded entirely by wealthy philanthropists to train fully professional musicians. Leonard Bernstein is one of their more famous graduates. Applicants are accepted there solely on the basis of artistic talent and promise. Nobody pays tuition there; you get full tuition scholarships; it's entirely merit based. When I told them about you, without hesitation they granted you a full four-year scholarship; that's tuition and all expenses paid. Neither you nor your parents have to pay anything." She went on, "Curtis Institute is in the center of downtown Philadelphia, on the Main

Line. That's where the blue bloods—I mean, the upper classes live, you know, the important people. They are the people with whom you will want to have connections. You really are cut out for a career as a professional concert musician, and this all expenses paid scholarship at Curtis Institute is your lifetime opportunity."

Heretofore at VSDB I had been pushing back against Mennonite disapproval of instrumental music (and against some other Mennonite boundaries, too). Now my Mennonite heritage stood firm. The idea of training for a professional career as a concert musician—that would be professional entertainment. That would not be compatible with service to God and church and mankind. All that travel would be incompatible with having a family. And, I had just read somewhere that an "occupational hazard for career musicians is venereal disease!" I suppose I was still a practical Mennonite farm boy after all. The prospect of a high-flying public life just didn't fit anywhere on my horizon. The whole idea of an institution committing itself to a four-year all-expenses-paid scholarship on the strength of one phone call—that seemed like a fairy tale. My Mennonite scruples rebelled. Maybe Mrs. Kiracofe hit me with too big an idea too fast. In any case I declined the offer; actually, I waved it aside about as casually as one would say, "No thanks, I don't really care to play golf."

Well, Mrs. Kiracofe didn't give up. She took me to the minister of music at First Presbyterian Church in Staunton, where she was the organist. He proceeded to help me understand, "It is your spiritual duty not to waste your God-given talents. Your spiritual duty is to serve God with whatever talents and gifts you have!" Well, yes of course, I knew one is supposed to serve God with all one's being, and the man is saying all that with the same kind of moral authority I was oh so familiar with in my Mennonite world.

He tapped his pipe on an ash tray; from behind a cloud of some-what pleasant smelling tobacco smoke he went on speaking with his strong voice of authority, "It's like this: if your talents are base-ball, then you must serve God by playing baseball with all your heart and mind; you play professional baseball to the honor and glory of God!" He also illustrated his point with professional act-ing in movies and theater. Wow, did that reference to professional baseball ever clarify things for me—only not the way he wanted. This naive Mennonite farm boy suddenly understood clearly, you don't serve God with just any old talent that strikes your fancy. Rather, you develop whatever talents are useful for God's King-dom purposes. Professional baseball and theater, and things like that don't serve God's purposes! So, well…there are just certain careers "true believers" don't do. I "suddenly knew" the world of pleasantly scented pipe tobacco and professional baseball to the honor and glory of God was not my home; my home was with the Mennonites. I was now immune to further reasoning.

My teacher still didn't give up. She took me to the organist who played my very favorite pipe organ in Staunton—that Taylor Booty tracker organ at Trinity Episcopal Church. The results were the same. She talked to my parents, and evidently, they dismissed the idea as casually as I did. After graduation that offer from Curtis Institute pretty well dropped out of conscious memory.

Some forty years later my daughter Diane was working at Whitesels Music in downtown Harrisonburg. She came home one day with this story:

> Today an elderly lady came into the store ex-plaining that she was a music teacher and needed certain music for her students at VSDB. I said, "VSDB?! My father went to VSDB."

She replied, "Oh, who was your father?"

"Dan Bowman."

At that the lady went off—"Danny Bowman! Danny Bowman was the best piano and organ student I ever had! And I got him this all-expenses-paid four-year scholarship to Curtis Institute in Philadelphia and he, both he and his parents just casually turned it down! They had no idea what they were refusing!"

It was Mrs. Kiracofe! As Diane reported this conversation to me, it all came back clearly, oh so clearly. I had virtually forgotten that scholarship business. Now it was all as fresh as though it happened yesterday. Now I plainly began hearing Mrs. Kiracofe's repeated lament through those last months at VSDB, to me directly and to others about me. Her laments ran like this: "Danny, and his parents too, were so naive and withdrawn and isolated from the world, they had no understanding of what they were casually refusing; they had no real understanding of what they were offered." She understood our Mennonite separation mentality well and didn't like it; it was causing me to waste my God-given talents. Presbyterian understanding of talents in service to God and Mennonite understanding of talents in service to God were indeed radically different.

Though I had pushed back against Mennonite disapproval of instrumental music and had accepted the "worldly" view of public performance, full-time professional entertainment was still beyond the pale. My beloved piano and organ teacher was sad, as I wrapped up my sojourn in the foreign land of VSDB as a staunch Mennonite. And forty years later she was still sad. I did call her after her encounter with Diane; she sounded very old.

My efforts to assure her that I was using my piano and organ talents around the community as a lay musician didn't really satisfy her; I had squandered my God-given talents.

Sitting here now I can see that, in addition to feeding my soul—and it certainly did that, music structured my life at VSDB in two significant ways: First, it made constructive use of my free time (and there was a lot of that). Second, music gave me solid standing in the VSDB social life even though I didn't participate in the all-important dances and movies. But music simply was never meant to be my life-time career.

As I entered Eastern Mennonite College in the Fall of 1961, I had a sense, "Ah, at last I'm coming home to my Mennonite roots." It felt so good. Again, my instrumental music structured my place in student life, though not in official academic life. There was a lot of buzz about the new blind student on campus (the first ever), and it was soon known he played piano and organ very well. "And he even has a reed organ up there in his dorm room!" (Dad had purchased that reed organ five years earlier from a local pawn shop for $5 and I had restored it to playable condition.)

Within days on the EMC campus I was fully aware that restlessness regarding Virginia Mennonite grumpiness about instrumental music was far more than my little personal issue—it was pervasive on campus. Some of the students were a bit rowdy asserting their musical independence. I found myself put forward in the first meeting of the Zelathian literary society that Fall to give a little "talk" on instrumental music. Among other things I averred that God could indeed be worshiped "with a drum." I meant that as a shocking assertion and it was heard as such.

Gradually over my four years at EMC I came to understand how that musical straightjacket which had been dogging me all along came about. It was systematically and officially imposed by strong personalities in Virginia Conference culture, among whom were the founding fathers of EMC. Why did they do that?

Well, they were not entirely out of touch with long-standing traditions in the larger Christian community. Throughout the history of Christendom there have been groups of fervent believers who have taken a dim view of instrumental music. In the early American scene, Puritan and Quaker opposition to musical instruments is well known. Amish and Mennonite emphasis on simplicity has always de-emphasized music instruments.

Then, in the late 19th century and early 20th century throughout United States and Canada, Mennonite church leaders were increasingly concerned about the impact of modern science and technology on Mennonite life. Young people were exiting the church in droves. The founding of Eastern Mennonite School/ College was a concerted effort by Virginia Mennonites to respond to these trends, specifically to "keep our young people safe." In 1913 a constitution for the new school was proposed. Among the stated aims and purposes for this new school are these words: "… to give due attention…to the peculiar doctrines of the Church, together with special training in vocal music—looking to the strengthening of that feature of divine worship [unaccompanied singing] in our CONGREGATIONS."[4] Note, the desire to maintain and promote unaccompanied congregational singing was actually listed alongside the desire to preserve the "peculiar doctrines of the church." Thus, prohibition of musical instruments on campus was actually built into the soul of the new school. From many witnesses, it's clear that four-part singing was in the curriculum, and was intentionally part of daily worship and other formal and informal events. It was intentionally part of recreation.

Interestingly, with the discipline of that musical straight-jacket, Mennonites did learn to sing very well! They actually developed unaccompanied four-part singing into a significant cultural treasure, something to be preserved for its own sake. J. Mark Stauffer codified this music philosophy in 1947 in his little book, *Mennonite Church Music—Its Theory and Practice.*[5] It was toward the end of Professor Stauffer's career at EMC that I signed up for a music appreciation class to be taught by him. I thought he seemed a little wary of me, a well-known proponent of instrumental music on campus; I certainly was wary of him—the official embodiment of exclusive a cappella music in church and on campus. In the first class period he grumbled good naturedly about the ironic fact that he of all people was assigned to teach this new class on music appreciation, meaning a serious college level study of INSTRU-MENTAL music. And, not only would he be teaching a class on instrumental music, but he would be using the official EMC record player, the purchase of which he had strenuously opposed. He went on to teach that class with real grace and professional finesse. I became excited as I caught on that he was to be taken seriously regarding all music, including instrumental music. By the end of the class my working knowledge of great music had been vastly expanded, and I was grateful to J. Mark Stauffer.

I do recall the sour thought in this class (and at other times on campus), "So, these conservative Mennonite professors go to all sorts of prestigious music schools (like Juilliard) to acquire academic credentials and have all these wonderful experiences with great music of all kinds and then come back here and tell us to be content with a cappella four-part hymn singing." (They were trying to "keep us safe!")

After that class, my annoyance at the musical straightjacket imposed by Virginia Conference leadership cooled considerably. The whole Mennonite community by then was opening up to the wider world of music and the other arts. My thoughts turned more to the philosophy of music and to the theological thinking underlying regimentation of the church's music.

As to philosophy of music: I came to see that music, instrumental music included, certainly is an important part of human existence. It is not a frivolous (unspiritual) waste of time and resources. Music employs the highest faculties of body, mind, and soul. With or without words it expresses the deepest human thoughts and emotions. It is essential to healthy community life and must be taken seriously by educators and community leaders. But as long ago as Plato and probably before, it's been understood that not only can music awaken and stir fine and noble sentiments, it can also arouse the crude, the ugly, the undesirable. Responsible educators and community leaders will thus inevitably be concerned with promoting or discouraging this or that kind of music within their understandings of culture and community.

As to the church's theology of music in my time: It's easy to see how a settled community of farmers with Anabaptist understandings of simplicity—farmers that were preoccupied with reversals in agricultural markets, disaffections by so many young folks, and pressures from their stance as conscientious objectors during World War I—it's easy to see how they might have little use for musical instruments and the fine arts generally. They found scripture prooftexts regarding musical instruments accordingly. Nevertheless, I find myself desperately wishing the architects of Virginia Conference would have heeded the prophetic words of the young Harold S. Bender to J. L. Stauffer in 1920. By 1920 Bender saw clearly where the church was going with its emphasis on separation from the world and felt the need to protest. Bender said to Stauffer, "I believe in being unspotted from *sin* but I do *not* believe in making Mennonites separate from the rest of the people in the world....I believe our strict regulations have done more harm than good." Bender went on to blame "the poverty of the average Mennonite in culture—things of music, literature, art, and beauty—on excessive separation from the world."[6]

My musical journey has ended with this question: How much regimentation and micromanagement of a religious group's spirituality is ever justified by even the "most correct" understandings of God and the Bible? Over the years I have listened with interest to the observations of retired church leaders; I have rummaged around in Harry Brunk's two-volume account of Virginia Mennonite Conference proceedings;[7, 8] and most recently I read Elwood Yoder's *History of Weaver's Mennonite Church*,[9] which is also a wonderful window into Virginia Conference as a whole—it has become my opinion that Virginia Conference leaders were reaching for too much direct control of our personal piety, too much direct control of the thoughts and deeds of our walk with God. That can sound like a rebellious conclusion, but rebellion isn't the bottom line of my thinking. The church historian in me won't allow me to toss out all notions of church discipline. For example, we pulled off a significant conscientious objector witness during and after World War II that revolutionized mental health in America[10]—could we have done that without serious church discipline? However one resolves that issue of church authority, it nevertheless seems that a system that made Netty Pearl Suter cry when they came and took away her reed organ, that made Daniel Lehman take the treasured reed organ he had received from his mother into the backyard and dismantle it, that made my Uncle Will take Aunt Mary's beloved reed organ into the backyard and chop it to pieces, that made my first cousin think he might prefer blindness so he could have records and radios, that unnecessarily barred kids like me from legitimate and healthy musical joy—that system was missing the mark.

9
MOTORCYCLES—REALLY!?

At Eastern Mennonite College, while diligently pursuing learning and wisdom, I guess I also indulged in the last of that rowdiness that started in fifth grade. Scholarly activities can weary a body; after a while a body needs some horsing around. One day I was walking down the hall in the boys' dorm (Ad Building, second floor north) and brushed past someone shoulder to shoulder. Feeling frisky, I grabbed his left arm and efficiently put a snug hammer lock on him. To my surprise he didn't act like a dorm horse player; he just patiently practiced nonresistance. A dignified and bemused voice said calmly, "Hello, Daniel." I quickly let go and assumed some manners. I said, "Oh, sorry, I thought you were one of the guys here in the dorm," and walked on. A minute later some of the guys grabbed me, "Dan, do you know who you did that hammer lock on? It was EMC PRESIDENT John R. Mumaw; he was showing some guests around." I always liked John R. Mumaw.

One of my best friends at EMC was Harry King. One day he showed up on a little 50 CC Yamaha motorcycle. This was when those cute little motorcycles were starting to flood into the country from Japan. I was enthralled with the thing. Harry was ever adventuresome. He soon had me up front on the cycle while he sat behind me and told me where to go. We tooled around the lawn in front of the Ad Building, around the fountain, across the hill, and up and down the hill. I was astonished at the power of that little engine. Compared to garden tractor and Cushman motor scooter technology that I had known earlier, this little thing, though it looked like a toy, was actually a sofisticated bit of merchandise from an economy that was "really coming on!" It was well designed, well constructed, and everything worked like it was supposed to.

In June 1965, I graduated from EMC and took a temporary job as a motorcycle mechanic. This was at Suburban Motors which was nearby in Park View. We sold Honda, BMW, and Triumph motorcycles. Again, I was impressed and delighted with the serious engineering and careful construction of these bikes, particularly Honda.

But more than fascination with the machinery, I was consumed with the desire to get out and run these things—I KNEW it would be FUN! At lunchtime when no one was around I would sit on this or that bike in the showroom and fairly lust after taking it out onto the open highway!

Around here in the Valley I still meet people who go off, "Oh, I heard stories about you riding bicycles and motorcycles ..." Well, those stories got a little blown up beyond reality. I did mess around with bicycles and an old Cushman scooter on the farm; and I puttered around with one or two 90 CC Honda trail bikes. Most of that was riding up and down a farm lane—the kind with two gravel tracks and a grass strip in the middle. The grass-gravel line gave me some reference points. This was enough riding to show what I was missing; it sort of undid whatever adjustment to blindness I had earlier achieved. Then I did have one good experience operating a regular motorcycle.

That summer an EMC grad would often come into the shop to work on his own cycle. It was Elvin Martin. He took a fancy to me and got ideas like Harry King, only with a MUCH bigger cycle. He had a BMW 600 with signal lights mounted on the ends of the handlebar. He was a big fellow. He had me get on the bike up front; he sat behind and reached past me to hold on to the signal lights. With this arrangement he could guide and balance the bike as usual, but I had control of everything else— the clutch, throttle, brakes and gear shifter. He did the feet-on-the-ground work when starting and stopping. We started in the middle of Park View and went out Mt. Clinton Pike. He told me when to start, stop, speed up, slow down—"Back off a bit, we're getting too close to that car up there," etc. After a while we turned around and went back. That's as close as I got to "cruising a free and open highway!" Sensing and controlling the power of that machine, shifting the gears—that was thrilling! I've often wondered what a state trooper would have done with us—to which of us would he have given the ticket, and for what?

10

DATING AND MARRIAGE—OF COURSE

E verybody, or at least many women in my life, insist on a chapter on dating and marriage. I've been hesitating. One day, after a lot of digging around in my VSDB and EMC memories, I realized that, as an old man, I can now indulge the luxury of reminiscing on high school flames and college dates without the regrets, without needing to discount the earlier loves in order to validate the last. So, let's see…

We were visiting Ferne's sister, Martha, in Kentucky. In the gathering time at their church, a woman walked up to me with a friendly greeting. I replied, "Hi, you must be Rosie" (Ferne's niece). Haley, a six- or seven-year-old standing nearby, asked Rosie, "Why did he say that? Can't he see who you are?" Rosie explained, "Dan is blind. He can't see, but he is married and has children just like everybody else." Haley's immediate response, "But how can he see to kiss the bride?"

Once when one of my piano tuning customers was driving me to my next appointment. She asked how I met my wife. I caught on that what she really wanted to know was, how I "chose her from all the others?" I told her, in the college dining room one evening, I liked the way one of the girls across the table laughed at something I said. She replied, "But how did you know what she looked like?"

At this point, I got a little mischievous. I said, "Now wait a minute, you and I are from the same faith and cultural background; you know very well we were told we should not be concerned about outward appearances, that beauty is vain, only skin deep. Right?" She brushed that aside. I said, "Being blind, I'm spared such distractions." She would have none of that either. I reminded her of those words from 1 Peter 3 about the hidden person of the heart, the gentle, quiet spirit within, etc. She indicated, yeah, yeah, she knew about those verses, but she wasn't interested in pious talk; "You know good and well physical appearance matters!" The conversation went back and forth some more, till she was getting annoyed with me and was starting to tell me I would have been foolish to date or marry someone I had no clue what she looked like. So then I gave in and admitted, "OK, yes, I did ask the guys in the dorm about the appearance of this or that girl of current interest." At that, she triumphed, "OK, I knew you would have some way of knowing what the girls you were dating looked like."

Everybody "knows" about those stereotypical preferences in the world of dating and marrying—women don't want to marry a guy shorter than she, men are not interested in girls that are too heavy, etc., etc. Many people, if not everybody, are also familiar with the way these stereotypical preferences are very important in the earlier stages of getting acquainted, but fade to non issues or just "stuff to laugh about" as the acquaintance deepens into a solid relationship. It's no different for blind people—I did try, covertly, of course, to get my friends to talk about (describe) this or that girl at first, but as the acquaintance deepened into a relationship, I was content to rely on my own judgements.

My earliest memories include crushes on various girls. I'm amazed at how early that boy-girl magic appears in childhood—

it is just there; it is not learned. In my first remembered Sunday school days, age four or five, this certain girl sitting right there in front of me, a complete stranger, was instantly THE ONE; nevermind the other girls. Amazingly, we are male and female well before the male and female hormones come in.

It was the same way in grade school, one crush after another, and sometimes, several at a time. Now as an old man, it's been fun at grade school reunions to compare notes with other schoolmates, also old and worn out, about who had crushes on whom—"What, you had a crush on her, too!?" "Yeah, yeah, all the boys had a crush on her."

Valentine's Day came along in fifth grade. I was sorting out my valentines, which one to send to whom. *Here's one, this big red heart with a picture of a friendly looking girl in very blue jeans. She's standing in a garden row, leaning on a hoe, saying something like, "I'd love to hoe a row with you." I think I'll send it to Sarah Margaret (the current crush). Well, wait a minute, that says it a little too strongly. I'd better tone it down a bit. I'll just take this pencil and make a barely visible X over the whole thing. There, that oughta do it.*

Well, when the Valentines were handed out the next day, the girls at the back of our fifth grade row started tittering and acting silly. Suddenly, Eldon, sitting behind me, banged me on the shoulder, "They found the X you put on Sarah Margaret's valentine!" That's when I learned what an X on cards and letters means! I couldn't figure out what kind of face to put on after discovering I had accidentally bespoken my true feelings.

Through my VSDB years, I had typical teenage crushes on various girls around me, some secret and some open. However, Juanita, the girl whose face was the last human face I saw, was always at least on the edge of my mind. I don't recall being sweet on her as with a crush, but she was always comfortable to be around. She was capable, pleasant and sociable, had good common sense and a ready sense of humor. She was kind and empathetic, but not mushy. In short, for me, she was a solid GOOD FRIEND! In our senior year I became aware we were both getting sweet on each other. Her erstwhile steady boyfriend had graduated the previous year and was nowhere in the picture as far as I could tell. Graduation was coming up; I had to think over some things. It was increasingly clear, Juanita and I could be happy together. I was sure she and my mom would hit it off, and, indeed my whole family would like Juanita. Would she be able to come join us Mennonites? Or, would I be able to leave my Mennonite people and join her world?

But then another issue came crowding in—at VSDB I soon began hearing stories and observing for myself various problems associated with intermarriage among blind people. When both partners in a marriage are blind, you have immediate and major issues with transportation/driving, reading myriads of necessary documents, looking after children, etc. These are not insolvable problems, especially when the couple is intelligent and resourceful. But why load up a marriage from the git go with all that extra difficulty when marrying a sighted partner would, supposedly, sweep all that away? We VSDB kids discussed all this openly; more than once I heard the declaration, "I don't want to marry another blind person." But we all witnessed our blind friends marrying a blind partner.

To be fair, there are reasons why blind people end up in-termarrying. One reason is the way blind people have been edu-cated in this country—the system of centralized institutions for educating blind children (now largely de-emphasized in favor of main streaming) has spawned powerful blind subcultures where intermarriages will readily occur. A second reason is the obvious fact that, thinking rationally and objectively, blindness is definitely not among the desirable traits or qualities for a prospective partner. Quite apart from irrational prejudices about blindness, a sighted person will and should hesitate and think objectively about marrying a blind partner. That of course narrows the field of possible choices for the blind person. Third, facing obstacles and difficulties (such as blindness) alongside another person can be a powerful bonding experience. Said another way, "being in the same boat" can be a powerful arrow in Cupid's quiver.

Juanita was partially sighted though legally blind; she could function with large print as well as Braille. However, she wouldn't be able to drive, and that was going to be a big deal for me. Well, you know how it is—at some point you just wave rationality aside and capitulate to the heart; you just go on and marry and begin tackling the very real problems as they come along. I have a strong hunch that, if Juanita and I had been together another six months, that's what we would have done, or that's what I would have tried to get her to do.

Then graduation day was upon us. Juanita began sitting in the stairwell to listen to me practice piano in the adjoining piano studio. Everybody in the senior class was getting sentimental—"We'll never see each other again!" As per usual, a school dance was planned for the last night before commencement. I decided to lean hard on my Mennonite scruples and go to that dance. I wanted a little more time with Juanita. I didn't dance; I sat or stood around talking to various friends when Juanita was off dancing. We left the dance early. In the lobby of the girls' dorm I tried to say a suitable goodbye; I gave her a "careful" hug; I wanted to kiss her goodbye but didn't. Then she was gone, into the inner recesses of that building. The next day at commencement, we seniors were all involved in photo sessions with our respective families and had little to no chance to say a final goodbye. So, before we knew it, we were all whisked off back into our home worlds and our VSDB days were all done. Juanita and I did exchange Braille letters once or so in the next several weeks, but her old boyfriend reappeared. They were soon married, and I was soon immersed in preparations to enroll at EMC that fall. So ended what might have become my first mature love.

Then, the EMC days—I had lots of dates, the typical college casual dating type. My blindness seemed to be no big issue in so far as casual dating; in fact, it was a point of interest for some girls. In my junior and senior years, though, I became increasingly restless and unsettled. I was completely naïve and unfocused with regard to vocational/professional direction; I had no clear idea how I would achieve a living income. This was becoming a big deal! I was discovering that it is very easy for a blind person to get a good higher-level education but quite difficult to gain AND MAINTAIN commensurate employment. Being thus vocationally uncrystallized, I was a boy, not yet a man. I couldn't present myself to this or that woman of interest as though I was "qualified" for her consideration. This problem came into clearer focus as my interests narrowed down to two interesting girls.

During summer school 1963 the whole EMC student body hiked from Skyline Drive in Shenandoah National Park down to South River Falls. Somehow, I ended up walking with a cluster of girls—I don't recall how or if I arranged this, but it was much to my liking. (The other guys could feign indifference toward the girls while secretly checking out the scenery from a distance.) One girl in that group, Leanna, caught my attention. She was a little quieter than the others, I suppose, a little mysterious. Some thirty or forty years later, I suddenly realized that, when encountering completely strange women at various public events over the years, I have correctly identified several as "Numann" (name changed). It's their demeanor, their speech, their singing—I don't know how I know, I just know they are "Numanns." Well, in the next several months after this hike, I learned that Leanna's mother was a Numann. So, was I attracted to Leanna by a "Numann mystique"? The reader can decide, or just wonder, or scoff. Anyway, I liked her. We dated casually through the rest of that summer. That Fall we did the annual EMC hike up Massanutten Peak. Through the next school year we dated other people, too.

Sometime later that year (1963-64) I met another interesting girl. That was the last year EMC did family-style seating in the dining room. They had this system that randomly seated three girls and three fellows at each table, and then changed the mix twice a week. That would be laughed out of court today, and indeed it would be difficult/impossible to implement for large student populations. That system did work well for me; I became acquainted with a lot of interesting people, fellows and girls, and most particularly, with Ferne Lapp.

One evening this girl across the table laughed at something I said; I really liked that laugh. It had something in it that signaled a pleasant personality and that she would be agreeable to getting further acquainted. I made sure I got her name correct—Ferne Lapp. Back in the dorm I feigned nonchalance getting the guys to talk about Ferne Lapp. They immediately blew my cover and started in on me with silly talk like, "Oh yeah, Dan, now there you are! She'd make a perfect wife for you! She's so tiny and...!" When I finally got past their foolishness, I had learned she was indeed short, seemed pleasant, was conservative (Mennonite style, but not too conservative), and had no obvious negatives. Beyond those basics, I would just trust my own judge-ments. So, I asked her to the EMC spring banquet.

On that first date Ferne got a really dramatic lesson on how to guide a blind person. As per the usual practice in those days, I went to the girls' dorm, North Lawn, and asked the girl at the receptionist's window to call for Ferne Lapp. When Ferne emerged from the mysterious innards of the building, and after suitable greetings, I took her left elbow in the standard sight-ed guide fashion. As we turned toward the outside door (which someone was holding open) I did a secret double take when I discovered how small she was. I was on the outside of the turn and had to step quickly to keep up with her. "CRAASHSH!!" That front entrance was a double-door system with a steel strike post in the middle, the kind that makes a lot of racket when those heavy doors close against it. I slammed full body up against that post! The noise DID NOT allow us to remain inconspicu-ous—there were lots of folks standing around! I was not hurt, just embarrassed, mostly on Ferne's behalf, and she was really embarrassed. She told me later she had gone to some of the girls I had dated earlier to learn how to walk with a blind person. They instructed her well, and then added, "You have to remember he's there beside you when going through doors and tight places! It's easy to forget that you have to allow clearance for him in addi-tion to yourself." Well, Ferne never again forgot that. We had one more date that year; I did enjoy her company. I remember wondering off and on about childbearing issues for a woman as small as Ferne; I kept those questions to myself.

Both Leanna and Ferne were seniors, I was a junior; they would be moving off my horizon. Most of my friends had a steady girl by now, or were engaged, or best of all, were getting married while still in school. They also had good employment prospects—that problem of being so unfocused as to how to achieve a living income was getting in my way. As the semester ended Leanna and I saw each other several more times—I was on the verge of pushing on to "Let's get serious" even though I had no job on the horizon and even though another guy was stepping into the picture. I was also aware she had an itch to "see the world" (maybe be a missionary) before settling down—she wasn't quite the traditional domestic Mennonite girl after all. Then, at that 1964 commencement Ferne pushed her way through the crowd to say a special "Goodbye" to me. She seemed to make a special point of introducing me to her sister, Martha, with her two daughters, Leta Fern and Rosie, ages nine and seven. In those few minutes I caught on that I meant something to Ferne and furthermore, that she had a fascinating family—while she was Mennonite, she had a neat Beachy Amish family cultural background. Thus my junior year ended with Leanna going abroad for a year and Ferne returning to teaching school in Lancaster County, and me in vocational limbo.

In my senior year, I became a little depressed—with no clear vocation or life calling in view, both my academic life and social life languished. My social life did quicken a bit with one girl, but for whatever reason, the spark didn't ignite. As the year ended, graduate school plans did fall together—I was accepted at two different universities for graduate level studies in sociology. Both schools would begin in September 1965, one at the Hartford Seminary Foundation in Connecticut and the other at Duke University in North Carolina. In June 1965 I graduated—my college days were done!

I took a job for the summer as a motorcycle mechanic. That job, though temporary and supposedly beneath my "intellectual dignity," gave me great satisfaction and reassurance—I could indeed get a job when I needed one! Later in the summer, on the eve of my final decision about which graduate program to opt for, I got a call from Richmond canceling my graduate school plans altogether (more about that elsewhere in the book). About the same time I got a note from Leanna saying that on her way home from her year abroad, she stopped in to visit Ferne (they were friends). She hinted broadly that Ferne would still be interested in hearing from me. (*Hmm, I still wonder what that conversation was all about.*) So it was that I was still working as a motorcycle mechanic when the next school year (1965) began, and a plan was starting to hatch in my head.

Every October EMC held a Christian Teachers Institute. I suspected Ferne would be there. Having that job now, I was ready. Although I had a black patch on one eye (due to recent eye surgery) I was in much better shape physically thanks to my work. So, that Friday evening I called the North Lawn dorm and sure enough got Ferne on the phone. We found time to visit and began planning future contacts. So, through that winter and spring (1965-66) I made several trips north to visit Ferne, and she made several trips south to see me. I discovered that Ferne had occasionally driven from Lancaster County, down through Virginia into the Kentucky mountains, to visit her sister—all by herself! This small woman, sitting on pillows, was driving a big used 1956 Chevy into those mountains, sometimes on snowy roads! I was impressed—"Now here's one capable woman!"

Two of those visits stand out. On the first, in early December, we spent the evening in her home. It was a small trailer, but it was homey and pleasant. There wasn't time to fix a full meal, so she set out beans with bacon soup, those round Ritz crackers with Velveeta cheese, and pickles—all on nice China on a pretty tablecloth. (To this day I like beans with bacon soup with

Velveeta cheese on Ritz crackers!) We listened to music—I liked her choices. It all felt right—*OK, let's go with this option!* When I returned to my friend Rodney Houser's place where I was staying overnight while visiting Ferne, he asked, "So, how did it go?" I replied, "I think this is it" (meaning, she's THE ONE). Somewhere in the midst of these events, I decided I could leave concerns about childbearing and small women to Ferne and modern medicine.

The other more memorable visit was that Spring—Ferne signed us up for one of those bus tours from Lancaster to an annual flower show in Philadelphia. Ferne went straight for the rear of the bus—there were empty seats back there; we had the rear of the bus to ourselves. To my astonishment, then delight she produced a book to read—*Green Eggs and Ham*, by Dr. Seuss! Well, Ferne was a schoolteacher and her forte was, and still is, children's literature—she knows where the good, fun stories are. She read that book to me and described the pictures; it was fun! As it turned out, that was the beginning of a lifetime of reading out loud together. Since onset of the empty nest stage, after clearing away the supper dishes, Ferne and I sit at the table and she reads an hour or so—book after book after book after... That after supper reading began when Ferne, per my birthday hint, got me the complete collection of the Joel Chandler Harris stories—you know, *Brer Rabbit, Brer Fox* and their gang, a BIG book, and she read the whole thing, all EIGHT HUNDRED PAGES! If you think Dr. Seuss and *Brer Rabbit* are too easy, we also have read the likes of Howard Zinn's *Voices of a People's History of the United States.*

That visit to the flower show was a harbinger of another thing to come. I would soon be discovering that Ferne had/has a very green thumb. You should see her house plants—her African violets, hanging ferns, Norfolk Island Pine, and her orchids! I told her soon after we were married, "The more the house looks like a green house, the better I'll like it."

In the middle of this long-distant dating, a new set of graduate school plans fell into place. This would lead almost directly to a good job. Classes would begin in September 1966 at Richmond Professional Institute in Richmond, Virginia. It was a master's degree program in vocational rehabilitation counseling. A good job and a lifetime partner were becoming real!

On completion of her school year, Ferne moved to Harrisonburg and took a summer job at Martin's Store. She rented an apartment from my Uncle Wade and Aunt Lois Bowman—that was wonderfully convenient for us. By the end of that summer, 1966, we were engaged; Ferne was returning to her teaching job in Pennsylvania, I was resigning from my mechanic's work and heading off to Richmond for grad school, and we would marry the next summer.

At this point I must include a little story on Ferne and two of her sisters—Martha and Sadie. Several years ago, Martha's daughter, Twila, drove Martha and Ferne and me up to Snyder County in Pennsylvania to visit Sadie. Twila and I sort of sat back and listened in as these three sisters began rehearsing old times. After a bit they began giggling and tittering like so many teenagers. Twila and I sat up and became all ears as we caught on to what they were saying. These three sisters, in their seventies and eighties, were disclosing to each other that, during their dating years, each had been secretly keeping a "date book," a record of all the men they had dated—names, dates, and activity. Then they began checking, "Do you still have yours?" Each still had her Date Book! Well, back at home, I got Ferne to go over her Date Book with me. Sure enough, there was my name in all the right places.

For the record, Leanna married two years later; she and her husband had successful careers, raised a family and had grand-children.

Somebody tell Haley, "I did kiss the bride, and it was not at all difficult."

11

LIBERATION FROM BLINDNESS, SORT OF

ORIENTATION AND MOBILITY TRAINING

The most important nonacademic training for me was orientation and mobility. That is training in the use of the long cane and certain other learned skills to independently get around in homes, public buildings, stores, city streets, college campuses, public transportation, etc. I got only a smattering of this training in my senior year at VSDB, but it was finished up six years later in Richmond, Virginia, where I was attending graduate level classes at Richmond Professional Institute (now Virginia Commonwealth University).

This orientation and mobility training for blind people is done by highly-trained specialists working one on one with the blind person. The training is intense, the stakes are high—if the trainee doesn't master the skills and scrupulously adhere to proper procedures, he/she can get killed; if he/she successfully completes the training, the sense of newfound freedom and independence is exhilarating, even wildly exhilarating!

Broad Street is the main street east and west through Richmond; it is six lanes of busy traffic, three lanes each way. For my last training session my instructor, Bill Springer, took me to the Medical College of Virginia building on the southeast corner of 12th and Broad. This was to be a completely solo performance, meaning that my instructor would not be at my elbow or several steps behind to get me out of trouble. My assignment was to cross Broad Street to the north side, turn left and cross 12th Street, then proceed west on Broad to 5th Street, crossing back and forth across Broad Street at each block. That meant eight blocks, eight times crossing Broad Street with its six lanes of traffic, eight times making an unerring right angle turn to cross eight side streets! At 5th and Broad I was to go into the Miller and Rhodes Department Store, take the escalators to the fifth floor and meet Mr. Springer there. This was a fiendish assignment—it would require correct performance of all that I had learned to date, and the instructor would not be available to pull me out of danger if I made a "normal student's mistake."

I would have to maintain the correct tapping procedure with the cane to avoid utility poles, parking meters, trash cans, open manholes, and up or down steps at curbs. Once your cane hits something, you have one step in which to stop or swerve.

I would have to maintain a straight course down the sidewalk. To do this I must use dead reckoning as from an imaginary internal compass, and I must make radar-like use of sounds echoing from surrounding buildings. I mustn't let traffic noise, crowds of people, curiosity about a nice whiff of perfume, etc., cause me to unknowingly veer left or right. If I stop to talk with someone or to wait for traffic, I must plant my feet, or at least one of them, immovably on the sidewalk. If I shift my feet while confabbing with someone (normal behavior for sighted people) my body will rotate a bit and I will be off course when I resume walking.

When approaching an intersection, I must study the sounds of moving traffic and idling car engines waiting at a red light in order to parse out when I have a red light or green light. The sounds and movements of people around me will also assist in "reading" those traffic lights. If someone grabs my arm intending to assist me across the street, I might have to execute that clever but graceful maneuver whereby I disengage his hand from my arm and instead take his arm while saying something like, "Thanks, but let me take your arm above your elbow like this. It'll work better that way."

And, since I was to cross Broad Street at each block, I had to make ACCURATE RIGHT-ANGLE TURNS at each intersection. This is where this training assignment turned fiendish. When approaching an intersection, whether you are planning to cross the side street and continue straight ahead or planning to turn and cross the main street and proceed on the side street, the critical problem is to keep four square to the intersection. YOU DON'T WANT TO VEER OFF INTO THE MIDDLE OF THAT INTERSECTION!! The standard procedure for keeping your bearings four square to the intersection is to square yourself with the curb by running your cane left and right along the edge of the curb just before you step off. But that squaring off against the curb is not foolproof. Sometimes that curving edge of the corner sidewalk is large, still curving well back into the crosswalk area. If you square off against that curving section, you WILL end up veering into the intersection, and once there you will likely freeze with fright and confusion—if you live long enough to experience fright and confusion. So, in the end, the blind pedestrian needs to rely on dead reckoning instincts to maintain a straight line when needed and to make accurate right angle turns when needed. All of these intersections on this section of Broad Street had those big corner curves well back into the crosswalk area—and this final exercise was to test/prove my ability to execute accurate right angle turns regardless. I had spent many hours with my mobility instructor learning and practicing these skills (as well as the other skills described above) and supposedly was ready for this acid test.

Well, believe it or not, I pulled off that assignment without a hitch. When I met Mr. Springer on the 5th floor of Miller and Rhodes, he shook my hand emphatically and said with matching emphasis, "Congratulations! You are on your own!" My excitement and sense of accomplishment matched his!

In the weeks as I was finishing up this mobility and orientation training, I was very aware of a growing sense of liberation from blindness. I no longer had to await someone else's convenience to go to the hardware store, the big Sears store, two different churches where I could practice on good pipe organs, the jewelry store and big department stores way downtown, or classes at RPI and MCV. I began to notice and delight in that breeze on my face, that low sound in my ears as I walked at a fast clip to and from classes—it was about three quarters of a mile from our apartment in the 2000 block of Park Avenue to the RPI class building in the 900 block. Most days I made two round trips daily. My instructor was amazed how fast I was wearing out the nylon tips on my cane—I was running up the mileage on that cane! This was FREEDOM! I made a one-day trip by bus, unaccompanied, to Harrisburg, Pennsylvania, and Newark, New Jersey, for job interviews. The Harrisburg interviewer took note of my independent travel skill; it helped me land the job.

I said this mobility training felt like liberation from blindness—yes it did. But then reality reached out and smacked me around a bit making me understand that blindness is still for real and ignoring that fact when you are a blind pedestrian can be dangerous. About a year after that training Ferne and I and our new baby daughter, Laura Mae, were living in Harrisburg, Pennsylvania, where I had landed my first job. One evening after a long day with a fussy baby, Ferne asked me to go to Oby's, a sandwich shop about two blocks away for some delicious sandwiches so she wouldn't have to make supper. This was about 7:00 on a February night; it was dark, but I "knew" the intersections were well lighted and I had no qualms. At the first intersection I waited for traffic sounds to clear, then started across. Halfway across I heard a car's engine and heard tires screech to a stop just as a headlight hit me on the right side. I landed on the pavement about 20 feet ahead of the car, on my left side crosswise in the street, propped up on my left elbow, facing up the street. I was conscious enough to understand I was lying on a city street at night and hearing another car coming down the street toward me. I "knew" the intersection was lighted and he would easily see me lying there, but I instinctively raised my right hand to signal, "Watch out for me lying here!" The car went on by, pretty close, I thought. Soon people were all around and I was gathered into a rescue vehicle and taken to an emergency room. A policeman picked up Ferne at the apartment and brought her to the hospital. A neighbor volunteered to watch Baby Laura. No broken bones were found. Ferne and I were then taken home in a police car.

No bones were broken—yeah, but every joint ached like two broken bones. In a day or two I was back in the office. One of my fellow employees then told me, "That night when you got hit I was in this nearby watering hole when a guy came in and told us there was an accident up the street where a guy was knocked down and lying in the street. He didn't see him at first, but his car would have creamed his head if he hadn't raised his hand." (So much for assuming people will see me.)

Here's what happened: As I started to cross the street, a car driven by an elderly man was coming up the street to my right.

He came across the intersection very slowly, looking off to his right for an address; I was on his left starting across his lane of travel in the full beam of his headlight but not in his diverted field of vision. I did not hear him coming because he was driving so slowly AND because I had not waited long enough for ALL of the traffic sounds to clear—the sounds of traffic fading into the distance still masked the sound of his softly idling engine. No charges were filed for the incident; his insurance covered my hospital bills. In my opinion we were both at fault—he shouldn't have diverted his eyes from his line of travel as long as his car was moving, and I should have waited longer for ALL traffic sounds to clear.

Upon reading this account, Ferne told me after that incident she made an "INDEPENDENT executive decision" that I WOULD NOT BE ALLOWED to walk the streets alone after dark. I barely recall this unilateral decision, and I don't recall any occasion that tested her metal on this matter.

There's still more to this story. Another of my fellow workers in that office was blind and used a guide dog. In the larger blind community, there was and still is a lot of contentious disputing about the relative merits of the cane versus the guide dog. Since my first days in that office this friend had been "after me" to "get a guide dog and quit relying on that cane." When I showed up in the office after the accident, he had to practically bite his tongue to keep from saying, "I told you so." I was secretly amused at that. Well, believe it or not, one week later to the day, he and his dog were knocked down on the same street several blocks further south. It was thought the dog didn't see the car coming because the late afternoon sun was in his face. As with me there were no broken bones for man or dog, just a lot of soreness. Now it was really "interesting" how careful and polite

BOTH he and I were when the conversation came anywhere near those accidents. Indeed, the whole office was polite, no, sober when any talk veered near this matter.

Within several days I contacted and began working with another mobility instructor to assess whether my hearing specifically and mobility skills generally were really adequate for navigating the streets as a blind pedestrian. I also wanted this training brush-up to help me get over the extreme gun shyness that had settled over me. For some time after the accident, when I heard screeching tires, my reflexes were indeed pre-conscious and uncontrollable. If I heard screeching tires when I was on the street, alone or accompanied, I would realize I had backed up and pushed anyone behind me out of the way BEFORE I was consciously aware I had heard screeching tires. The instructor soon assured me my hearing and skills were indeed up to par, but it took some time for the gun shyness to dissipate.

Some years later reality again knocked on my head for attention regarding safety of blind pedestrians. I learned from mutual friends that Joe Shankle, whom I had known as "an older, more experienced blind boy" at VSDB was killed while crossing 12th and Broad Streets in Richmond; that's the same intersection where I started that last mobility training assignment.

Back in my first months at VSDB when I was a very inexperienced blind navigator, Joe took an interest in me and began to show me how to get around without a lot of groping—how to "not look so blind." I was ready enough to "not look so blind," but I did think he was pushing me into ways of getting around in hallways and doorways that were too risky—for me at least. Joe could walk down a long hall without touching anything, turn and walk confidently through a doorway without groping to find the opening or to see if the door was open or closed. I had to trail my fingers along the wall to stay on course and to find the doorway and reach to see if the door was open or closed. Joe could do all that—walk around confidently without "looking so blind"— using his "blind radar"; my blind radar was still wimpy and actually never did develop as keenly as his. When I got the news of his death, they also told me his friends for some time had been warning him, "Joe, you need to slow down. With the way you charge out into traffic the second you think you have the right of way, you're gonna get killed."

So how many blind pedestrians actually get hurt? One Internet source says at least 70 legally blind persons are involved in pedestrian accidents each year. You can check this link: (https://www.hg.org/legal-articles/pedestrian-safety-enhancement-act-to-protect-the-blind-from-personal-injury-22515)

There are media stories about blind pedestrians and the new silent electric cars and sometimes silent hybrids—the blind community, legal community, and car manufacturers are "discussing" what to do about all this. In one of these news stories some wag sniffed, "Blind people have no business being on the streets by themselves." Boy, would I ever love to give him a talking to! Prejudices like that can only promote "entitlement," like this: "OK then, we blind people will just sit at home at taxpayer expense."

Let's end this chapter with a lighter tone. Everyone has heard and used the phrase, "The blind leading the blind." I have had two experiences with this—literally. Ordinarily, when a blind person walks with a sighted person as guide, he takes the sighted person's elbow. That puts the sighted guide in front where he belongs. That is the correct procedure. If you offer to guide a blind person, by all means offer your elbow; do not grab his arm (or any other body part) and try to guide him from behind. Once in a while, though, it falls out that the sighted person is guiding from behind, and that can work, sort of, for special circumstances, but that can also lead to trouble.

If you've attended conventions of professional associations, you are familiar with the way strangers standing around the check-in area will begin chatting and getting acquainted. As a rehabilitation counselor and later as a piano technician I have participated in such conventions many times. Since many blind people work in those professions, numbers of blind people will be circulating around the front desk and convention hall. On two occasions I found myself getting acquainted with an interesting stranger, neither of us knowing the other was blind. As per the usual course of such getting acquainted, one of us says, "Let's go down to the bar to get something to eat," or "Let's go over to the exhibit hall and check out the new tools." The other guy says, "Good idea," and grabs the first guy's elbow. We set out, one thinking he is walking with a sighted guide in the normal front position, the other thinking he's walking with a sighted guide in the wrong but sort of workable rear position. Each is responding to the body movements of the other as leading movements. In a few steps the "guidance system" for the pair of us begins drifting and going hay wire; we start to start and stop, wander this way and that. This confusion of leading signals and following signals is very disorienting! Even though the episode is just a fleeting few seconds, the loss of bearings is profound; the feeling is strange, weird, even sickening. In both my experiences we caught on quickly; in the one case we laughed, decided who was going to be the guide, and went on; in the other we were embarrassed and quickly split from the scene hoping no one saw us looking so stupid.

This disorientation phenomenon is fascinating to me from the standpoint of brain science—the brain desperately needs to be "always oriented in space." In these experiences the two brains desperately needed to know, which was leader and, which was follower. Confusion on that point resulted quickly in loss of "orientation in space;" it was as bad as vertigo.

One day soon after finishing that mobility training in Richmond, I was out on Broad Street on some errand or other—by now I was enjoying any excuse to navigate Broad Street. As I stepped up to the curb preparing to cross Broad, I realized other folks were clustered around there and I was shoulder to shoulder with someone. Requesting sighted assistance from nearby bystanders is one of the standard techniques blind people use when crossing streets. So, I said something like, "Hi, would you mind if I take your elbow while crossing the street?" The gentleman sort of jumped, then replied, "Uh, er, oh, wul, yeah, I'll hep you across." While crossing the street I became aware of some kind of lightweight cloth draped over the man's shoulder and flapping in the breeze against my arm. On the other side of the street I thanked him and went my way and he went his. Several days later a friend called to me across a parking lot, "Hey Dan, I saw you out there on Broad Street the other day. Did you realize that man walking you across the street was a KKK guy IN FULL REGALIA?! "Wha-a-aT?" I stammered. He went on, "Yeah Dan, you didn't know, but you had walked right into the middle of a Ku Klux Klan demonstration—they were all in full regalia!" Now wouldn't that make quite the picture on today's Facebook—a KKK demonstrator in full regalia kindly helping a blind man cross a busy street! To this day, whenever I recall this incident, I wonder what that man would have done if it had been a black blind young man that walked up beside him?

One thing more needs to be discussed in this chapter—sighted people have often confided to me embarrassed uncertainty about whether and how to offer help to a blind person they encounter on the street, in an office, at church, in an airport, etc. The public can see that the blind pedestrian is focusing intently on what she's doing, and they know they shouldn't distract her concentration. Yet, there's the anxious fretting, "Shouldn't I offer to help in some way?" Stories are out there where offers to help have been impolitely rebuffed by blind people who are entirely too prickly. Stories are also out there where blind people have been "handled" by insensitive, even crude "helpers." For myself, I would prefer you to err on the side of offering help when none is needed. It's my responsibility to COURTEOUSLY explain what help I need or don't need, and I usually add, "Thanks for checking." One easy thing to remember is this: When approaching a blind person to be of assistance, position yourself so that your elbow is available if needed; don't take hold of the blind person, let her take hold of your arm at or just above your elbow.

12

HARRISBURG AND HARRISONBURG—
THE ADULT YEARS

REHABILITATION COUNSELOR, THEOLOGIAN AT HEART, PIANO TECHNICIAN WITHOUT APOLOGY

"That's a pretty little town, the way it lies along the Susquehanna River and all!" exclaimed a rehab counselor friend of mine in early 1968 when I announced I'd likely be landing a job in Harrisburg, Pennsylvania.

We were still living in Richmond, Virginia, where I had finished a master's degree program in Vocational Rehabilitation Counseling. Ferne Lapp and I were married the preceding June. We were wrapping up what would be a wonderful nine-month time in Richmond.

Before the wedding I had rented a neat second floor apartment at 2014 Park Avenue. This had two bedrooms, a living room with French doors that opened onto a second floor screened-in balcony. That balcony overlooked several backyards full of flowers like you see in gardening magazines and greeting cards! Ferne fell in love with the place when she saw it. That second bedroom was perfect for a guest bed, my study, and my woodworking shop—and the landlord was OK with all that!

Vocational Rehabilitation was a Federal-state program to enable handicapped people to achieve gainful employment.

In 1954 this program was greatly expanded to include, among other things, generous stipends to train personnel (rehabilitation counselors) to run the program. At that time, I was still a simple Mennonite farm boy, just out of college with no debt, no expensive habits like smoking, drinking, carousing in bars or other "worldly entertainments," and no car—just occasional bus tickets. After paying tuition and living expenses, I had $50 per month, which became seed money for my woodworking hobby—I started buying woodworking tools and equipment. I had two mentors to help me with these purchases. Back when my life merged into Ferne's I had gotten acquainted with two of her brothers-in-law—Wesley Stoltzfus and Bill Chupp. Wesley was a skilled furniture maker and Bill was a skilled construction carpenter. Both knew their way around GOOD woodworking tools and equipment; both loved to talk shop with me and eagerly guided my tool purchases. Both delighted in helping me find ways of doing things without vision.

After we were married and settled into the apartment, I made my big purchase—a Craftsman 10-inch table saw, the kind with a solid machine tooled top. It was a beauty! Ferne blessed it. I still use that saw.

Thus it was, in early 1968, I had finished a graduate level training program that qualified me for professional employment; a wonderful woman had come alongside as a lifetime partner; I was launched on a very useful hobby; and I was riding high on a newfound sense of personal independence thanks to all that training in the use of the long cane. Now in this interval waiting for final arrangements on the new job in Harrisburg, I was finding how ideally situated we were in Richmond—I was in walking distance of the Sears store on West Broad Street with its wonderful hardware department, Pleasants Hardware with more good hardware, and St. James Episcopal Church where I was welcome to practice on their very good pipe organ. There were good bus connections to anywhere else I wanted to go in Richmond. Ferne had a pleasant job in the city library; the bookmobile. We were discovering that Richmond was a beautiful city with a high esprit decor. But now we had to leave it. I did get that job in Harrisburg and Ferne was pregnant.

While checking out ads for apartments to rent in Harrisburg, I had my first experience on the wrong side of racial prejudice.

"Hello, I'm calling about an apartment you have listed for rent in Harrisburg," I said.

The reply, "I don't want to discuss that apartment on the phone. From your accent, I need to see you in person first."

Ferne and I were astounded at this—we thought we were moving north where people weren't prejudiced. I didn't have to think twice—I wasn't about to give that guy the chance to inspect my skin color. We almost immediately found another nice apartment at 258 Peffer Street about two blocks from where I would work.

Well, observing regional accents turned out to be a two-way street. Ferne and I both immediately noticed what Ferne liked to call "Dutchiness" in Harrisburg English. She grew up amidst Lancaster County Dutch culture, but she had lived long enough in Richmond to become attuned to "proper" English— Southern style English, of course. What really made her laugh— politely, of course—was hearing black folks talking like they came right out of Lancaster County.

When the girls at the office began listening to my dictation through their earbuds, I really got a ribbing. "Where in the world are you from? We've never heard anybody talk like that!"

Finally, I figured out what had shaped my "dulcet tones." "I grew up in the Shenandoah Valley," I explained. "There's a sizeable German culture there—Mennonites, Brethren, and descendants of Hessian soldiers who moved into the area after the Revolutionary War. Their "dutchy accents" comingled with the "southern twang" of their Scotch Irish and English neighbors. The result was/is a distinctive regional accent. Somebody immediately dubbed my speech as "Southern Dutch," and the label has stuck to this day.

The apartment we found—three rooms plus a basement that I could use for my shop—was near the corner of Green and Peffer Streets in the heart of the Old Uptown Historic District of Harrisburg. This was about two blocks back from the river, a block or so back of the governor's mansion. The riverbank along there was a neatly terraced riverside park, perfect for nature walks and family outings. It showed a lot of civic pride. The houses in this Old Uptown area were once grand, upscale homes of people of means but most were now subdivided into apartments. Our apartment was right at ground level with a doorway that opened onto a small concrete stoop with two steps down to the very public sidewalk. Our bedroom window and living room bay windows were at eye level of passersby who were willing enough to morph into lookers-in. Ferne quickly became an efficient manager of curtains and venetian blinds so we could have both a view outside and privacy. I had to build a louvered grill for our big window fan in the bedroom so we could have both fresh air and privacy.

In this area there wasn't enough soil anywhere to support even one blade of something green. Ferne was a farm girl and that had to be remedied. So, I built her a flower garden—a wooden box five feet by eighteen inches by twelve inches deep.

We painted it a proper flower box green, then put it in our car's trunk and visited a farmer friend across the river. He happily filled it with good farm soil and then wondered how I was going to get that thing out of the car—the back of the car was squatting low. When we got back to the apartment, I soon wondered too how I was going to get that box out of the car. Ferne rounded up boxes and buckets into which we scooped most of the dirt from the flower box. We then placed it on the sidewalk back against the house next to the doorstep and returned the soil to the box. Ferne soon had a very attractive little flower garden there. Passersby began to stop and admire and comment favorably. That little flower garden provided a much-needed accent to the neighborhood.

It was also immediately apparent we needed a kitchen/dining room table sized to fit a certain place in the kitchen. So, I got some pipe clamps and put the new table saw to good use. I assembled the legs and skirt boards with five dowel pins and lots of glue at each joint—three dowels per joint would have been enough. Ferne brushed on a polyurethane finish. We wanted a Formica top; I networked with friends on how to work with Formica. The end result was a solid, homely but serviceable, 51 by 35-inch table with a nice Formica top that our daughter, Diane, is still using today.

Ferne quickly found a good job as a ward clerk at the Polyclinic Hospital, but that soon ended when Baby Laura arrived in late December 1968. We were soon learning it is true as the books say, "Parents of newborn babies don't get much sleep"—more on those days later. From about age five months, Laura liked to sit on her mother's lap out on that little porch right on the sidewalk; she would make eye contact, smile, wave and generally make a friendly display to anyone coming up the walk from as much as half a block away. Perhaps the final most memorable scene from the Peffer Street chapter was that perfect autumn day in early October when Baby Laura was about 10 months old; I took her to the office—with Laura on one arm and my cane in the other hand I walked the two blocks to the office. (Yes, I saw to it my blind mobility techniques were hyper correct.) Coming off the elevator I stood Laura up on the counter beside the reception-ist's desk where she could see and be seen. I kept my arm lightly about her for obvious reasons but suddenly realized she was ac-tually standing there perfectly poised and balanced with no as-sistance from me—her first upright stand with no hand hold. She stood there like a calm professional model—with her little bonnet like cap, light blue (I think) sweater, pink dress and white hard soled shoes. I was SO proud; the office staff responded like people do to a baby! Ferne then arrived to pick up Laura and headed off on some errands. I went back to work.

Later that October 1969, we bought the house at 2914 Croyden Road in Wilson Park, a post-World War II housing de-velopment about 25 blocks east of the River. That neighborhood was right next to the Klein Village Shopping Center. These homes were small, well-built brick duplexes perfect for young families with small children. The streets were lined on both sides with big elm trees. The houses, each with a little front porch or stoop, were set back from the sidewalk about 20 feet—a perfect set up for sit-ting on the porch to monitor the children and visit with neighbors passing by. Most of the driveways and sidewalks were perfect for roller skates and ride-'em toys. The next eight years were HAPPY YEARS for us all—just like the Dick and Jane books!

(Since blind people are always interested in employment and job experiences of other blind people, I'm including more detail in the rest of this chapter than perhaps otherwise needed.)

How did I get into Vocational Rehabilitation in the first place? Back when I graduated from EMC in 1965, I had been accepted into two different graduate level programs in sociology of religion—one at the Hartford Seminary Foundation in Connecticut, the other at Duke University in North Carolina. Before I could finalize the decision, those plans got derailed. The Virginia Commission for the blind was at that time sponsoring my college expenses as a Vocational Rehabilitation client. After cheerfully covering my expenses at the very religious EMC for four years, somebody in Richmond suddenly decreed that government money cannot be spent at religious institutions, not even for Vocational Rehabilitation training leading to employment; I was told to cancel my plans for grad school, plans that they had earlier approved. So it was that I worked for a year as a motorcycle mechanic. It was as a motorcycle mechanic who happened also to play the organ that a friend, John S. Wenger, arranged for me to play the pipe organ for Sunday evening chapel at the Woodrow Wilson Rehabilitation Center in Fishersville, Virginia. It was through contacts there that I learned about and then enrolled in the master's degree program in Vocational Rehabilitation Counseling in Richmond. That, as already noted, led directly to employment in 1968 as a rehab counselor in Pennsylvania. Several years later, at a regional rehab counselor convention, I met someone from Richmond who knew of me as a rehab client back in 1965. I asked him about that "stupid ruling" that forced me to drop my graduate school plans. "Oh my goodness," he exclaimed, "that was a misinterpretation that was cleared up a week later! And nobody got back to you?!" Well, that "little" bureaucratic fumble did turn me into a path leading directly to employment—a critical issue for me then because I was wanting to get serious about marriage. (What's that about "God moving in mysterious ways...."?)

The eight years I worked in Harrisburg as a Vocational Rehabilitation Counselor were rich and unforgettable. We counselors were to visit visually-impaired clients in their homes, prospective employers, school counselors, etc. We blind staff would hire drivers for this "field work"; we sometimes covered more than 200 miles in a day. We also put in much office time reading medical reports and case records, dictating case notes, working up and dictating rehabilitation plans, etc. We blind staff used volunteer readers for most of this reading.

From the ranks of these hired drivers and voluntary readers came some wonderful acquaintances and even some lifelong friendships. The ladies at the local Jewish synagogue had made a serious commitment to supplying volunteer readers for blind workers in government offices around Harrisburg; some of these reading sessions blossomed into neat friendships. The lady who became my regular driver, Mrs. Eleanor Borek, also became a wonderful "Grandma" for our family—rocking our babies, attending their birthday parties, graduations, weddings, and our anniversaries. Mrs. Borek often reminded me of the following two stories.

We were looking for an address in rural Franklin County. We finally found it in a wooded mountainous location—a cabin-like home on the other side of a rather deep ravine or gully. The only way to get to that cabin from our car was to cross the gully on a one-plank footbridge—a single wooden plank about ten or twelve inches wide and maybe fifteen or twenty feet long with no handrail! We stopped and pondered our options, then screwed up our courage to go for it! We went side stepping across that plank, she first, with me following; I held her arm both to steady her and to guide me; I had my cane and notebook in the other hand. That plank bounced up and down A LOT! We got across! What we found was a man in his forties, very ill and losing vision due to complications from diabetes, and a young woman, maybe in her early twenties, with nice long legs in shorts—calm down now, Mrs. Borek so informed me later. The scene had all the appearances of a very sick man retreating to a secluded spot to spend his last days with a beautiful young woman. The man wanted nothing from our agency, no referrals for medical help. We respectfully took our leave and side stepped back across that plank—no, we didn't take anything to settle our pounding hearts! I've often wondered what became of that pair.

One day we were eating lunch in a restaurant on Manor Road between Lancaster and Millersville. I happened to comment that I didn't really know the Peter Rabbit story. Mrs. Borek proceeded to tell me the whole story. She told me later that we got a lot of quizzical glances from other diners, obviously puzzled at this scene—a well-dressed portly middle-aged woman sitting in a restaurant telling the story of Peter Rabbit to a professionally dressed, intelligent looking young man across the table!

Vocational Rehabilitation was highly focused on enabling disabled people to achieve "substantial gainful employment." That was supposed to mean "taxpaying, self-supporting employment." Generous funds were available for medical services, adaptive gadgets, adjustment training, vocational training, even college education—most anything that would prepare/equip a disabled person for suitable employment. We counselors had the tasks of persuading the disabled person to begin the rehabilitation process, then supervise the process for each client, then persuade an employer to "try a disabled but now quite capable person," and then persuade the disabled person to actually take the job. Those last two steps were not easy! Coming up with a willing and ready employer just when we have a willing and ready client—good luck!

In the midst of all this hustle and hassle, we counselors did have some profoundly human experiences, like this one: I was visiting a couple in Lancaster; they were around age 60; he was losing vision, could no longer read but still had significant mobility vision. They were unhappy. She was saying, "He uses poor vision to duck out of doing things around the house." He was saying, "She won't believe me when I say I can't see this or that." I recognized and began to explain, "This is a typical scenario with partial vision—partial vision is often more frustrating or at least more confusing than total blindness for both the individual and the family. You can quickly comprehend total blindness—just close your eyes and you'll see. But with partial vision, it's obvious to folks around you that you can see this here, so why are you claiming you can't see that over there?" Light bulbs started coming on in their heads. I suspected that the man was also pulling that little prank on his wife that I tried on Eldon that afternoon when I came home from school with a retina detachment in process. So I told them how I tried to "improve on the facts" when Eldon wouldn't accept my claim that I couldn't see well enough to do my share of the chores." (The reader can find that story on page xv of this book.) I told this story humorously and allowed that such "improving on the facts" in order to convince a skeptical family member is not all that unusual. They sort of laughed; more light bulbs were coming on. Several weeks later I got a phone call from the gentleman; he said, "I'm calling to tell you that my wife and I really appreciate your help, especially that story about you and your brother. It really has changed things around here!"

So then, why did I leave that good job in Harrisburg eight years later? When I first took the job, I had in mind working there five to eight years, then moving on to church-related work—probably not preaching but maybe in church academia or in church social services. For the first five years I liked the job well enough; the pay and benefits were good; I was settling into this work as a comfortable lifelong career. At six-and-a-half years, I was restless. At eight years, I was out. Vocational Rehabilitation did have on paper clearly stated purposes and methods that aligned well with my personal values, but I was increasingly disillusioned with the way so much of our working energy was focused on internal bureaucratic wrangling as distinct from delivery of client centered services. Adequate secretarial support for blind professional staff was a chronic issue. Our agency's public image with some groups and persons in the communities we were serving was POOR—I was nonplused to repeatedly hear accusing words like, "...you bureaucrats from Harrisburg!" Office management changed—what had been seen as my strengths, were now seen as "problematic." Turnover among the rehab counselor staff was high—eleven people cycled through four rehab counselor positions in eight years. I checked my retirement pension; I checked my eligibility for Social Security Disability payments to be used as a launchpad to another livelihood; I then resigned.

The problem people in that office are all dead now except me. Part of me would love to take some pop shots at their ghosts, but, I suppose we will all be best served if I just pretend to be a wise old man, one who nods knowingly, then turns to more important matters. Besides, that deteriorating office situation did serve to put me back onto my original career track. Also, that eight years in state civil service got our retirement nest egg off to a good start; Ferne was able eventually to parlay that up into an adequate retirement reserve.

This crossroads where I now stood in the Spring of 1976 was interesting. Which of my several very different interests should I now pursue for a livelihood? I considered woodworking, making quality furniture —no, not that for a living income. What about computer programming?

The thought of computer programming took me back to the Fall of 1962, my sophomore year at EMC; my rehabilitation counselor from the Virginia Commission for the Blind, Mr. Hardy, came to EMC to talk with me. Standing on the front steps of the old Ad Building, Mr. Hardy told me excitedly, "We want to pull you out of this place [EMC] and send you to Cincinnati to study cybernetics." When I caught on that cybernetics was working with computers—we now call it "computer programming"—I instantly vetoed the idea. I explained that computers are almost all connected, directly or indirectly with the military; with my religious convictions, I would not be interested in that training. I didn't tell him I also didn't want to leave the Mennonite world again; my time at VSDB was enough. Mr. Hardy was very upset with me. Now as a professional rehab counselor myself, I could view myself as Mr. Hardy saw me back then. That 1962 Cincinnati training program was a brilliant and timely move by someone in the rehabilitation system; the idea was to get blind workers into the earliest jobs of a new profession that was about to explode into many good job opportunities. And, the military connection was not an issue. I was turning down what would have been an ideal vocational option for me. After turning down that Curtis Institute scholarship, this computer programming opportunity would be my second Great Road Not Taken.

So now, at this 1976 junction, I reconsidered the computer programming option. I knew I would be good at that. I ordered several recorded textbooks on the subject. In the end, though, the idea didn't really take root. The thought of seminary training got hold of me and persisted.

It was with relief and excitement that I began preparing to attend Eastern Mennonite Seminary back on my old stomping grounds in Harrisonburg. Academic requirements for admission to seminary included one year of college level New Testament Greek. I opted for a do-it-yourself home study project to meet that requirement. Through the Pittsburgh Theological Seminary, I found a good home study course based on audio cassettes. Through the Library of Congress, wonder of wonders, I found a Braille Greek textbook from which I could learn the Braille Greek characters. One of the secretaries who earlier resigned from the same office where I had worked, Lorraine Sersch, was doing some volunteer reading for me. One day, as a joke, I told her she should learn the Greek alphabet so she could read Greek for me. To my astonishment, she quickly learned the Greek characters and began dictating Greek vocabulary words while I made up Braille index cards for study. A lesson here: If you're going to be blind, you do well to make it fun for people helping or working with you. Lorraine and I had a ball learning Greek.

So it was, for the rest of 1976 and the first half of 1977, I studied Greek, looked after the girls, and learned a lot of house husbanding. Ferne found a job that she really liked in a flower shop. Then during the summer of 1977, we sold the house on Croyden Road and moved to Harrisonburg, supervised the building of our new house on Rockingham Drive, and enrolled the older girls in Waterman Elementary School. I did some work setting up my shop equipment. Finally I got the verdict on what I had accomplished with my Greek studies—Dr. G. Irvin Lehman at Eastern Mennonite Seminary reviewed my work and gave me credit for six hours of college Greek. I then enrolled at Eastern Mennonite Seminary that September.

Four years of seminary, graduating with an MDiv degree in 1981—so what? My learning went like this: When we understand the human scene more deeply, we can see more clearly how profoundly the Bible speaks to that scene. It was through reading great secular humanists that I came to understand more deeply the workings of our human nature; my appreciation of the Biblical story deepened commensurately. Alongside all that reading came language study. Studying the Bible, or at least parts of it, through the original languages opened many windows into the cultural settings and the minds of the original writers. As those insights grow, we begin to see the greatness in many creeds and denominational doctrines; we also begin to see the pettiness of many creeds and denominational doctrines. We can even begin, with fear and trembling, to reformulate those creeds and doctrines into useful statements for our own times. Frankly, I was totally unprepared for the way reading secular humanists, and non-Mennonite scholars along with traditional Biblical studies, would deepen my appreciation for the Bible and even for my own Mennonite heritage. Now I cringe when I hear people say, "I don't pay any attention to all that other human stuff, I read just the Bible and go by that."

At the end of those four years I was at another crossroads. I had been planning to move to Richmond for PhD studies, the goal being employment somewhere in church academia. But now wouldn't be a good time to move the girls again—they were coming up on junior high age. Academic fatigue was lurking around the edges. A move to Richmond would mean still more time on Disability. It was feeling like high time to get a real income going again.

"...high time to get a real income going again!?"—my thinking was getting complicated. Numbers of folks around me were, so to speak, trying to console me with words like, "There's nothing wrong with simply living out the rest of your life on Disability." I didn't see myself in that kind of way—I had signed on to Social Security Disability as a temporary steppingstone, a way to launch to another job.

Right at this time, I chanced to get into an "animated discussion" with an acquaintance; suddenly he dismissed my argument by saying, "Your opinion doesn't count since you are on welfare!" (For the record, Social Security Disability is not public welfare.) Well now, that angered me! About the same time someone else offered the opinion that "the vote should be limited to those with at least $10,000 in property." Well, with notions like that around me I was fuming, and to be truthful, my attitudes still stir when their two names are mentioned.

Now that I have retired from 36 years as an independent, self-employed businessman; now that I (we) have bought and sold one home and built, paid for and sold another; now that I (we) have put two daughters through college (with student loans) and helped the third with the down payment on her home, now that I've (we've) produced enough income for Ferne to build up a retirement nest egg (Ferne had various part-time jobs during this time)—now that I've done all that without vision (doing a job without vision usually means less net income than when doing the same job with vision), maybe my opinion now COUNTS! So here it is: My considered opinion is that those two people making those remarks exhibited a woefully impoverished understanding of what democracy in the United States is all about. More specifically, those for whom life circumstances have not gone so well as mine—those who are on public welfare, those who have no property—they are citizens, too; they all have a right to be heard, to be taken seriously. Is that not what "all men are created equal" means? Their single vote must have the same weight in the ballot box as the single vote of the billionaire. THIS IS ESPECIALLY IMPORTANT since THE WEALTHY AND POWERFUL TEND to VOTE FOR WARS THAT INEVITABLY SEND THE POOR AND POWER-LESS OFF TO DO THE DIRTY WORK! Hmm, maybe I'd better get back to my original subject—which way to turn after completing seminary?

Piano tuning? Since high school days I had been picking up pocket money here and there with occasional tunings. Now, as I was finishing up seminary, out of the blue, more and more people were calling for tuning. It turned out there was indeed a shortage of piano tuners in the central Valley area—one of the really good tuners had moved to Florida; another was laid up for some time due to a car accident; and, the public was discovering, "You don't want to call that third guy, he'll leave your piano in worse shape." Was a ready-made piano tuning business falling right into my lap?! I would have little competition! But, did I want a manual trade? I was now, some would say, highly educated—college and two graduate degrees; I had come to love the academic world! Yes, I had come to love books and the life of the mind, but I also loved woodworking and things mechanical; I never scorned the idea of earning one's living through skilled manual work!

Dad's philosophy of labor and money, I can see now, were deeply ingrained in me. I heard Dad argue these points many times, but never so forcefully as that day back in 1968 when Dad was helping Ferne and me move into that Peffer Street apartment in Harrisburg. An acquaintance of ours from Virginia who speculated in "declining neighborhood real estate" stopped in to welcome Ferne and me to the neighborhood, but also, as we caught on, to scout out the area. Dad lit in—"Earning money by simply investing and speculating is contrary to Bible teaching," Dad said. He went on, "The only honorable way to earn a living is with the labor of one's own hands and with the sweat of one's brow. The Bible says the sleep of the laboring man is sweet. If you give an honest day's work for a fair wage, and if you help out your neighbors when they're in trouble, you won't die filthy rich, but you will have enough." Dad's argument, especially the words "filthy rich" cut to the quick—our friend responded with matching heat. Mennonites aren't supposed to speak angrily to each other, but the voices of both men were trembling with emotion as they went their separate ways.

Well, I didn't (and don't) disparage investing and "shrewd money management" like Dad did, but I did (and do) see manual labor as honorable. That made it easier for me to see that a major key to successful employment for blind people is FLEXIBILITY OR WILLINGNESS to take advantage of job opportunities that happen to come your way. In the end, I decided to study up and tool up and go for it—"it" being a one-man business as a fully-qualified piano technician.

Well, actually the decision to "go for it" sort of slipped and flopped into place piecemeal as the transportation issue resolved itself. Transportation from job to job is a make or break issue for blind tuners. Whenever blind piano technicians get together, they're soon comparing notes about how they handle that transportation issue—hire drivers? have the wife or other family members do the driving? use public transportation such as bus or taxi? have the piano owner pick up the tuner in exchange for reduced fees? just side step the transportation hassle by working only at a large university or large music store? and, well yeah, by hitching rides with friends who, for the moment at least, enjoy driving you around? Ferne saw immediately, and I soon saw, whatever I was going to do for a living, Ferne could not be doing the driving—she was a full-time home administrator! It quickly settled out that, whatever business volume I was going to achieve, it would be limited by what I could do by using the expensive city cab or having the customer pick me up for a reduced fee. That would reduce my net income—yeah, well, that just goes with the territory of being blind.

As I sort of timidly launched my business, two events put me in high gear. First, coincidentally with that shortage of tuners in the Valley, the city implemented a $1 cab fare anywhere in city limits for handicapped passengers. If the destination was outside city limits, you paid that $1 plus just the mileage in the county. That meant for the first lean years I could easily afford the convenience of cab transportation. The city dropped that $1 fare about the time my business had picked up enough to afford full cab fares. Second, many piano owners began stepping up to help with the transportation. One would pick me up first thing in the morning; when I finished her piano, she would drive me to the second appointment; when I finished there, that customer would run me to the third appointment; when I finished there, I might call a cab, or the customer might run me home—or variations of that pattern. I was surprised and humbled with how willing many piano owners were to go to so much trouble to get their piano tuned—some actually drove as much as an hour one way to fetch me. I was also surprised and pleased with how fast word-of-mouth advertising worked—owner involvement with my transportation seemed to stir still more word-of-mouth advertising.

With transportation resolving itself thus, I got really serious about preparation for professional piano service. My training in piano technology at VSDB was a good start, but I needed more. I embarked on one more do-it-yourself study project—

this time to master the considerable body of technical data on pianos. Through the Library of Congress I got all the Braille textbooks on piano service that the Library could locate plus all the issues of a then-defunct Braille magazine called *The Braille Piano Technician*. I also subscribed to *The Piano Technician's Journal*—THE official technical monthly magazine published by the Piano Technicians Guild (PTG). Making copious notes on all this reading became a high priority. I began purchasing or building proper tools and equipment for the trade. I began attending the monthly meetings of the Richmond Chapter of PTG. Before long I took and passed the exams required to become a member of PTG as a "Registered Piano Technician." The letters "RPT" after my name on business letterhead, yellow page ads, etc. would GET ATTENTION! I became very active in the Richmond Chapter of PTG, taking my turn presenting technical lectures, and serving a while as vice president (meaning I planned the chapter programs). The PTG *Journal* published several of my articles and I did a six-month term as "contributing editor" for that magazine.

When it was all said and done, I had completed 36 years as a full-service piano technician. I liked the work itself—woodworking, things mechanical, and things musical all rolled together. I liked the people, good conversations, and special friendships that sprang up.

About those monthly trips to PTG meetings in Richmond—those were four-hour round trips plus meeting time; I hired drivers for that. I specifically looked for drivers who could maintain good conversations, which made the road time itself useful! That big investment of time and money in the Piano Technician's Guild was repaid handsomely. If you want to be serious about any profession or trade, you will want to join the relevant professional association and attend trade shows and conventions. This is especially important if you are blind or have other disadvantages.

Even if I say so myself, that's an interesting work history for a blind man—starting out as a motorcycle mechanic, then Vocational Rehabilitation Counselor, ending up as a theologian and church historian at heart and piano technician without apology.

My family insists I include some interesting stories from my tuning days. Here are two that are NOT typical and therefore unforgettable:

> One morning I arrived at a home to tune the piano. A friendly woman with an infant in her arms met me at the door and escorted me to the piano. Somehow, she caught on I was seminary trained. She was immediately alert, saying she was a strict Fundamentalist. She went on, "I gotta nurse my baby, but I want to talk to you. I'm gonna go to the next room, leave the door partly open and turn the chair so my back is to you. That way I can ask you some questions while I nurse my baby." When she got settled and I got to work, she sure enough started quizzing me systematically on the "Five Points of Fundamentalism"—one point at a time. I answered carefully—after all, I was talking to a nursing mother—I didn't want to upset mother or baby. I seemed to have passed her examination, albeit with some reservations; maybe she didn't want to upset her piano tuner. She did get in a little dig when she informed me that her church group referred to "seminary" as "cemetery."

The following story is adapted from something I wrote for my family early in my tuning days; identifying details and names are disguised.

The tuning appointment was for an address in Harrisonburg.

Miss Piano Owner had told me she wouldn't be there, but her roommate would let me in. With a cab I arrived at the appointed 2:00 p.m., but there was no roommate or any other body. This was annoying; I had just carried my 77 pounds of equipment up a long, very narrow and rickety set of outside stairs. This meant going right back down those stairs and another cab fare back home with no tuning fee to show for the trouble. I called Piano Owner at her work. The girl on the phone said, "Oh, she's not here today. She's at the Charlottesville store." After some urgent explanation I got the girl persuaded to call Piano Owner and tell her to call her piano tuner. Finally, Piano Owner called and was all perplexed—"I can't imagine where my roommate is; she knew you were coming and the time." I asked if her landlord could let me in. The landlord turned out to be someone I knew, and "Yes, they will let you in." So, I went back (another cab fare) and was met by Mrs. Landlord and Roommate who had now shown up.

Roommate immediately insisted she would carry the cases up the stairs and I should take her arm in proper sighted guide fashion—she wanted me to know that she knew proper sighted guide technique! I had to talk loud and fast to get her to see that I could and should carry both cases and she should simply take my arm to guide me. That settled, both Roommate and Mrs. Landlord proceeded to escort me across the lawn to the rickety stairs. Those stairs—I now wasn't all that confident they could handle me and my 77 pounds of equipment—now Roommate was proceeding up with me, and Mrs. Landlord, too. I managed to kindly explain to Mrs. Landlord that she was no longer needed. Well, those steps didn't collapse before I got up (nor when I went back down later).

As Roommate was helping me get settled in, she seemed awfully casual about the inconvenience she had caused me—two extra cab fares plus an extra trip up and down that long flight of rickety steps with my 77 pounds. "I just knew you were coming this afternoon, and I had to go get some blood work done for my passport stuff. I'm in seminary and am going to Africa." Suddenly she caught on and offered an apology suitable to the offense, and said she would run me home.

While the tuning was underway, a man-type person came in and he and Roommate began having a loud, animated conversation; I kept tuning. Later, Roommate explained, "He's not my boyfriend, he's another roommate's boyfriend. He comes to cook for us." When I was 20 minutes from finishing up, Roommate came and said that she and Other Roommate's boyfriend had to go get some groceries. She said, "We'll be back in less than 20 minutes." I had serious doubts. Almost an hour later—that's right, I sat and played with the kitten 40 minutes—Roommate breezed in saying they had all their groceries at the check-out and then discovered she didn't have her checkbook. I've forgotten how she solved that problem.

Well, finally, we were headed home. But first, about that kitten—he was tiny; he had no idea how puny and vulnerable he was around a blind man's feet. If I waved my cane over him, he would jump for it. I kept raising the cane to see how high he could jump; he hit it at 20 inches or more. He would attack that cane like some mighty tiger!

When we finally got in the car, it lurched and bumped around while Roommate was trying to get it into gear. She explained, "Oh, I'd better warn you. When I put this car in gear, I never know whether it will go forward or backward. Sometimes, when I want reverse, it goes forward; when I want forward it backs up. The other day it lunged about 30 feet before I got it stopped." Well, I checked my seat belt and looked around for the handholds. We did get home; I never heard whether she got home forward or backward.

But that's not all! When I got home, I realized I had left my red sweater there. I called that evening and they said, "Yes, it's here." I told them to keep it there and Ferne would come pick it up one evening the next week. When Ferne got there, they gave her a red sweater, a better quality one. "Wait, this isn't my husband's red sweater." "That's the only red sweater here." After some checking around they said, "Oh that other red sweater went to Salvation Army. Just take this one." So now I had a far better red sweater, and I wore it for years!

Now, I want to alert the reader to two things in these stories. First, in both stories I'm sort of laughing at the way sighted folks sometimes do funny things with and around blind people. Yes, when the sighted world intersects with a world where people do everything without vision, funny or sometimes awkward things will happen. Blind people love to share stories among themselves about these funny and sometimes stupid incidents. I cringe at this, but yes, I do participate in it. My method of operation, though, has been to handle these incidents in ways that put the other person at ease, ideally such that both persons can laugh about it. For example, when people show me to the bathroom in a home or public place, they often, no, usually they reach in and switch on the light then get all embarrassed and say, "Oh, I'm sorry, I shouldn't have done that!" I always respond with, "You needn't be embarrassed, you were being a good host."

Second, in the second story, I'm alerting the public to what happens when you don't take the tuner's appointments and schedule seriously. When you screw up your tuner's appointment schedule he gets just as upset and bent out of shape as your doctor and dentist do. Those appointment slots are the key to our income. HANDLE THEM COURTEOUSLY, PLEASE.

13

WOODWORKING—YEAH, AND THAT TOO!

At this point I'm going to risk boring some readers with a lot of detail regarding various woodworking and home improvement projects I did; the point is to illustrate what can be done without vision. It may well sound like bragging but, oh well, so be it.

HOME IMPROVEMENTS

Before moving into the new house on Croyden Road we had the living and dining room floor sanded and refinished—it became a very attractive hardwood floor. Immediately upon moving in Ferne announced she needed more light in the living room. I installed valance lighting across the front wall and one end wall of the living room using four 4-foot fluorescent fixtures—and Ferne has wanted that much light in every place where we've lived since.

We got serious about outdoor landscaping—we had a professional landscaper install new sod and a dogwood tree in the front yard, two maple trees and a fir tree in the backyard, several new shrubs here and there, and heavily prune existing shrubs. I was totally involved in planning and supervising this work.

To correct a problem with water in the basement I set two good splash troughs under the down spouts and carefully graded the ground to insure proper water runoff. I spaded up the ground in the left back corner of the lot and installed a vegetable garden with a brick border. I formed up and prepared the gravel bed for a concrete pad in the right back corner of the lot on which I erected a 10-by-14-foot aluminum lawn shed (I had a friend pour and work the concrete).

I tore away the old wooden back porch and an old wooden lean-to shed and used an 80-pound electric jack hammer to break up the old sidewalk and porch step—now that was heavy work! I then set up the form for a new concrete back porch with a step going around a corner. (The friend who poured and worked the concrete liked my forming job.) Next, I dug out topsoil, prepared a gravel bed and formed up for a concrete patio surrounding two sides of the back porch. That patio job included a sidewalk with a slope (just right for landscaping aesthetics) over to the driveway.

My brother, Bernie, did the concrete work for that patio. As he was finishing it up, he began to protest and lament loudly—the center of the patio was low, allowing water to stand there about a ½-inch deep. The concrete truck was already gone, so we couldn't correct the problem. He was DISGUSTED! He needn't have fretted. That puddle in the middle of that patio added to the play value of that backyard many times over! It was a "clean mud puddle" and children from tiny toddler to age eight or so LOVED the thing! When they splashed it dry, they would get out the garden hose and add more water. Eventually we did graduate to those backyard "kiddie pools," but they needed parental supervision. That puddle didn't. To this day, if I end up planning a patio for a family with young children, I will try to plan a low area for a "clean mud puddle." I will make sure, though, to avoid locating it where you step down onto the patio from a porch or doorstep—you very much don't want SLICK ICE at that spot every time the temperature goes below freezing before you get it swept dry!

We needed several more items in that backyard. I built a 6-foot picnic table; it was equipped for a shade umbrella. (It was with that picnic table project that I learned that Ferne was right—you don't need four coats of polyurethane finish; two will do.) We got the next biggest swing/gym set available from Sears and I set that up. With bamboo poles and bailer twine I added a trellis to one end of the swing set and tried to get some kind of vine to grow there. That vine was for shade but it didn't cooperate well. I also set up a sliding board that we got from Sears.

We wanted some really nice roses. We researched what kind to get and how to care for them. We got four top quality rose plants, a lot of peat moss, and the just right fertilizer. On a nice Sunday afternoon, I set to work planting those roses across the back end of the driveway. Well, that was THE HARDEST SOIL I ever worked in! The digging iron blistered my hands severely. I was exhausted by half done, but I kept working. I got the roses set in place and Ferne dutifully watered them as per the books. I was stiff and sore for several days. Those roses bloomed BEAUTIFULLY for several years—until Ferne got tired of all the spraying for bugs and I got tired of all the fertilizing with a root feeder that you had to attach to a garden hose. I did enjoy those roses, they were worth the work, but I vowed never again to work that hard on a sabbath day—and I have kept that promise.

As I said earlier, our street was lined with big elm trees on both sides. That meant a lot of shade, but it also meant a lot of unevenness in the sidewalk where the roots pushed the various concrete slabs up in higgledy-piggledy ways. In front of our house one of the slabs was cocked up about four inches at one end. This was a tripping hazard for pedestrians and a nuisance for roller skates and ride-'em toys. The city seemed in no hurry to tackle the problem. I thought for a while, then decided to try something myself. I dug out the soil at one side of the slab, deep enough to get our car jack down in there and work it under the edge of the slab. As I began pumping, the jack fairly groaned under the load; I was afraid I was overloading the thing. The slab did start coming up. When that side of the slab was up high enough, I wedged some boards under there to make a ramp. (By the way, I MADE SURE I didn't get hands or feet under the edge of that slab at any time—the thing was about 4-by-5 feet and 4-by-5 inches thick; it was heavy!) I then backed the jack down, lowering the slab onto the ramp. I took my six-foot digging iron to the other side of the slab and socked it into the ground right next to the slab and leaned it forward hard against the concrete. The slab scooted forward a bit. I kept working thus and actually managed to scoot that slab up the ramp and out onto the grass on the other side! This made it easy to remove the offending roots and relevel the ground under the slab. I then used the digging iron in the same prying fashion to return it, inch by inch, to its place. I could hardly believe back then, and I can hardly believe now how easily that big heavy slab went back into place! The walk was now wondrously level! The city never thanked me for my labors (that was a public sidewalk). For the record, those elm trees succumbed to Dutch Elm disease and the city cleaned them out by the time we moved away. What a pity!

Who did the lawn care chores? I did. I did all the lawn mowing with a good quality hand push reel mower. I sometimes mowed at 10:00 at night. Ferne only occasionally had to clean up skippers. I did all the edging and trimming along the sidewalk and drive—whenever Ferne insisted it needed to be done. I'll never again put a brick border around a garden—I had to trim the grass along those bricks too many times. Every spring I spaded the garden for Ferne to rake and plant her seeds. In the Fall I raked the leaves to the front curb for city pick up. We had to look after a huge, overgrown privet hedge at the back of the lot. Ferne trimmed the thing with electric hedge trimmers and kept the poison ivy under control. I ground the trimmings to mulch with a five-horsepower shredder.

Inside the house I had to remount the bannister for the main stairs. The masonry and plaster wall in that area had been damaged by abuse and improper use of wall anchors. I had to fasten a 1-by-4 rail to the wall to which I then fastened the bannister brackets and then the banister itself. That bannister was SOLID! (Solidity of bannister rails is something I check inconspicuously to this day when I approach a flight of stairs.) I installed baby gates at the top and bottom of those stairs.

The basement needed a lot of work. To make the basement stairs safe for small children I added an extra rail to the two-by-four railing that was already there. To properly vent the new dryer to the outside I opted to not go through the masonry wall. Instead, I removed a glass pane from one of the basement windows. In its place I put a wooden panel with a housing for the dryer vent pipe. To make the basement workable for a workshop, I built a 12-foot by 30-inch workbench along one wall with two 12-foot shelves above it. To make a solid top for that bench I laminated two layers of ¾-inch plywood and topped it with a 12-foot by ¼-inch thick Masonite panel—yes, that was overkill but it worked wondrously!

TOYS AND FURNITURE

Toys for the kids—oh yes, any family with a shred of Dutch culture has to have a marble roller in the house. I built five and sold four. These were lightweight and too flimsy construction that turned out to be a prototype for the really well-crafted marble rollers I made years later for the Virginia Mennonite Relief Sale.

Yes, any household with kids (any age) has to have a good set of blocks. Making those blocks—that was A LOT of fun for both Ferne and me! I made the blocks; she painted them. This blind man insisted on BRIGHT, bold Crayon box colors—red, yellow, green, blue, pink, and orange (recall my love for Crayon box colors back in Dale Enterprise School days), and Ferne happily agreed. I first cut the lumber into 36 by 1½ by ¾-inch strips. Ferne then painted those strips—carefully, with good quality enamel paints, one undercoat followed by two regular coats. I then cut the strips into mostly 3-inch blocks, some square 1½-inch blocks, some 6-inch blocks, and a few 12-inch blocks, etc. Ferne then painted the ends of each block with an undercoat and two regular coats. There were more than 250 of them. Those blocks were beautiful (and, despite chips and scuffs, they still are)! I then made a block box with a seat on top suitable for little butts. Ferne then painted that and added decorative decals. A LOT of play hours came out of that box!

Working with Braille requires the same desk or table height as the old typewriter tables. I decided to build myself a desk accordingly. The end result was, and still is, a three-piece desk, which when assembled is 8½-feet long by 28 inches wide and 27 inches high. The two end units look like low kitchen cabinets, each with a Formica top, a cabinet style door opening into a big storage area, and four drawers on roller bearing tracks. These two end cabinets are positioned against the wall of the study, spaced apart to accommodate the third unit. This third unit is a simple panel suspended between the two cabinets to make the main work area; it also has a Formica top. This leaves a nice kneehole in the middle of things. On top of this long desk, back against the wall, is a large bookshelf system. The configuration and size of the bookcase accommodates my big Braille volumes, telephone, calculator, and other desktop impedimenta. There's plenty of room to work and room for important clutter in which to lose stuff. If I sound pleased with this desk, I was and still am.

Part of the challenge of building that desk was my cramped 20-foot by 20-foot basement workshop with an immoveable gas furnace in the middle. I had to carefully plan all my moves for handling big 4-by-8-foot panels, partially constructed pieces, and individual parts of all kinds. I hated and still HATE dents and scratches in my furniture before it even leaves the shop! Shut your eyes the next time you handle a four-by-eight-foot panel— you'll see what I'm talking about. (If you try that, I hereby disclaim any responsibility if your wife screams at you for knocking some precious heirloom off the shelf!)

The next big furniture project was a sewing machine cabinet for Ferne's new Pfaff sewing machine. On all the store-bought cabinets we looked at, the machine was positioned above the kneehole such that the needle was off to the left of the operator. Ferne wanted that needle directly in front of her when seated at the kneehole, and the rest of the cabinet had to accommodate that! Of all my furniture projects, this one probably involved the most intense exercise of shear imagination and visualization to do the planning.

I first took note of the way the drawers were mounted on Ferne's old Singer treadle sewing machine—two drawers were suspended under each end of the tabletop in a lightweight OPEN rack. No lumber was wasted trying to conceal the drawers' sides. The intent was for the drawer boxes to be seen as an integral part of the exterior case. For Ferne's cabinet I decided to make these racks more rugged and extend them to the floor, thus making them the pedestals for the cabinet. Each pedestal would hold four drawers, and those drawer boxes would have the same nice finish as the main case. We wanted to be able to fold the machine down out of sight and close the top when not in use. When closed, the cabinet would look a little like a kneehole desk, like a nice piece of furniture in the living room.

This project required A LOT of intricate joinery. It was done with solid oak lumber (and I didn't have enough lumber for many mistakes). The joints were all dovetail, mortice and tenon, or dado. The drawers all had little compartments for Ferne's vast collection of sewing impedimenta. I'm afraid I fitted that case too closely to Ferne's specific sewing machine. That machine is going to wear out before the case does, and it will be a BIG job retrofitting that case to another sewing machine. At this writing it is 46 years old and working fine; so is the machine.

Ferne and I experimented for a while to find a wood finish the two of us could handle. Aside from the fact that I wasn't about to try painting or varnishing without vision, My shop was, and still is, too dusty to use brush-on finishes—I despised, and still do, dust settling onto my finish before it is dry. We found several finish products where you simply brush the stuff onto the wood surface and keep it wet for the prescribed amount of time. No great skill is required; you keep brushing on more as needed to keep it wet. When the time is up, you rub it dry with clean rags. You can repeat this process as many times as you want. Ferne brushed the oil onto the wood and kept it wet for 30 minutes or so. After that she was free to go; I rubbed the piece dry—an ideal procedure for a blind craftsman and sighted partner. We achieved good quality DUST FREE finishes. Proper and skillful sanding is the main determinant for a quality finish with this procedure; and sanding I could, and still can, do.

MORE HOME IMPROVEMENTS

The attic in that house on Croyden Road had no floor. You just walked on the beams or on a few skimpy catwalk boards. Recalling my experience climbing around on the beams in Dad's barn when they were adding the new end—I decided to climb up in that attic to reconnoiter. I did and immediately decided to put down an attic floor. First, I took up those old catwalk pine boards and stored them out of the way. Brother-in-law Bill Chupp agreed to cut through the upstairs ceiling and install a pull-down folding staircase. When he had the opening ready and before he installed the stairs, I climbed up there. Bill pushed the 4-by-8 flooring panels up through the hole to me; I pulled them up and stacked them conveniently—all the while making sure I didn't step down between the beams or down through the stair opening! Bill then installed the stairs, and, as per plans, went home and left me to lay the flooring. I had to plan my moves carefully handling those panels, but I got the job done, surprisingly quickly. I installed handrails around three sides of that stair hole for obvious reasons. To prevent items from rolling or falling off the floor edge down into the space between the joists I nailed a narrow strip along the edge of the floor, way out under the roof rafters. I felt like a professional—and, boy, did we all like that attic!

In the summer of 1977, we moved back to my hometown of Harrisonburg, Virginia. We built a house at 300 Rockingham

Drive and moved in at the end of August. I was totally involved with the contractor in all decisions from the day we stood on the empty lot back in March—my blindness didn't seem to "blind" the contractor to the fact that I would be a competent homeowner. To this day he likes to reminisce about the day we stood in the grass and weeds on that hillside lot; I positioned myself just so to show him precisely how we wanted the house situated so the dining room window would have a good view of Massanutten Peak. I also insisted that he plan the elevation of the house to MAKE SURE the top car length of the driveway, which would be steep, was level—I didn't want any cars drifting back down into those apartments across the street!

Often during construction Ferne and I visited the site to witness the progress, to learn how things are done, to monitor quality—you know, to be an informed homeowner. One day, after the vinyl flooring was installed in the dining room and before the toe rail was put down, I got down on my hands and knees to examine AND ADMIRE how closely they had made the vinyl fit against the baseboard and back into corners. Just then the construction foreman walked in, "Aha," he crowed, "I caught you checking up on my work!" I don't think I ever convinced him I was ADMIRING his work.

During the 41 years we owned that house, I was often up on the roof to check things like the flashing around the chimney and to clean out the gutters. I liked to stand at the peak of the roof and imagine the view way across to Summit Drive atop the hill in Park View. I suppose I secretly hoped somebody would notice that "crazy blind guy" standing up there on the peak of his roof acting like he was king of all he surveyed—but don't tell anybody I said that. Finally, the day came when I got too old for such foolishness, so I made something Ferne and I called the "gutter gitter." By the way, when I was cleaning those gutters manually, I would have Ferne stand down on the ground to keep me informed how close I was getting to the roof edge—and I have butterflies now as I'm writing this almost as bad as back then when I was easing down that slanted roof to the gutter.

The objective of this "gutter gitter" was to reach up over the gutter and down into the trough and grab a "handful" of gutter trash, lift it out over the edge and drop it. I wanted to work from the ground—no ladders. I found a 9-inch spring clamp—the kind that looks like an overgrown clothespin. I added wooden paddles to the jaws to make it grab a bigger "handful." I mounted this along with a rope and pulley system on the end of one of those long extension handles that painters use to reach high places. With that rig I could reach up over the edge of a gutter, pull on the rope to open the jaws, bring the jaws down into the gutter on top of whatever was in there, release the rope allowing the jaws to close on whatever was there, lift the debris out over the gutter edge, pull on the rope again to open the jaws and drop the "handful." This thing worked!—sort of.

Standing on the patio at the back of the house, the gutter there was about 10 feet up, and I could make the thing work with some effort. Down front, though, things were different. Standing on a bank near the downspout, which was the critical area, the gutter was about 16 feet overhead. A hemlock tree spread its branches into that area. I had to stand amidst those branches, push the gitter (with its long unwieldy handle) up through those branches, nudging branches left and right as needed. I got Ferne to stand nearby like a spotter to call out directions—"A little more to the left! Now, forward a bit...no, not that far, come back a little and to the right. Now nudge that branch to the left a bit and push on up. Now there's another branch you have to push to the right. Stop! You have the jaws above the gutter; now move it forward and down to get the jaws into the gutter! Etc. and etc." At this point I was near exhaustion—I was maneuvering that gitter on the end of its long pole with my arms fully extended overhead! I pulled the rope to open and close the jaws on whatever was up there. I brought the "handful" back over the edge of the gutter and dropped it; I did this once or twice more. Suddenly, there was a rush of water down the downspout! Whoopee! We had the gutter opened!

Now, there's one thing I haven't told you yet. I did not know when I started this gutter cleaner business that when a gutter is clogged for a while, it gets full of "water!" That "water" is not nice, clean rainwater! It's more like a little stagnant pond full of mosquito larvae, putrefied vegetation, and bird poop! That debris I pulled out over the edge of the gutter came down over my head and shoulders AND STANK TO HIGH HEAVEN! It splattered on Ferne, too—remember, she was standing there looking straight up overhead! We did that job again several months later—me wearing a hard hat and old shirt, Ferne standing back out of the way. We did get the gutter cleared, with water rushing down the spout, but that was enough. I was too old for this particular kind of foolishness. Ferne was too. Actually, she got a serious "crick" in her neck from all that looking straight up. We rustled up the money and had a good gutter guard system installed—problem solved! That "gutter gitter" was banished to a corner in my shop where it made an interesting conversation piece for a long time.

This house on Rockingham Drive was set into the flank of a hill—meaning there was more hillside up back to channel water right down into our basement. We immediately set out to grade the topsoil such that the water would run to either side and down along the sides of the house. We borrowed Dad's little 1970s Datsun pickup truck; I overloaded it with topsoil from Dad's farm. Ferne drove that overloaded truck to town, and—I still can't believe this—she maneuvered it up across our steep front yard and up alongside the house and into the backyard! The clutch was smoking but Dad told us later he noticed no ill effects from that abuse! I did the grading—by walking around I could tell immediately which way the water would run—and Ferne soon got a good stand of grass going. Then we decided to dig it all out and put in a 12-by-24-foot concrete patio.

I did the digging and Ferne and I pulled many cartloads of soil down the street to where we could dump it down a bank into some woods. Laura and Diane were by then old enough—somewhere in the seven to ten age range—to thoroughly enjoy reading the line levels for me as I set up the forms. The shale rock layer under where the patio would be was slanted downhill toward the house—just right for channeling any water that got under the concrete slab down to our basement. So, I dug a trench under what would be the front edge of the patio to carry any such water off to the side and into the roof water disposal system. Laura and Diane enjoyed helping me test this arrangement with the garden hose. Then I covered the whole area with the prescribed gravel bed, put down reinforcement wire, prepared the screed rails, and somehow rounded up a bunch of friends to work the concrete—it sure is nice to have a lot of friends, especially when you're blind!

Soon after that, I built a better picnic table with good redwood, and with wheels so we could chase the shade around on the patio. Then we bought and I assembled a basketball hoop for one end of the patio. I reassembled and set up the old swing set and sliding board. Eventually I put a swing in the maple tree. That patio and backyard served our family and friends WELL!

As you no doubt know, any middle-class family with all those toys plus yard and garden equipment needs a backyard shed. This time, instead of buying and assembling a kit, I built an 8-by-14-foot shed from scratch. I studied the design and engineering of several sheds, paying a lot of attention to the roof rafter or truss system and researching snow load issues. I got out my Braille trigonometry tables and worked out the angles of the saw cuts and lengths for the roof trusses. This was my first experience with carpentry where assembly was with hammer and nails rather than screws and glue. I don't think I hammered my thumb more than any other good carpenter.

When the man from the lumber company was carrying the 4-by-8 plywood panels from the delivery truck up to the backyard for the shed, I asked, "Do you guys ever compete to see who can carry the most panels at once?" He stopped in his tracks, thumped the panel down, turned to me and said with all deliberate, solemn anger, "I work like I'm paid." He picked up his panel and went on. That for me became a sacred moment— that glimpse into the "common laborer's" world! I respected him and still do.

A backyard neighbor began taking an interest in this shed project. He got to worrying and fussing when I was up on the roof nailing down the shingles. At one point he called to Ferne, "Don't you worry when he's up there hammering those nails like that?" She replied, "I don't watch."

During those 41 years on Rockingham Drive, Ferne had various garden projects around the yard. I dug an awful lot of holes and prepared them for shrubbery. Ferne got a mini cultivator she could handle so I didn't have to spade up the garden anymore. At one point she decided to try elevated strawberry beds. We had some railroad ties delivered to the front yard. By now Karen was old enough to help me get those timbers up to the backyard and generally horse them around. Cutting them to length (with a handsaw) and bedding them into place was a big deal! When we were finished and Ferne had her strawberries and other plants growing, we had a well landscaped backyard— it was beautiful! Encroaching shade from surrounding trees, inadequate soil moisture, and probably also creosote from those railroad ties brought this raised bed project to naught.

WOODWORKING WITHOUT VISION

At this point I'm going to interrupt my narrative to discuss the basic issues of doing woodworking without vision. Then I'll come back to my indoor projects on Rockingham Drive.

Should blind people be allowed to use all that dangerous woodworking equipment!? That, or variants of it, is a frequent question. Since parents, teachers, and counselors of blind youngsters may be reading this, I want to comment seriously on this issue.

Over the years I have had several friends who call out every time we meet, "Hey Dan, hold up your hands, do you still have all your fingers?" I do. Rather than taking offense at the question, I have begun thanking them for their concern. Whenever I'm thinking privately or talking publicly about this, I make a point to not be cocky or braggadocious, as in, "Oh, I know what I'm doing, it'll never happen to me!" I try to "have butterflies," be a little scared, every time I reach for that power switch.

When you stop and think about it, the equipment and safety precautions for operating table saws, jointers, skill saws, routers, shapers, drill presses, etc. by blind workers are not all that different from those for sighted workers. Recall, almost always the work piece is guided by fences, crosscut miters, pilot pins or pilot wheels, or carriages; the hand movements are guided and controlled by these mechanics, not by vision. The standard rules are like these: ALWAYS UNDERSTAND your equipment before diving in to work. ALWAYS KNOW, before reaching for the power switch, where your hands are going to move relative to the cutter. ALWAYS KNOW before reaching for the switch, where the work piece or cutoffs are going to fly if something gets caught or jammed. ALWAYS KNOW, before reaching for the switch, where your hands are going to go if something is jerked out of your grip. ALWAYS WAIT for the machinery to completely stop before reaching in to pick up pieces.

When I'm preparing to perform an operation, I place the work piece on the machine table, lining it up just so. Then I plan how to hold it STEADY with one hand while reaching for the power switch with the other. Then I plan (practically choreograph) how I'm going to move that hand back from the switch to the work piece without jiggling the piece AND WITHOUT GETTING that hand INTO THE CUTTER. In this kind of world with these kinds of rules, the work can be done without sight.

Work with band saws and jigsaws is, of course, usually done free hand by visually tracking along pattern lines drawn on the work piece. So, making all that fancy scroll work and those sexy curvy pieces was out for me—until I discovered how to use flush cut router bits with patterns or templates. I discovered I can get patterns by removing pieces from my wife's furniture, using it for a pattern, then returning it to its right place (hoping the router bit's wheel didn't leave marks in the finish). I even laid a dresser on its back, used C-clamps to fasten a work piece to the scroll work at the bottom edge, then used the flush cut bit to cut my piece—it worked! I've gotten friends to make patterns for me. I've started saving a copy of any curvy piece I can get my hands on for future use.

Shaping pieces on a bench belt sander is the only freehand

work I do—and I pay A LOT of attention to where my hand is going to go if the work piece gets jerked out from under my hands—you can guess why.

Lathe work—I experimented with that a bit and gave it up. First of all, trying to hold and control the chisel on the tool rest with one hand while "looking" at the spinning work piece with the other hand—that doesn't work, at least not well enough for those nice turnings. Second, without vision, you can't tell exactly where that chisel is going to remove wood until it removes some wood. If it's not exactly right, and it often isn't, you have to change your mind about what you wanted to do in the first place or throw the piece away.

Dovetails—they are easy to do with a router and dovetail template. I've never tried hand cut dovetails—my skill with hand chisels and small saws is atrocious.

Sighted assistance? Blind people like to be independent. Sometimes, though, they think that means never asking for sighted assistance. Actually, they are MORE independent if they develop the social skill to call for sighted assistance when needed. With really fine wood crafting where display and orientation of the wood grain is part of the art, the blind craftsman must get sighted assistance. Ferne has become very attuned to wood grain patterns; she starts making "expert comments" as she walks up to any crafted wooden piece. When I ask her to come to the shop to help decide how to cut out pieces for best grain display in some project, I prepare to lose the argument.

"I want to get two 3-foot pieces from this 7-foot board. Which end should I favor?"

"OK, you get just one 3-foot piece out of this board. There's a beautiful cathedral grain pattern right here in the middle; that belongs in the middle of the top shelf of this desk."

I holler and protest, knowing all the while she must have the last word. "But that will leave me two useless scraps! This is good cherry lumber! I don't want to waste this stuff!"

She won't budge. "You get one shelf out of this board, right here in the middle."

I give up, thank her for her expertise, and keep on grumbling about the waste of good cherry wood.

Within a year or so after getting my table saw, I was totally frustrated with that cross-cut miter. I ended up making a pair of sleds, one for either side of the saw blade. These sleds are used in place of the cross-cut miter, but they use the same miter grooves in the tabletop. A sled is like a carriage that carries your work piece past the saw blade MUCH MORE SECURELY AND ACCURATELY AND SAFELY than you can achieve with the cross-cut miter. It has become my dogmatic opinion that a pair of these sleds is absolutely essential for a table saw. You can handle small pieces and very large work pieces with ease and safety. You can build all sorts of jigs and fixtures onto the sled for specialized work. They solve all sorts of blindness issues, but also make the table saw much more versatile to both sighted and blind users. Search the internet for "table saw sleds." You will see all kinds of ideas for useful sleds and how to make them.

With these sleds you can cut accurate circles with your table saw—blind or sighted. Search the internet for "Cutting circles with a table saw" to see how it's done. It's easy but DANGEROUS. Be alert to the problem of kickback. You can also use hole saws to cut accurate circles. Circles made either of these two ways will be more accurate than cutting them with a band saw.

One last problem—how do blind woodworkers make accurate measurements? Search the internet for "measuring devices for blind woodworkers." There are MANY devices, some simple, some very complicated. Probably the most important single measuring device is the "telescopic click-rule." You'll find it listed and explained among the other devices.

So, should a blind teenager be encouraged to take up woodworking? The starting questions and answers should be the same for the blind person as for the sighted person: Does this person have the basic intelligence and manual dexterity, the temperament to master the tools and trade of woodworking? Some people, blind or sighted, simply do not have those qualities and should not be encouraged in that direction. Others clearly are qualified to become craftsmen and should be encouraged and enabled to move ahead. In short, the question is not whether the person is blind or sighted; the question is whether the person has the craftsman's temperament. If so, the blindness issues are solvable.

MORE TOYS AND FURNITURE, AND THE MENNONITE RELIEF SALE

Back to my woodworking projects on Rockingham Drive—my indoor projects on Rockingham Drive mostly centered around furniture pieces, toys, and special tools and equipment for my piano tech business.

When Ferne decided to get serious about raising orchids, she needed a lighted orchid shelf system. Her specific requirements were: (1) two 4-foot florescent fixtures each with two grow light tubes suspended over; (2) two adjustable 22-inch shelf/trays; and (3) no visible electrical wiring. The rest of the design was up to me—ah, the joy of creative design and build projects! So now, we have a nice orchid case—the light fixtures are out of sight, up under what appears to be a Formica tabletop with skirt boards. Ventilator slots at the top of the skirt boards prevent heat buildup under the top. The adjustable trays accommodate plants of different sizes—like orchids and African violets, philodendron, too—it's a nice little indoor garden. And the Formica top is a convenient dining room counter.

In the course of time our daughters needed study desks in their rooms. I eventually built six study desks scaled like those in the EMC dorms in the 1960s but with solid maple and fussy craftsmanship. Later our grandsons needed personal bedroom furniture. I built a bedside cabinet for each—ash construction, fussy workmanship.

In the year 2007 I got involved with the annual Virginia Mennonite Relief Sale with an unlikely big splash. I had decided to make a "high quality" marble roller for each of the girls, then added an extra one to the project for the Relief Sale. A marble roller is a wooden toy found in many if not most homes with Pennsylvania Dutch roots. You drop the marbles into a bin at the top, preferably a handful at a time; the marbles go cascading back and forth down wooden tracks to a box at the bottom. The noise is horrendous but children love it and will play with the thing for hours; adults hold their ears. To be a wood crafter in the Pennsylvania Duch world, you have to build one. Marble rollers of all sizes and shapes show up at the Relief Sale every year. Search the internet for "marble roller" and you'll find a plethora of creative designs.

When I built those earlier marble rollers years before in Harrisburg, I opted for lightweight pine wood, slender pieces, and, I suppose you could say, minimalist engineering. They did not endure. This time I opted for the best wood crafting I could achieve. I wanted playability, durability, aesthetics, but also a demonstration of fine woodcrafting. This involved finding good quality maple wood and having it planed to precise dimensions, planning for grain display, careful planning and cutting and fitting of parts, and even finding craftsman-like ways for correcting or working around mistakes. Ferne was a merciless inspector for glue stains. She and I managed a nice rub-on finish after a local cabinet shop sensibly declined to do a lacquer finish because their spray equipment would not work with all those little nooks and inside corners; and a brush-on finish wouldn't work either. When I took the roller to the exhibit hall the evening before the sale, the sale workers were instantly delighted. I was not prepared, though, for the way things went the next day.

The marble roller came up for auction the following morning. The bidding quickly went past $1000. *Good,* I thought, *I'm satisfied.* The bidding went past $2000 and kept going. I started to fidget. *Come on guys, that thing isn't worth that kind of money!* The bidding went past $3000 and kept going. I knew people were now watching me and I was trying to figure out what kind of look to put on my face. The bidding stopped at $3700! The place went wild! A mere marble roller, a toy for $3700?! My Mennonite scruples about simple living and fair pricing were stirring. Then I relaxed, *Well OK, if people want to get carried away like that raising money for a good cause, actually my favorite charity, the Mennonite Central Committee, well, I won't complain. I'll be glad to help!*

Later that morning someone reached across several chairs and grabbed my arm. It was Rosemary King. Rosemary and her husband, Harry, and I were old college best friends. Harry died several years before this Relief Sale in a plane crash. It was she who bought that marble roller. She said, "I did it for you and Harry!" I felt good inside.

Two years later I took another marble roller to the Sale; it brought $2500. Paul Christophel bought it; he was the man bidding against Rosemary two years earlier. Interestingly, Paul's family bought a farm back the road from my home place when he was age twelve; he grew up much involved with my younger sibs amidst the joys and toils of community farm life. He and I became friends later when we were attending Ridgeway Mennonite Church.

Over the next couple years, I took several more rollers to the Relief Sale; the public excitement, the prices, and my ego all got scaled down to realistic dimensions. Thus began eleven years of active participation in the Virginia Mennonite Relief Sale. Each year I contributed something, sometimes a serious piece of furniture, sometimes a simple toy or footstool. This gave meaning and purpose to my hobby time throughout the year. At the risk of committing the sin of bragging, but in order to illustrate what one person can sometimes do, I'll go ahead and say that my woodcraft items over those years raised a total of $13,035. Now mind you, that's only a fraction of the total raised by other contributors.

About that annual Virginia Mennonite Relief Sale—I want to commend that event! It happens annually on the well-equipped Rockingham County Fair Ground. It's much more than a simple fundraiser; it's a day-and-a-half FESTIVAL displaying and appreciating the cultural and religious heritage of Mennonite folks of different ethnic and religious streams. The auctioneer's chant—a delightful bit of cultural audio, goes on for hours, different auctioneers spelling each other off every 15 minutes or so. Beautiful handmade quilts and woodcrafted items of all kinds go across the auction block. Sometimes keen competition or friendly rivalry gets into the bidding. Sometimes folks hesitate to run the bidding up and up because of concerns about the appearance of showing off wealth (some good old Mennonite humility here?), but then they capitulate to the game and go for it! And the foods—some, like dough-nuts, kettle corn, Laotian egg rolls, and ice cream, are made on site for immediate consumption; others, like apple butter and pies are made to take home to your pantry! On Friday evening you can sit down to a beef barbecue; on Saturday morning you can choose pancakes and sausage or an egg omelet or biscuits and gravy for breakfast. Or you can opt for a quart or so of Brunswick stew. Friendly banter, old friends meeting, music by different kinds of local talent, an old yellow and red MM trac-tor running a little mill to grind cornmeal for you, old "hit and miss" gas engines demonstrating their racket, people pedaling a stationary bike to power an ice cream freezer, rides around the fairground in an authentic stagecoach—these kinds of things keep the sights and sounds interesting. Yes, it is a festival with lots of fun and excitement, but one can quickly sense a serious, very serious commitment to the workings of the Kingdom of God in this world. Periodically speeches come over the sound system regarding world hunger and refugee needs. Years later when Paul Christophel and I were rehashing that marble roller incident, he said to me, "I did it for the glory of God!" That's a stock phrase but it was heart spoken! It takes more than a thou-sand volunteers to produce these sales, and they go home very tired. Other Mennonite communities around the U.S. and Canada do similar relief sales. It is wonderful that such a fun-filled event can raise so much money for effective world relief!

OK, back to my woodworking—since fourth grade I have wanted to build a water wheel. Since middle age I have been just as fascinated with the way the brain works setting up and manipulating visual images. I'm talking about the processing of visual images without visual input from the eyes.

Over those nine years when we lived in Harrisburg, I

"wasted" much time standing on street corners waiting for a bus; over those 36 years here in Harrisonburg when I worked as a piano technician, I "wasted" ever so much more time waiting for a cab! (That's what you get when you're blind—you're always WAITING for somebody.) Well, that old propensity for day-dreaming and fantasizing, which I discovered in the year after losing vision as a twelve-year-old got put to good use. While doing all that "waiting for somebody" I began visualizing those water wheels I had seen in real life and in books. By fits and starts I began working out how to solve this or that problem—how to make the gear wheels, their proper ratios, how to arrange their shafts and trunnions (bearing blocks), etc.—all in my head while waiting and WAITING for something. Could I actually make a pair of pinion gears? Could I get the paddles curved and angled right for the water wheel? As I began retiring from my piano tech business I got more serious about all this. I began search-ing the internet for technical specifications and dimensions. I got my brother-in-law, Wesley Stoltzfus, and my brother, Eldon, to help me get my hands on real gristmills and water wheels. I talked shop with a machinist friend, Gordon Shantz, about gear technology. An Old Order Mennonite machinist friend looked through his catalogues to find an indexing rotary table with dividing plates, which maybe, just maybe I could use without sight. (A rotary table is what you use to cut evenly-spaced gear teeth, among other things.) I found one on the internet, bought it, and settled into learning how to use the thing.

Well, a rotary table is not something you just pull out of the box and proceed to use like you know what you're doing! You have to LEARN A LOT before achieving evenly-spaced gear teeth! It took a lot of visualizing to "see" just how the teeth of two gears would interact as tooth pushed tooth; I wanted to shape the teeth accordingly. When it came to making those curved grooves for the paddles in the rims of the water wheel, I was indeed as fascinated with my "seeing" those grooves as with the physical object itself. I tried to do mental videos showing how the water would drop into and then pour out of those water wheel buckets; I wanted to shape the paddles accordingly. It was all frustrating—those visual images kept shifting around or disappearing altogether—but it was also fun; I got the job done and it was gratifying!

Now, sitting in my shop is a working model of the basic machinery of a gristmill. The scale is one inch to the foot—my 10-inch water wheel represents a 10-foot wheel; my 4-inch disk represents a 4-foot mill stone. The speeds of the wheel and stone on the model are true to the speeds of the wheel and stone of a real gristmill. The rate of the water flow over the wheel is true to life. I want to add more working machinery—like a grain cleaner; this project will probably remain a work in progress for a long time.

Well, OK, woodworking has been a serious hobby for me (and for many)—it defines who I am. But there was, and still is, more to me than woodworking.

14
A FAMILY—OF COURSE

From the time I began assuming I would marry and then actively planning for it, children were just part of the package. It never occurred to me to stop and think, *Wait a minute, as a blind person, can I manage parenting? Can I actually achieve an income that will support more than just a wife?* How many folks really stop and seriously think through such questions before capitulating to romance and marriage? Fortunately, Ferne was as naive as I was, or she saw qualifications and possibilities I never conceived.

My notions of an ideal family included lots of kids, ideally 12 of them! Twelve? Where did that number come from? There were nine of us, plus Mom and Dad. It was the book *Cheaper by the Dozen*, by Frank Bunker Gilbreth Jr. and Ernestine Gilbreth Carey (1948), one of the many books Dad read to us, that set twelve kids as the ideal family model. I had a happy childhood with all my eight sibs. I was proud of the image we cut, all piled into our white, two-door '49 Ford, and later in our '57 Ford station wagon. When Ferne and I started planning family size, I thought maybe five to eight kids would do. By the time we had three—girls!—three was plenty, and if they had been boys, I wonder what would have become of me.

Our children were born at Harrisburg Hospital on South Front Street in Harrisburg. The city bus routes to and from the hospital and the floor plans of the building were ideal for independent navigation without vision. That made it easy for me to look like a young father quite capable of the role. At least the nurses and the pediatrician, after initial hesitation, became persuaded thus.

Ferne was pregnant. Her water broke one evening soon after Christmas, 1968. After getting her settled into the hospital, the nurses dismissed me, saying, "You may as well go home for the night. It will be a while yet, labor has not started." When I got back early the next morning, I found that Ferne had been in labor all night. They "allowed" me to see her for a few minutes, then banished me to the waiting room. I was dismayed at what I had just seen—Ferne was conscious but sweaty and all washed out, all limp and wimpy. I waited all morning. By noon I was sure I was losing Ferne! About 2:00 p.m. the doctor came and told me they decided to do a Caesarean delivery. More waiting. Finally, at 4:00 they wheeled her past the waiting room, heading for surgery; they "allowed" me to talk to her a bit. A rag doll has more substance than what Ferne seemed to have! I was distraught, what had I done to her?! More waiting. Finally, at 6:00, a nurse "just passing by" casually dropped the information that we had a baby girl. I pronounced her name to be "Laura May."

Jesus referred to the way a woman soon forgets all that travail when she's full of joy WITH the new baby. Ferne says that's the way it was for her. Well, I shared in the joy of the new baby alright, but I never forgot Ferne's travail!! I would have been a poor Lamaze partner! I don't think there would have been "three little girls" if I did not have the assurance that all future births could and would be Caesarean.

The next afternoon, Sunday, I went back to the hospital with our pastor friend, Don Martin. We were "allowed" to view Baby Laura through a hallway window into the preemie nursery—she was a month early. I was a little embarrassed to ask, but I got Don to make sure all the fingers and toes were correct in number. He assured me Baby Laura looked really good.

Monday morning I was back in the hospital; the maternity ward nurses seemed done with keeping me at a safe distance. They sent me down to the nursery to scrub up so that MAYBE I could hold the baby. What a production—these preemie nurses had to start all over comprehending that a blind man could/ would be a capable father for that tiny baby. Two or three nurses scrubbed me up and put that gown over me just so! They got me seated and brought Baby Laura to me. I felt them relax and step back as they saw I knew how to hold a baby.

Well, the bug bit; I guess today they call it "bonding." There she was, on my left forearm, her round head in the palm of my hand, her little butt snug into my elbow (five pounds, 2 ounces). Stirring and pushing around in her blanket, she was clearly a living being; her face so perfect to my touch—yes, the bug bit! I sit here now pondering the wonder of it—that little creature back then on my arm would one day be telling me what to do!

Over the next days I visited Ferne and Laura at the hospital frequently—navigation about the place was easy; I liked "appearing competent." The nurses were always happy to see me; down in the nursery they just kept a gown by the sink and let me go over there to scrub up and put it on whenever I came in. The pediatrician, though plagued with notions about young first-time fathers, was finally comfortable with me.

It was when we got Ferne and Laura home from the hospital that my ordeal began—Ferne's ordeal was the birthing, mine was sleeplessness! At night Laura would sleep two hours, wake up and want to be fed and changed, then play (want social interaction) for an hour, then sleep two hours and wake up again—

all night long, all day long. We had been warned about this in those "expectant new parents" books; I was surprised, though, to discover how big and real this problem can be, and I was cha-grinned at how poorly I coped with it. Thank goodness for my sister Miriam's help during those days. Laura did begin sleeping all night and we soon forgot about the sleeplessness.

As soon as Laura could hold her head up and look around, she was clearly a social creature. She would make eye contact, smile, and draw people—strangers, anybody—into her orbit. Ferne immediately noticed that Laura was indifferent to toys unless play with toys was part of social interaction with people.

Laura began to sing as she began to talk—and it was good singing. Once, after her afternoon nap at eighteen months I found her in her crib, holding onto the top rail, jumping up and down, singing "Jesus Loves Me" with all her might, ON PITCH! And she danced, too, swinging her little butt around to any mu-sic—we had no TV and we weren't around people who danced. That dancing came from her innocent nature! That was my first inkling that Mennonite scruples about dancing were overdone.

Two years later Little Diane came along, also a month early. The nurses all remembered me and made a fuss over me. This time I wasn't just ALLOWED to go hold my baby; rather, I was ORDERED to "Go down there and play with that baby!" I went down and scrubbed and gowned, and then, there she was, in her blanket, on my left forearm, her round head in the palm of my hand and her little butt tucked into my elbow—another five pounder. She pushed and shoved and fussed a bit, and, yes, the bug bit all over again! When we took Baby Diane home, we made a special point of presenting her to big two-year-old sister, Laura. Laura was just up from her nap; she stood there smiling and rubbing her tummy.

Sometime in that first week my brother Jim came to visit. My sister Elva was helping us at that time. She had raked the leaves in the front yard. The property line between us and the neighbors in the other half of our house was exactly down the middle of a grassy area between the two front sidewalks. Elva had dutifully raked the leaves off our half of that section. Jim stopped and looked at that, then asked, "Did you cut the leaves in half that were lying on the property line!?" He was most impressed. We've enjoyed seeing that as a harbinger of Diane's precise, meticulous nature. And I've always thought Diane was/is very much like Aunt Elva.

As we settled into the new baby routines, Ferne involved Laura where possible; that was easy because Laura was so sociable. When Diane was old enough to sit up to the table in her highchair, Ferne looked after Laura and I fed Diane. I hesitated at first—I didn't want to be coming at her little face with a spoonful of messy baby food not seeing exactly where her mouth was—I didn't want to mess up her face, and what if I got it in her eye? I needn't have worried. As soon as the spoon was anywhere in her vicinity, she opened her mouth and went for it!

When Diane was old enough to sit and play independently on the floor, and before she was talking, Ferne could plainly see from the way she moved her Play School people around that she was creating a lively "pretend world." When she got older, she would make up games for herself and her two sisters.

By age three months I suspected Diane was nearsighted. By five months I was sure of it.

Before going further, I need to explain—by this time we had a folding baby crib in which you could raise the mattress to about table height; the side railings were then about eight inches above that. Ferne had made a really neat curtain or covering for those rails, sort of bassinet style. This put the baby on display for all to monitor and admire and adore—and big sister Laura did. Little Diane was so cute lying in there, smiling at her big red rattle.

Well, that big red rattle proved what I was suspecting. It had an abstract smiley face (just two dots and a smiley curved line) on one side and a blank surface on the other. When lying on her tummy, if we placed the smiley face up close to her face, she would smile and keep smiling at it. If we turned the blank side toward her, her smile disappeared. Turn the smiley face back to her, she smiled again—clearly, she was relating to that abstract face! If we moved the rattle further away from her, she paid no attention to the smiley face nor the blank side. Seeing all this, and noticing the way she reacted as I moved objects into and out of her field of vision, I knew she was very nearsighted. At eight months our ophthalmologist confirmed extreme nearsightedness. At fifteen months we put glasses on her.

Recall, I had been very nearsighted as a child; I knew what glasses would do. So, I was intensely interested in what would happen as the optician slipped those glasses onto Diane's face. I made it a point to be holding her on my lap for this event. As the lady's hands came toward Diane's face, she pulled back shyly. When the glasses went on, I felt her start to relax; her head bobbed slightly (I was sure she was blinking); she looked a little this way and that, coming more erect; then, there on my lap, she was clearly taking in a new much larger world!

Back when Laura was a baby, we had gotten one of those baby carriers that puts the baby on your back. With that I could easily carry the baby when shopping or whatever with little danger of bumping her. This model carried the child facing forward. I had noticed that when Laura was in that carrier, she was head up and interested in the world around her. In contrast, when Diane was in that carrier, she just rested her head on my shoulder as though bored. Now, with those glasses, she was head up and alert, keenly interested in her new world just like Laura.

I had doubted that we could keep glasses on a one or two-year-old. We never once had trouble keeping those glasses on Diane!

Four years after Diane's birth, Karen decided to come—two months early. We went to the hospital. After examining Ferne, the doctor came to me in the waiting room and explained, "There's no use trying to stop the labor even though it's 2 months early. It won't make a better baby. The chances are fifty-fifty. Keep your fingers crossed." When the baby was delivered, a nurse came by the waiting room and told me we had a baby girl; they were afraid she had hyaline membrane disease due to her very immature lungs, but they were "down there working on her." Finally, I think late evening, someone came and told me the baby was going to be OK. She would be Karen Sue.

When I got back to the maternity floor the next morning, the nurses were looking for me. They wanted me to hustle down to the nursery to play with the baby in the isolette. After scrubbing up, a nurse took me to the isolette, showed me the access holes and explained the tubes in the baby's nose—one for feeding, one for oxygen. Then she discretely left.

I reached in. There she was—tiny and skinny (three pounds, seven ounces). I was surprised how long and lanky she was. She wore only a diaper (it was warm in there) and was lying on a smooth pad. She was on her tummy, her arms and legs and head spread to the five winds. When I put my hand on her back, she immediately curled up into the fetal position. When I removed my hand, she sprawled out again. I returned my hand to her back, she curled up again—several times, back and forth. I realized she was experiencing my hand as security—she was supposed to be snug in her mother's tummy another two months; lying out in the open like that would be anything but comforting. When I first heard her cry, it really scared me—so tiny and kitten like! (That may have been later after the breathing tube was removed.) I wouldn't have had to worry considering the voice she came up with later. She was clearly interacting and responding to me; she was a functioning human being—but she was supposed to be in her mother's tummy another two months!

The next day I found little Karen in her isolette, still on her tummy with her head turned toward her right, the tubes arranged in orderly fashion. When I put my hand on her back, she curled up as before. When I put my finger in her hand, her fingers would slowly close on it and she would slowly, with little seemingly random movements eventually get it to her mouth! I took care not to give her little "hints" with my own hand movements as to which way to go—she got my finger to her mouth by herself! When she got my finger to her mouth, she would suck strongly on it! I reported this to the nurse. I was afraid the nurse would dismiss my report as exaggerations of a proud father. Instead, she turned to me and said, "Now say that again." I repeated my story. She said, "Well, really now! We'll have to see if we can get her on a bottle!"

A day or two later when I went in, the nurse announced excitedly, "Mr. Bowman, we have Karen on a bottle!" Soon after that, the breathing tube was taken out. A week later, the pediatrician called to me from the far end of the hall, "Oh, Mr. Bowman, your baby is doing wonderfully. I'm calling her my 'Mighty Mite.'" He had earlier stressed to me, "Don't even think of getting that baby home before six weeks." Karen came home in four weeks!

Karen was our smallest baby at birth, but she became our biggest, strongest, and most athletic teenager. At eighteen months she would climb to the top of the backyard sliding board by herself and sail down with both hands in the air—that scared the daylights out of our next-door elderly neighbors but delighted me! Eventually she rode a unicycle while juggling three balls.

Those nine years on Croyden Road were a happy time—our Dick and Jane years. We put a lot of priority time and resources to making the house and yard suitable for children. Outdoors we fenced in the backyard, set up swings and a sliding board, built a picnic table with shade umbrella, and installed a concrete patio. We resurfaced the driveway, not for the car but for an assortment of ride-'em toys, roller skates, trikes, and bicycles. I especially enjoyed teaching the girls to skate and ride bike. The other families on the block also had kids the same ages as ours—so there were lots of playmates. The street was lined with shade trees and the front porches, actually stoops, were just right for parents to sit out and visit with neighbors while supervising the kids.

One of the bumps in the road the girls had to deal with was my blindness. It was age three-and-a-half when each, in turn, actually caught on to what blindness is, and that "Daddy is blind." Each went through a short period of sadness and solicitous concern on my behalf (mourning). Each soon got on with a normal, busy childhood where Daddy's blindness was just a part of daily living.

To understand blindness, the girls had to sort out the problem, "If Daddy can't see, how can he always find me when we play chase?" Well, as long as I could keep them giggling and yelling, I could chase them like any father. By the time they understood, "If I just keep quiet, he can't find me," they were old enough to lose interest in chase.

Once at age 5, Laura and her friends were playing on the backyard swing set. They got into that typical childhood bragging about what all their daddies can do. "My daddy can fix the TV." "My daddy can drive the truck." "My daddy can drive the car." Without missing a beat, Laura chimed in with the same pride, "My daddy can't drive, he can't see." My blindness was just one more fact of her life.

One day when Diane was age 4, I came home from the office tired and just flopped down onto the sofa. Diane came over to tell me something. Both to tease her and because I was tired, I pretended to ignore her. She pushed at me several times— "Daddy, DADDY...!" She knew I wasn't sleeping. Suddenly she flounced off, flinging back over her shoulder, "Oh Daddy, you're hear blind!"

When Karen was age three, she announced to someone, "My daddy's a good blinder. He can close the garage door!"

One thing I noticed early on as I got into the world of growing babies is the way you can "see" the child's nervous system laying itself out and getting all hooked up. I never got over my fascination with that. With the baby on my lap facing forward (as soon as she could sit erect and control head movements), I would move my right hand from behind and alongside her head and watch what happened as my hand came into her field of vision. At first, the head might bob or move just enough that I could tell she "saw" it. A day or two later she would definitely turn her head toward my hand. A little later she would turn toward my hand and also reach for it, tentatively, sort of groping for it with her right hand. Then, still later, she would turn her head more quickly and reach and actually take hold of my hand with her right hand. Then came the day when she would actively arouse herself, turn and reach for my hand with her left hand

and take firm hold—the eye-hand coordination circuit was now all hooked up, ready to go! I thrilled at that!

It was the same way with roller skates and bicycles. When I first got Laura on skates, or the bike, she was totally clumsy, uncoordinated, graceless, and scared silly. In due time she became competent, graceful, in control of her wheels, and happy! The neurological system of equilibrium for us two-legged creatures is truly amazing—the brain processing just to stand upright and walk and run about smoothly and efficiently has to be ENORMOUS. Put that creature on wheels—skates or bicycle—and the brain processing volume has to increase another ENORMOUS amount! And, to do that the brain has to physically lay down new connections or pathways—we call that "learning."

Diane was an interesting study here. She was the least coordinated of our girls; totally unathletic in school phys ed. But she became the smoothest and most graceful skater I ever saw—and I "saw" lots of skaters in my time at VSDB. Getting Diane on the bicycle was even more interesting...

We started our girls on a 16-inch girl's bike. After the training wheel stage, I would walk/trot alongside holding the kid up till her balance mechanism kicked in. With Diane (we were now living on Rockingham Drive in Harrisonburg), we got to the point where I could plainly see she was right on the verge of launching forth on her own. She was stuck; she would panic every time I lessened my hold on the bike in order to "allow" her to learn the art of balancing the bike. She was getting desperately frustrated. Finally, I caught on—my holding the bike upright was somehow confusing her nervous system as to how to use the bike's steering to keep it upright. She needed a bike small enough for her to sit squarely on the seat and still get both feet flat on the ground and then launch from there—all with no assistance from me. My sister graciously loaned us a 10-inch bike. That thing was way too small per the usual rules for fitting a bike to the child's size, but well, "Let's try it."

I got her on that little bike and explained, "Just practice pushing off with one foot, turn the handlebar the direction you start to fall; you can catch yourself with one foot as needed. Just keep playing around like that and see what happens." To my delight, within a minute or two she was riding up and down the street in front of me. Inside of 10 minutes she abandoned the little bike and got on the 16-inch bike and rode off like she had always been riding that thing! (Yes, there's fatherly pride in this account, but I didn't stretch those time estimates.)

Around 1982, when the girls were 14, 12, and 8, I found a very used Schwinn tandem bicycle in a local pawn shop for $80. I fixed it up and began casting about for people to ride up front. I was curious and a bit worried—can a front rider on a tandem bike with much less body weight than the rear rider handle balancing that load? I needn't have worried. Ferne could do it but biking really wasn't her cup of tea. Laura, who was small for her age, handled it like a trooper and she would oblige her daddy from time to time, but she had her own social interests. Diane, well it wasn't her cup of tea either. It was Karen, age 8, who proved, much to my surprise and delight, that it's not body weight but a good sense of balance and coordination that makes a good front rider on a tandem bike!

At age 8, Karen was already a good bicyclist. Could she be my front rider? Her weight would have been about a third of mine. I got on the rear seat and held the bike while Karen climbed up front. Her feet didn't reach the pedals; I instructed her to put them up on the bike frame, out of the way of the pedals. I made sure her hands were strong enough to pull the break levers decisively. We launched forth—on a very quiet street. To my amazement and awe, it worked—we could do it! I was delighted and grateful on two counts—I was observing firsthand the workings of the human equilibrium, and I had found a capable front rider who liked bike riding as much as I did. I wonder how many miles we put on that bike. In the course of time I found other folks who liked to ride tandem. Of course, I know now that a small person can handle a big motorcycle many times their own body weight, but I'm still fascinated with the phenomenon of equilibrium and balance in two-legged creatures on wheels! As already noted, Karen went on to master the unicycle—I stayed well out of her way with that.

I need to go back to Harrisburg when Diane was around age 4 or 5. We had one of those little pedal cars—the kind scaled for kids age 4 to around 10. It had realistic automotive steering. Diane could ride it just fine. Sometimes I would have her put her feet on the side rails rather than the pedals. I would then push from behind—the seat back served as a perfect push handle. There was purpose in my madness—I wanted to see if her nearsighted vision might limit her future driving skills. The sidewalk was extremely rough and uneven due to tree roots—lots of obstacles to steer around. I ran faster and faster; she kept zigging and zagging flawlessly around those obstacles! It was easy to "feel" her getting the hang of the steering on that little car; she judged distances perfectly as she kept trying to smooth out the swerving between zigs and zags. Once again, I was fascinated with brain development. Even for handling a little car like that, it requires A LOT of brain processing to judge distances and speeds, and time your control moves accordingly. We assume those abilities to seamlessly process speeds and distances and control movements are just the obvious and normal way things are, but actually, that brain processing is a wondrous phenomenon in the cosmos!! That's just as true for driving the little pedal car as for driving the Indianapolis racer.

Well, these three little girls grew up, and each became quite capable of telling me what to do! More than that, two of them produced six grandkids who soon will be capable of telling me what to do.

15
SUCCESS WITHOUT VISION

SOME THOUGHTS ON WHY AND WHY NOT AND HOW

Working on this book has again and again brought me to the question, What accounts for my "success" in life? And I'm aware there are other blind persons who have eclipsed what I accomplished. So how is it that some of us blind folks accomplish so much when it just doesn't go that way for most blind people? At VSDB we were told many times that 80% of blind people are and remain unemployed. That was in the 1950s; I don't know what that figure would be now. That statistic, of course, relates specifically to employment, but I think it also reflects reality in the broader picture of life. So how did little ol' me end up in the fortunate 20% crowd? The more I ruminate on all this, the more I see that almost all of the "causes" of my success were/are not of my choosing. I simply cannot toot my own horn on these matters.

My original intent in this book was to tell stories of human interest to the general reader. However, insights have surfaced that might be informative and helpful to parents and educators of blind children. I fancy I know what I'm talking about, but the reader must be aware my story is very dated; young blind people today will do things differently from the way I did. Blind people now have reading and mobility technologies plus education and training resources I never dreamed of. Parents and educators must stay abreast with these changes.

First of all, I was born into a Mennonite farm culture, on a farm with a long history. That meant lots of useful lumber salvaged from old buildings and fences, lots of old bolts and nuts and washers, lots of screws and nails and cotter keys, lots of ropes and chains and wire and used bailer twine—all lying around for use in adult projects as well as little boy projects. Familiarity with and basic skills in using hammers, wood saws, hacksaws, drills, pliers, screwdrivers, and wrenches of many different kinds was part of daily life. The girls had their tools and skills, too. Some of this technology was conveyed to us kids by actual adult instruction; more often it was by simple imitation of adults, like "Monkey see, monkey do." I remember so well as a small child seeing Dad heaving and sweating over a big wrench—I instantly knew how to use that wrench, and I even knew what to say when the wrench slipped and barked my knuckles. It was in those first days at VSDB when I showed my Erector Set that I discovered such basic knowledge of hand tools was NOT universal—when I put a screwdriver in the hand of a new friend, he had no clue what to do with it! I wasn't just surprised, I was astounded.

Another equally important part of my farm culture background was a prodigious family work ethic involving even small children. This is a well-known part of Mennonite and Amish farm culture. Mom caught on almost immediately after my unsuccessful eye surgery that I could still dry the dishes. And, from my quarreling with my sibs for not washing the dishes clean enough, she correctly deduced that I could jolly well wash the dishes, too! And shell garden peas right along with the other kids—no question, "Get to work." And, "Polish the family's shoes every Saturday afternoon." She set me to mowing the yard with the old push reel mower and working parts of the garden with the two-wheeled garden tractor. Dad, apparently catching on to what I could still see, set me to harrowing the field above the barn with the Case tractor and spring toothed harrow. As I got into piano and organ lessons, my folks supported and promoted that, too. At one point Dad bought an old junker reed organ for $5 from a local pawn shop and turned it over to me to keep me busy. (I got it working and still have it!)

Little did I realize this facility with tools and family work ethic was something special. From 1969 to 1976 I worked as a Vocational Rehabilitation Counselor for Pennsylvania's Bureau for the Visually Handicapped. From that professional vantage point I discovered that many, if not most families with handicapped children, simply do not have meaningful work suitable for children; they don't even have the wherewithal for meaningful hobbies that could develop useful skills. And on top of that, there is sometimes a "Pity, pity" attitude toward the handicapped child—"Oh, you poor unfortunate child... " Parental pity is unhealthy generally, and in particular it can keep the child from useful work and hobby experiences. I don't think I ever felt a single note of such pity.

On my rehab caseload there were several conservative Mennonite and Amish kids. It jumped out at me—these kids had no sense that they were handicapped! I particularly remember one 15 or 16-year-old boy with really poor vision who regularly forked manure from the stable alongside his dad and brothers. I would have been wary of working alongside someone wielding a pitchfork with poor vision like his. He just couldn't understand why I, a state official for handicapped people, was calling on him. At one point I concluded, Mennonite and Amish farm culture just does not produce handicapped I'm-a-special-case personalities. (Eventually, though, I caught on that is not always the case.)

A most important variable producing successful outcomes is age of onset of blindness. If I had to name the ideal time to lose vision, I would say, age 12, or just before puberty. By age 12, I had mastered the basic skills described above. By age 12, I had made good use, very good use of my seeing years. Curiosity drove me to looking at and studying anything and everything around me. I constantly crawled over and peered into farm machinery, especially when Dad had it disassembled for repairs, to see how it worked. I took apart any old clocks or mechanical gadgets Dad would let me have and even my own precious toys to see how they worked. I LOOKED and LOOKED through magazines, catalogues, books, encyclopedias—anything with pictures, diagrams and schematics of how things worked or were put together. I browsed maps of the world near at hand and the world far away. From the *Sears* and *Montgomery Ward* catalogues I got some basic understandings of human anatomy and gender differences. I spent hours perusing Mom's old biology drawings and geography books and studied the maps in Dad's big Bible. I watched and studied how carpenters and builders built forms for pouring concrete and joined beams and struts to frame up a building. To this day I draw constantly on all that visual imagery.

Before going on I want to single out CURIOSITY. Through writing this book I've come to see that curiosity and a certain forward inclination toward life along with at least a modicum of intelligence, is a most important personality trait predicting how one will cope with serious disability. I can plainly see now, that for me, curiosity often overrode any bashfulness or reticence or even some social conventions. My wife says that is still the way it is with me. Curiosity keeps one "up and at 'em," fully engaged with life.

Thus by age 12, I was well grounded in the visual world. Then vision was shut down. But, though I did not think of it at that time, all was not lost. Look at the playing field before me: At age 12 I still had plenty of time and mental agility to learn the blindness skills. Being still in the home nest I did not have to worry about food, clothing, or shelter. Not yet dating, I did not have the dreadful prospect of rejection by some favorite girl. I had no wife and children to support. I had no shaky marriage that might be stressed to the breaking point by maladaptive behavior. I was not threatened with derailment of a job or career. I was not to the age where many folks find it harder, sometimes much harder to learn new skills. As a rehab counselor I witnessed struggle and drama with all of these issues by various of my clients.

Though we were part of a tight-knit Mennonite subculture, my parents did not hesitate to send me AWAY to a place where I could learn the new blindness skills—VSDB (Virginia School for the Deaf and Blind) in Staunton, Virginia. And, I remained curious as ever—curiosity actually made the learning of new skills fun.

So, what are these blindness skills? The more traditional blindness skills have been Braille, typing or keyboarding, and the use of the long cane or a guide dog. I talked about my experiences with mobility and orientation training with the long cane in an earlier chapter. By "typing," I'm referring to standard touch typing on a typewriter or computer keyboards—the QWERTY keyboards. Good facility with standard touch typing is imperative for education or rehabilitation programs for the blind. It's Braille that I want to discuss at length, but first I want to single out the newest blindness skills because that will govern what I say about Braille.

In this modern age a most important blindness skill has come to be facility with computers and digital technology generally. Our vast electronics industry is converting, or can convert, virtually our whole print culture to digital format. Once in digital format, nearly any text materials can be accessed by blind people. For example, with a computer equipped with a screen reader, a word processor, and an internet connection, a blind person (child or adult) can easily type Emails, write short or long documents or even books (like this one), or do recreational research or serious research on the internet. By adding a scanner and OCR software to the computer, blind people can pick up print books, magazines, billing statements, instruction manuals for new tools, etc., and read them. With eReaders like the Kindle reader, blind people have access to VAST libraries of eBooks. Handheld scanners with speech output can be used to read labels on canned goods and food packages in the pantry. Believe it or not, smart phones with those touch screens are proving quite useable and popular with blind users. There is at least one GPS navigator system designed for use by blind pedestrians on the street. Just recently I discovered that the latest upgrade for my computer's screen reader (JAWS, from Freedom Scientific.com) has introduced a primitive effort to make the screen reader DESCRIBE PICTURES over and beyond just reading text. WONDERFUL, WONDERFUL it seems to me from browsing the internet, manufacturers of digital devices of all kinds seem to be competing to make their products ever more accessible to blind people and to disability groups generally. So, a most important blindness skill has, in our lifetime, come to be familiarity with and considerable skill in the use of all this computer based digital technology.

Now, about Braille—A LOT of books (textbooks, books on technical, professional, and leisure subjects), magazines, religious works, recipe collections, computer manuals, music, etc., are available in Braille or, they can be custom Brailled on special order by a number of volunteer or commercial agencies. Braille is used to label anything and everything about the house—food containers, records and CDs and DVDs, clothing, glues and lubes and tools and parts compartments in the shop, and dials on household appliances and microwaves. Braille is used for personal notes and records, shopping lists, address and phone number files, collecting recipes, recording special notes and dimensions for shop projects, etc. (And, Braille is wonderful for keeping secret notes or records—if you need such.) All newer public restroom doors are labeled in Braille (so blind men have no excuse for walking into a women's room). All modern elevators have Braille labels on the buttons and on the door frame (so you can know for sure what floor you're getting off on). Proficiency in Braille remains an essential skill for successful living without vision and so MUST remain a top priority in the education of blind children and rehabilitation of people blinded later in life. Poor Braille literacy will be a lifelong bottleneck for the blind person just as surely as poor print literacy will limit the accomplishments of the sighted person.

But, from various sources I'm aware that Braille literacy in the blind population is declining sharply. I see two obvious reasons for this. First of all, alternatives to Braille are very good and getting better. Audio books have always been an alternative to Braille; they have very good readers and very good sound quality. But for serious scholarly study, Braille has always been preferred because with Braille you have immediate access to spelling, punctuation and formatting. Now, however, modern synthesized speech used for reading with computers and other digital systems includes ready access to spelling and punctuation as well as to print fonts and general page formatting. Furthermore, the clarity and sound quality of synthesized speech is rivaling audio books and is getting better. Probably the decisive reason for declining Braille literacy is simply that the newer methods of using digital technology with speech synthesizers are ever so much cheaper and FASTER than putting those materials into Braille. In short, digital technology for blind people is here to stay and for good reasons.

The second reason for declining Braille literacy is the switch from centralized residential schools for the blind to the mainstreaming system where the blind student is kept in the public school classroom; support services are provided for him there. Modern society is in general turning away from institutionalizing disability groups—blind, deaf, mental, etc. The emphasis now is to avoid isolation and keep the person in their home community by providing support services for them there. But, while there are good, very good reasons for mainstreaming, that approach, for the blind at least, has come up short in two important respects. First, that massive array of Braille resources and special devices that can be assembled in a centralized residential school cannot be reproduced in every public school where there is just one or several blind students. It's also easier to assemble a highly-qualified staff of teachers and instructors in a central location. Second, in a mainstreaming approach, a lot of special attention is obviously needed for the one or two blind students in a sighted student body. But parents and teachers and sometimes the students themselves recognize a certain unhealthy something in this constant special attention. I think of it as a "center of attention syndrome." Academic studies can get shortchanged in these efforts to provide the needed special attention.

Normal peer group experiences can also get shortchanged in the mainstreaming approach—and that is an IMPORTANT issue I want to discuss.

Children, right up through their teenage years, need a peer group—a crowd where they experience the give and take, the comradery, the crushes, the rough and tumble of life with people like themselves. Handicapped kids need life in a group where they don't stand out as a special case requiring special exceptions every time they turn around. Often I have heard blind individuals say, upon entering a group of blind people, "Hey, here we're all in the same boat! We all have the same problems! This is neat!" That means the kids can get on with normal peer group interactions like bragging about the bass sound on my radio, being jealous of that guy's fantastic tape recorder, angling for the attention of a certain girl, listening to classical music with a buddy who likes to explain the different instruments, trying to settle things by fistcuffs with an insufferable bully, discussing religion with some who are actually interested, learning to take a stand when others want to cheat, laughing at and telling dirty jokes, helping a fellow student study for a hard biology test, sitting in the organ practice room listening to someone else practice, competing for standing in the pecking order—you know, normal teenage life where you have to stand or fall based on your own social skills, not on what you "need because you're handicapped." I noticed this "all in the same boat" feeling in my first days at VSDB, especially when I got into that sixth grade classroom; it was like, *Wow, I will be able to have a normal life even if I can't see!*

As a Rehabilitation Counselor I became acquainted with students from a well-run mainstreaming program and students from two good residential schools for the blind. The youngsters from the residential schools seemed to me to be more socially mature, more ready to take on real life, more able to adapt to the seeing world, more ready for employment. Though the intent of mainstreaming is to avoid segregating the child in an "institution," he ends up being isolated as "different" right there in his home community. In some cases, he ends up being resented as an impediment to normal classroom activities.

There have been good reasons why society turned away from centralized institutions, but I won't be surprised if centralized residential schools for the blind are rediscovered. In any case, high school education in a central residential school is, without doubt, a key factor in my life success.

If I had a blind child nowadays, I would start by searching the internet for information regarding relative merits of any residential schools and mainstreaming programs in my area. Things being as they are now, mainstreaming would likely be the option of choice. I would then search for any summer programs, camps, seminars, workshops, study groups, or any extracurricular settings where blindness skills can be honed up and peer group experiences can occur. I would devote serious resources to helping the kid into useful hobbies or even into part-time/temporary jobs.

OK, back to my story—Braille became a most important key to my life success. Though most of my reading before the advent of personal computers was with Talking Books and various audio devices, I became a prodigious Braille user. Through my college, graduate school and seminary years my textbooks were all in audio format except for language classes. For German classes in college and for Greek and Hebrew classes in seminary everything was in Braille—RSV and King James Bibles, a TEV New Testament, Greek New Testament and Hebrew Old Testament, Greek and Hebrew grammars and lexicons, plus various Braille manuals.

Braille is BULKY! It is cumbersome; it requires TOO MUCH space—eighteen 3-inch thick volumes for the RSV Bible, twenty similar volumes for the Hebrew Old Testament, etc.—BUT IT DOES WORK. I rapidly accumulated many big Braille notebooks of my own study notes. And on top of that, we needed space for tape recorders, Talking Book players, a Brailler, a typewriter, etc. I had earlier built a desk more than eight feet long. Then we converted a bedroom into my study. I installed five 8-foot shelves in what had been the clothes closet and added two more 8-foot shelves plus some smaller shelves above my desk—about 60 feet of shelf space altogether!

Then as I began developing my business as a piano technician, I filled more big binders with Braille notes on piano technology, piano service tools and supplies, lecture notes for presentations at the Richmond Chapter of the Piano Technician's Guild, and my customer database. I stuffed eight file drawers with 4-by-6 notecards with Braille notes on all kinds of phone numbers, addresses, and general information. Two-and-a-half of those drawers held the card file portion of my customer database—one card for each of my 2,200 customers. I did my appointment calendar in Braille on 3-by-5 Rol-o-dex cards.

All the while I was also accumulating Braille music, Braille music manuals and catalogues, etc. And I was filling note binders with Braille notes on shop tools and projects.

In the late 1980s, came my computer with the screen reader to read the screen to me. This meant more Braille binders with my notes on how to use the thing, and stacks of Braille computer manuals. My 60 feet of shelf space was overflowing. Amidst a big learning curve, I switched my business service notes from Braille to a computer database. I began using email and doing all my correspondence with the word processer. I could work much more quickly and efficiently!

Now as a retired old man I'm aware that various digital reading and recording devices available now would have transformed the way I ran my business back then. But I'm still not inclined to back off from my urgent recommendation that proficiency in Braille is an essential blindness skill. It's bulky and clumsy, but it still serves essential purposes. It was/is a key factor in my life success.

Yet, even with all this marvelous adaptive technology, blindness is not reduced to a mere nuisance. It is a loss, not a mere difference. It is for real; you never escape it. But with mastery of blindness skills and adaptive technologies, with curiosity and a forward inclination toward life, with at least some economic and cultural advantages, and with time to get oriented to your new life boundaries, you can live a full and complete life, maybe in narrower boundaries, but still rich and full.

But blindness skills, adaptive technologies, curiosity, etc., are not the last word on the subject of success without vision. A most important dimension of success is friendship. It is a given that blind people will now and then need sighted assistance. Sighted assistance can become an occasion for great friendships; good friendship is needed for good quality sighted assistance. So, the ability to make and keep good friends is critical to the success of a blind person. The social skill to make things pleasant and fun for those who are helping you is an asset worth its weight in gold! If you are blind and also cranky and unpleasant, you'll never get the sighted assistance you need. Sighted assistance has, for me, been the occasion for many great memories…

To start with, I have eight sibs—Eldon, Shirley, Jim, Bernie, Miriam, Elva, Esther, Emily—who, while we were still at home, were all great at sighted assistance when needed. Our three daughters—Laura, Diane, Karen—also were happy sighted assisters in the shop, especially when I paid them well.

In my adult business years, seven people, initially casual sighted helpers, became life-long friends—the sort of friends that make life rich and full, that make "success" almost inevitable. Eleanor Borek drove for me in Harrisburg and became a surrogate grandma for our girls. Betty Kniss read many hours for me when I was in seminary. Paul Christopher did a lot of the driving to those monthly PTG meetings in Richmond. He also helped with shopping for good quality lumber. Holly Watts and Mary Veglahn provided great sighted assistance in the shop and in customer homes when vision or extra hands were needed. Robert Mast practically pushed his way into my life helping me break into the world of computers and internet surfing. Gordon Shantz, a first-rate machinist, helped me develop a variety of tools and gadgets for my piano service work. These friends made "success" possible; they made life rich and full even while living without vision. I have many other friends who made and still make life rich and full; I mention these seven specifically in connection with formal sighted assistance.

Two more people must be mentioned. Eldon was an ideal "brother alongside" as I restarted in a new kind of world. He never seemed annoyed or encumbered by having to "look after" a blind brother, or by having me hanging on his arm everywhere we went. One summer afternoon we walked across fields and climbed over fences with a neighbor boy to swim in Lloyd Trissel's farm pond. On the way home the neighbor kid started going off to Eldon, "How in the world can you stand him hanging on your arm like that?! That would drive me crazy!" Once in recent weeks an adult friend told me he asked Eldon, "Did you ever feel tied down or bothered having to look after Dan in those growing-up years?" In both these instances Eldon was surprised and puzzled by the thought that I might be a burden. I don't recall any incident where a "sense of obligation" figured in our doings. We were well matched in size and stride. We did have a lot of common interests—balsa model airplanes for one. Whenever he helped, say, by reading assembly instructions, it was always matter of fact, part of the fun; he liked my airplane as well as his. When helping with any hobby projects, he never took charge to make it "right" according to HIS notions; he helped me get it right according to MY notions. He enjoyed helping me climb around those farm construction projects, not for the do-gooder brownie points of it; he liked to climb around those things as much as I did. He was as interested as I was in figuring out how to do things without vision. He never got over our Bowman tendency to tease, pick, and argue. (Neither did I.) He certainly was no Goody Two Shoes. In fact, a chief pleasure for him once was planting empty beer cans around the EMC campus at a time when such pranks would stir up a paroxysm of holy consternation! If someone has to go blind, they need a BROTHER ALONGSIDE like Eldon!

And last, I need to say this about Ferne, my wife: From the beginning Ferne has been adept at providing lots of sighted assistance without getting co-opted into "merely being my vision." She has handled things in ways that maintained autonomy for both of us. This was especially critical as I began my piano tech business. As I explained earlier, she immediately realized, and then I caught on, that the transportation problem could not be solved by having her do the driving. I simply had to bite the bullet and pay public transportation or hire drivers. Also I hired sighted assistance when vision or extra hands were needed in the shop. Indeed, when I called on our daughters for sighted assistance in the shop, I paid them well, too. This of course meant less net income, but it allowed/promoted healthy, workable family life. Ferne came alongside as a partner—the business manager, seeing to banking, bills, financial records, taxes, saving and investments, etc. This worked well. It certainly was a key to my/ our success.

16

CONCLUSIONS—SOME THOUGHTS FROM THE BACK PASTURE

I am now an old man; it is hard to stand up straight. Like the old horse that has done his time, I'm starting to spend time in the back pasture. I have had a good and full life. There is a wild and wondrous joy in just being alive. But when our senses and conscious awareness get dull with age, we, and seemingly all living creatures (witness the tired old dog) can lose contact with a lot of that joy. Or maybe it's the "wild" we lose while the joy remains. Maybe it's like the musical tune that is still a perfectly good tune but doesn't sound so good anymore because the violin on which it is played is getting old and cracked.

Amidst a rich treasure of memories, there are past actions and roads taken that I would now choose differently, but I don't shut down past memories; I continue to learn from them. Yes, Peter Walsh, Virginia Wolf's character quoted in the INTRODUCTION to this book, is right; I will modify his words to fit me: The compensation of growing old is that while the passions remain quite strong, one had gained at last the power which adds the supreme flavor to existence—the power of taking hold of experience and turning it round slowly in the light, in the sunshine of the back pasture. In moments of waiting for a cab, or for a concert to begin, I enjoy these memories but often end up just contemplating the wonder of conscious intelligence, intelligence that is aware of itself as a living being!

I have lots of bright, colorful scenes from my seeing years, fifteen months to age twelve, and I have lots of scenes that have been pieced together from people's descriptions, from reading audio books and magazines, and from browsing the internet. I can contemplate the Grand Canyon, Niagara Falls, the Shenandoah Valley seen from the Skyline Drive atop the Blue Ridge Mountains, the Kalahari in Africa, or the landscape on Mars. I made good use of Emily Dickinson's frigate (book) to travel the world. And now I have the internet and Google.

A lot of those travels on Emily Dickinson's frigate have been with Ferne—for years, after the supper dishes are put away, we sit at the table and read for an hour or so; we have traveled a lot that way, and we still do. I find myself sometimes sitting around with a quiet sense of gratitude for a good life, and a good partnership with a great woman—which got better with time. She still seemed to get something for herself out of living with me. Nowadays we still use Emily Dickinson's frigate, but we also use a little "rowboat"—a four-wheel, side-by-side tandem bicycle to "travel" our quiet neighborhood streets (no, we don't ride on the cow paths).

That concludes my memoir. My friends know I tend to trot out opinions and insights at the drop of a hat, bidden or unbidden. They also know, and I sometimes come to agree, I don't always have it right, or maybe the timing is all wrong. Yet sitting here at the end of my life it does seem that some of what I have come to "see" is worth sharing before ending the book.

SOME THOUGHTS ON THE TWO GREAT COMMANDMENTS

I grew up in a culture where religion-based rules structured much of daily life and virtually all of our interactions with the surrounding community. Sociologists would say I grew up in a sectarian religious community. My nature, being what it was, I spent a lot of time mulling over church rules, trying to delineate between what God said and what man says He said. I know what it is to be a defender of the faith and say, "It's terrible the way some folks won't stay true to our Bible based rules." And I know the "fun" of joining in the fray dismantling those too-strict Mennonite church rules and regulations. At one point when I was active as a lay church leader, I took note from Jeremiah 1:10 that sometimes we have to pluck up and break down, destroy and overthrow, and sometimes build and plant. I thought I was attending the building and planting, but I certainly was starting to relish the plucking up and tearing down—those old ways had to be swept aside so the new can take root. One night I had a long conversation with Dan Smucker, then pastor of Ridgeway Mennonite Church, about these very things. About the same time, I heard this story on radio news:

> A crane operator in New York City received an order to go to a certain address and demolish the house. He hooked up his wrecking ball, went and knocked down the house. He then discovered he had gone to the wrong address.

Instantly, that story became a parable to me—if it has fallen to you to wield the wrecking ball, you need to be sure you have the right address!

OK, now I'm going to sit here and act like an old man who thinks he has figured out some things.

Regarding customs, cultural conventions, church rules and regulations, laws, sacred commandments, secular constitutions—these are essential for life together in community. They are cumulative over time; they become dated, sometimes burdensome, and need to be updated; they are often, maybe usually interpreted and administered by the strong, the powerful, sometimes with unjust results. From time to time we need a fresh grasp on values and principles that cut through these accumulations and reclarify life purposes and goals; we need to uproot and replant. These fresh understandings then guide cultural reformations and new cultural creations, which in turn guide individual life decisions and daily activities.

Repeatedly I have come back to the **Two Great Commandments** of Jesus as seen in Matthew 22:36-40. This pair of ideas is unbeatable for refocusing our thinking on life's main purposes and how to live. They serve well to guide us when we need to "interpret" our rules or even make sweeping changes. Eventually I worked up my own interpretive paraphrase of these Two Great Commandments. For whatever they're worth, here they are, starting with the Second Great Commandment.

The Second Great Commandment in Jesus' words: "… love your neighbor as yourself." (Matt. 22:39, RSV) An expanded explanatory paraphrase could read like this: *"Thou shalt respect your neighbor's right to survive and to flourish like yourself, and be willing to give him a leg up now and then as needed."* A corollary to that is: *"Thou shalt monitor, pay attention to what happens in your wake when you pass by."* Is there blessing and wellbeing, or is there cursing, despair, dysfunction after you've been there and done your thing? A great metaphor for this is a speedboat.

When we lived in Harrisburg we occasionally walked down to the Susquehanna River. One time a speedboat far out in the main channel went charging up the river, exuberantly exercising its Constitutional right, or better yet, its God-given right to cruise the public waters. It was soon gone, out of sight, out of sound, out of mind. In a minute or so I heard water slap, slapping at my feet. Ferne explained, "Oh, that's the wake from that boat that went up the river a bit ago." A boat's or ship's wake spreads a long way and does affect other boaters and even families and children on the beaches.

So it is with life. To love our neighbor as ourselves we will be concerned, careful about our wake.

Both this Second Commandment and its corollary apply not just to you as an individual, but also to your cultural institutions, your church, your business corporation, or your nation state. Two hundred and forty-four years ago our fathers brought forth on this continent a new nation. Yes, but what did our wake do to the indigenous people who were here first?

Humility is an essential element in this paraphrase—it takes humility to acknowledge the other guy has a right to survive AND FLOURISH, too. It takes humility to take responsibility for what one's wake does to others.

The First Great Commandment in Jesus' words: "You shall love the Lord your God with all your heart, and with all your soul, and with all your mind." (Matt. 22:37, RSV) That can easily be shortened to, "Love God with all your being." When we begin talking about loving God with all our being, our conversation often if not usually goes down the road of doing more religious things—more efforts to focus our thoughts on God, more prayer, more going to church, more studies in spiritual formation. Important as these things are, they do not get to the heart of what loving God with all our being is about. I've come to believe that King David gives us the key to what loving God with all our being truly is. In Psalm 51, verses 6 and 16, we see that what God really wants is not more religiousness but "truth in the inward being." This means that loving God with all our being is first and foremost about honesty and integrity within oneself. Otherwise our effort to respond to this First Great Commandment is an exercise in hypocrisy.

We humans play games with the truth, and it has ever been so. We have a chronic problem with casual attitudes toward truthfulness. We devote tremendous cultural energy toward coping with this casualness as a major problem. Think of the vast cultural resources tied up in keys and locks, safes, passwords, signed and notarized contracts, swearing of oaths, and court trials strenuously centered around getting at "the truth, the whole truth, and nothing but the truth." Think of those congressional hearings where the witness is sternly put under penalty of perjury. Recall those huge professional legal fees! All that is to hedge against universal human dishonesty. We play truth games in national and international affairs with official propaganda and carefully crafted disinformation for "reasons of state." In business and commerce, we are always wary of advertising claims. We see truth casualness in cultural practices such as "inferior schools are good enough for people of color." We see truth casualness in matters of personal conscience, such as "How I treated that girl last night—she actually wanted it." Think of all that psychological literature, marriage counseling, and Dear Abby columns that seek to sort out matters of truth in our interpersonal relations and even in our own heads. When you stop and think about it, the issue of truthfulness goes to the heart of what kind of creature we are.

So what does the First Great Commandment to love God with all one's being, have to do with all that? I've come to believe it sharply raps our knuckles regarding casual attitudes toward truthfulness. As David said in Psalm 51:6, what God wants is truth, honesty, and integrity in the inward being. We can't love God without coming to terms with that.

Here is my effort to understand this First Great Commandment by means of interpretive paraphrase: "*Thou shalt always maintain integrity and inner honesty and openness to any truth from any source regardless of how it may cut across your personal interests.*" This loving God with all one's being, this truth in the inward parts means humility, purity of motives. It means an end to dishonest thinking such as lying and self-deceit, denial, rationalization, pretext, willful ignorance; it means a willingness to stand vulnerable as though naked in the searchlight of any truth. Sometimes it's as simple as this: Loving God with all our being moves us toward acknowledging what we already know, or have come to know, in our heart of hearts to be true. To open up our inner being in this way to any truth can be scary. I sometimes get the feeling I'm standing in a temple before the God of the cosmos, the author, sustainer and knower of all things. We do well to recall the Christian testimony that, when we stand thus honest before Almighty God, there is grace. To open up our inner being to any truth can also bring us to stand humbly before our neighbor—a "different" person or even an enemy. That too can be scary. The New Testament witness here is to go ahead and get acquainted with that "different" person or even go ahead and love that enemy—new community, new fellowship and joy are there! To thus "love God with all one's being," sets one up to hear and respond to the Second Great Commandment.

SOME THOUGHTS ON PRAYER

Here at the end of my life I've been thinking more about prayer. A few years ago in our church congregation we had several events in close succession where prayers seemed dramatically not answered. Three of these were infants who did not survive birth defects; another was the death of a senior citizen who requested anointing with oil. Great prayer vigils were organized; much earnest prayer by sincere believers was sent heavenward. For me the Divine silence was deafening, though somehow, I still was not inclined to dismiss prayer. This was not at all my first encounter with this sort of thing, but this time I wanted to think seriously about prayer. Prayer seems to make sense independently from considerations of supernatural power and miraculous answers. How so? I certainly haven't figured it all out, but, for whatever they're worth, here are some thoughts.

When we spend all our time searching for the "right way" to pray so that God will answer every time, when we are preoccupied with proving to skeptics, or ourselves, that prayer really works, when we think of praying as a way to maneuver supernatural power to intervene in events in the natural world, when we think in terms of "blanketing a situation in prayer"—when we think along those lines, we don't get very deep into what prayer is really about.

To get deeply into prayer, we need to go deeply into life. To go deeply into life, we need to understand that troubles, sorrow, suffering, disappointment, insult, despair, anxiety, and fear regarding one's imminent demise are all actually part and parcel of being alive. The measure of "answered prayer" is not that these bad things were removed, though in popular imagination that's what prayer is all about. Prayer is a matter of going deeply into life, all of it, the good and the bad "in the presence of God," whether we know anything about Him or not.

Prayer is life getting in touch with the Wellspring of Life, the creature reaching back to its Creator. Prayer is also straining forward to One who is that same Creator, that same Wellspring of Life who is now way out there in front, beckoning us toward a Destination!

My prayers have become much less theologically specific, much more meditative. My prayers are more contemplation on the whole of life. My prayers are life looking up and turning toward a call from that Other which seems to be out there. They are life turning back, seeking to comprehend from whence it came. They are life savoring the present sheer joy of aliveness. They are life lamenting and weeping and protesting life's injustices and insults. They are life facing that moral divide in our human soul, acknowledging and regretting our sins and misdeeds. They are life being anxious about our continued existence. They are life straining into the future to fathom the possibility that we are truly on a journey to a Destination. That flicker of light way out there—is it sure enough a signal that death, even wanton destruction and cosmic violence is not the last word on life? Is there sure enough more to come!?

Prayer is not something that prescientific minds or defective brains do. Prayer is part of the very nature of intelligence; it predates theology. Prayer appeared in the cosmos when intelligent brains appeared in the cosmos. Since intelligence first appeared, it has been very aware that it exists in a chaotic and violent place; it knows that at any time it can be snuffed out and reduced to the inanimate material from whence it came. Awareness of this contingency, this existential angst, is integral to intelligence. It is this existential angst, whether subconscious or conscious, that explains our predisposition to pray. Prayers of petition bust out of our mouths before we intelligently determine whether there is a God out there to hear. Likewise, for prayers of thanksgiving—we let fly words of gratitude for the little we do have and for narrow escapes even before we know there is a God to say, "Glad to help." We beg, even grovel for forgiveness for misdeeds even before we know there is a Merciful One out there who will hear and forgive. From everything we know of the thinking of primitive man, from the dawn of his time he has prayed prayers of petition, thanksgiving, and penitence. Only with the emergence of modern science and education has it occurred to us to wonder if there really is a God out there to respond to those prayers. And interestingly, while we question whether there is such a God, we keep on praying—it's our nature.

It seems that a theology of prayer that emphasizes God's deliverance FROM troubles (miracles) does not have the staying power of a prayer theology that emphasizes God's going THROUGH the difficulty with us. Is it not true that prayers and thinking where we wrestle with our existential angst are the wellspring of gratitude?

SOME OTHER BOOKS
BY MY FAMILY MEMBERS

Haarar, Miriam, *The Covenant*, Tate Publishing and Enterprises, LLC, Mustang Oklahoma, 2008.

Bowman, Bernard, *George and Barbara Bowman: Immigrants and Bowman House Builders*, Anundsen Publishing Company, Decorah, Iowa, 2009.

Bowman, Eldon, *I am Eldon Bowman*. Published and bound by Eldon in 2012. It is publicly available at Massanutten Regional Library, the Harrisonburg Rockingham Historical Society, and in the Bowman Family Special Collection at the James Madison University Library.

Bowman, Bernard, *A Tribute to Oma Wenger Bowman (and Her Valley Wenger Ancestors)*, Lot's Wife Publishing, Staunton, Virginia, 2015.

Bowman, Ferne Lapp, *Song of the Redwing Blackbird: An Amish Mennonite Girl Grows Up, a Memoir*, Lot's Wife Publishing, Staunton, VA, 2015.

Bowman, Bernie, *A Mennonite Boy's Odyssey*, Wipf and Stock, Eugene, Oregon, 2016.

Bowman, Jim, *Saigon to Singers Glen: One Hundred Moments in the Life of a Mennonite Farm Boy*, Friese Press, Vancouver, BC, Canada, 2017.

ENDNOTES

[1] Virginia Woolf, *Mrs. Dalloway*, in *Aging Well: Surprising Guideposts ...*, George E. Vaillant. (Boston, New York, London: Little Brown and Company, 2002), 249.

[2] Emily Dickinson, "A Book," *Favorite Poems, Old and New*. Selected by Helen Ferris. (Broadway, N.Y.: Published by Delacorte Press, Bantam, Doubleday, Dell Publishing Group, Inc.,1957), 13.

[3] Elwood E. Yoder, *How Firm a Foundation: a History of Weavers Mennonite Church* (Harrisonburg: Campbell Print Center, 2015 by Weavers Mennonite Church), 135.

[4] Hubert R. Pellman, *Eastern Mennonite College, 1917-1967: a History* (Harrisonburg: Eastern Mennonite College, 1967), 17.

[5] J. Mark Stauffer, *Mennonite Church Music—Its Theory and Practice* (Scottdale: Mennonite Publishing House, 1947).

[6] Donald B. Kraybill, *Eastern Mennonite University: A Century of Counter Cultural Education* (University Park: Pennsylvania State University Press, 2017), 94.

[7] Harry Anthony Brunk, *History of Mennonites in Virginia—1727-1900, Vol. I* (Harrisonburg, Park View: H. A. Brunk, 1959).

[8] Harry Anthony Brunk, *History of Mennonites in Virginia—1900-1960, Vol. II* (Verona, Virginia: McClure Printing Company, Inc., 1972).

[9] Elwood E. Yoder, "How Firm a Foundation," in *History of Weaver's Mennonite Church*, 129-135.

[10] Steven J. Taylor, *Acts of Conscience; World War II, Mental Institutions, and Religious Objectors* (Syracuse: Syracuse University Press, First Edition, 2009).